MARCION AND PROMETHEUS

MARCION AND PROMETHEUS

Balthasar Against the Expulsion of Jewish Origins
in Modern Religious Thought

BY ANTHONY C. SCIGLITANO, JR.

A Herder & Herder Book
The Crossroad Publishing Company
New York

The Crossroad Publishing Company
www.crossroadpublishing.com
Printed in 2016
©2014 by Anthony C. Sciglitano, Jr.

Crossroad, Herder & Herder, and the crossed C logo/colophon are registered trademarks of The Crossroad Publishing Company

All rights reserved. No part of this book may be copied, scanned, reproduced in any way, or stored in a retrieval system, or transmitted, in any form or by any means, electronic, mechanical, photocopying, recording, or otherwise, without the written permission of The Crossroad Publishing Company. For permission please write to rights@crossroadpublishing.com

In continuation of our 200-year tradition of independent publishing, The Crossroad Publishing Company proudly offers a variety of books with strong, original voices and diverse perspectives. The viewpoints expressed in our books are not necessarily those of The Crossroad Publishing Company, any of its imprints or of its employees. No claims are made or responsibility assumed for any health or other benefits.

Library of Congress Cataloging-in-Publication Data available from the Library of Congress.

ISBN 978-0-8245-2016-8

Books published by The Crossroad Publishing Company may be purchased at special quantity discount rates for classes and institutional use. For information, please e-mail info@crossroadpublishing.com.

*For the Sciglitanos, especially Jeanine,
Anthony, Chris and Julie:
With you I am better than I would be otherwise.*

Table of Contents

Introduction		ix
1.	**An Anti-Marcionite Theological Aesthetic**	**1**
1.a	Balthasar and the Genealogy of Modern Marcionism	6
1.b	The Hermeneutics of Anti-Marcionism	25
1.c	Israel's Apophatic Pedagogy	37
	Conclusion	40
2.	**Against the Idols: Divine Encounter, Prophetic Covenant**	**43**
2.a	Encounter with Glory	46
2.b	Biblical Encounter versus Hegelian Prometheanism	50
2.c	The Central Plot and the Forms of Glory	53
2.d	Theophany and Covenant	57
2.e	Theological Anthropology	62
	Conclusion	78
3.	**Balthasar and the Encounter with Post-Biblical Judaism**	**81**
3.a	Kenotic Continuity: Encounter and Recapitulation	83
3.b	*Kenosis* and Discontinuity	89
3.c	Post-biblical Israel: Israel's Redemption	94
3.d	A Lonely Dialogue: Christianity and Judaism in the Context of Prometheanism	100
	Conclusion	106
4	**Judaism, the Nations, and Christological Hospitality**	**111**
4.a	Incarnation as Erotic Integration	112
4.b	Excursus on *The Truth of the World*: A Covenantal Ontology	126
4.c	Judaism and the Nations	136
4.d	A Cruciform Theology of Religions	146
	Conclusion	150
Conclusion		**153**
Notes		**163**

Introduction

MARCION AND PROMETHEUS is a book about Hans Urs von Balthasar's Christian theology of religions, but as may be obvious from the title, the focus here is on the special theological relationship between Christianity and Judaism, a relationship emphasized in the Second Vatican Council's *Nostra Aetate*.[1] For Balthasar, I will argue, Cross and Resurrection do not end Israel's covenant, but rather make relationship with the God of the Covenant available to all the world. This starting point for the text explains its somewhat odd order, that is, from the particular instance of Jewish-Christian relation to Christianity's relations with other religious-cultural forms. By ordering my text in this way, I want to stress that Balthasar does not work from a definition of religion and then view Judaism and Christianity as subsets of this larger category, but rather begins from an ecclesial point of view which sees God's covenantal faithfulness and love working through Israel and the Church for the world. Yet it is from within this ecclesial Christian point of view that Balthasar succeeds, I think, in offering a remarkably hospitable and capacious Christian theology of religions without sacrificing Christian content. Put otherwise, Balthasar's theology of religions suggests that Christian doctrine can present criteria for "discerning the spirits" and for perceiving the work of the Holy Spirit beyond ecclesial borders. So I set out to accomplish essentially three tasks.

First, like Balthasar commentators such as Kevin Mongrain[2], Cyril O'Regan, Ben Quash, and Raymond Gawronski[3], I regard Balthasar as responding to what he sees as a return of the Marcionite heresy in modern times. A substantial aspect of Balthasar's thought, whether on religion or any other topic, involves an attempt to depict a Christianity that is set against what he considers its abridgement and deformation by this Marcionite resurgence. Marcionism, for Balthasar, is a major cultural sign of the times that must be read, and read against, in light of the Gospel. Thus, Balthasar's "anti-Marcionism serves genealogically to purify the theological landscape so as to allow for a Christian theological discourse genuinely hospitable to Israel's covenant.

Second, I want to express the capacious nature of Balthasar's integrative approach to theology of religions discourse. Balthasar's theology, I will argue, is far more hospitable to truth and holiness found throughout the religions of the world than one would be led to believe from a cursory reading or from a reading of his detractors. Moreover, this hospitality receives its particular character through Balthasar's intensive engagement with the form of revelation as discovered in the Old and New Covenants and their relation. In other words, a perhaps counter-intuitive claim is being made: Balthasar's extensive reading of the Hebrew Scriptures opens up areas of engagement with other religions to which many other theological treatments of religion pay scant attention.

A third task of the present work is to present Balthasar's approach to a Christian theology of religions as an alternative model to many now populating the field. This claim actually springs from the first two, that is to say that Balthasar's theological viability as an alternative model emerges out of what I will argue is his capacious view of Christianity, and this capaciousness is directly related to his anti-Marcionite agenda. Of course, to say that Balthasar offers a helpful alternative model is not to say that one must follow him in all his details. Instead, what I am arguing is that the basic form of Balthasar's thought allows for a genuine dialogue with other religious traditions in all their own breadth and depth without relinquishing fundamental Christian convictions that support Christian belief, practice, and praise. A stronger formation of my thesis is possible: Balthasar's construal of Christian faith itself makes possible a hospitable form of ecclesial Christian theological discourse.

In making this argument, however, I am aware that *Marcion and Prometheus* runs counter to expectations. As capacious as Balthasar's covenant-grounded and Vatican II-oriented theology is, Francis Clooney[4] is no doubt correct to observe that his voice has by and large been viewed as unhelpful within theology of religions discourse. At the outset, then, it would seem important to explore several possible reasons Balthasar's voice has been so neglected (A). After this discussion, I will specify how the term "Marcionism" is to be used in my text (B). Finally, I will give a brief overview of Balthasar's theology of religions (C).

A. Neglect of Balthasar in Theology of Religions Discourse

Assuming that Clooney is correct in his judgment, I want to address what come to mind as the three most relevant reasons for this neglect: (1) the unique nature of Balthasar's work itself; (2) the development of theology of religions discourse; and (3) a sense that high Christology cannot be paired with openness to truth and goodness outside of Christianity. We will treat these in order.

(1) Balthasar's work confronts the theologian as an unwieldy and strange animal that rarely addresses a theological issue from start to finish in any one place. So one can find statements on religion or religions throughout his major and minor works and still never find a clear, step-by-step argument made in any one place in a form similar to what we find in Rahner's *Theological Investigations* or in more recent discussions such as Joseph DiNoia's *Diversity of Religions: A Christian Perspective*.[5] His style is more nearly patristic than Thomistic or analytical. He seeks to lead his readers into the mystery of Christ by circling it and depicting it from different vantage points rather than making a series of tightly deductive or inductive arguments. This does not mean that arguments cannot be found and adduced, or that there is no system to his work. Mongrain has shown that in fact Balthasar does have a formal structure or underlying "architectonic" to his thought.[6] But Balthasar judges that modern renditions of Christian faith have left its full depth and breadth so obscured, and often deformed, that adding another theological system to the lot, without first presenting a rich rendition of the Christian form (*Gestalt*), and also a variety of ways in which this form has been expressed, will only add to the problem.

The upshot of Balthasar's un-systematic system is that if one happens upon his more acerbic comments regarding non-Christian religions, then he will tend to get tossed into the "exclusivist" camp and dismissed as irrelevant or even malevolent. And there is no denying that Balthasar can be acerbic.[7] The danger here comes from reading brief excerpts from a volume or two of his major works and not grasping the broader form of his thought. For example, Francis Clooney[8] refers to a passage in the first volume of *Glory of the Lord* that appears to indicate that Balthasar sees no possible way to grasp God's relation to the world outside of an explicit reading of the New Testament or ecclesial catechesis. Volume four of the same *Glory of the Lord*, however, makes clear that for Balthasar metaphysical reason, whether poetic, philosophical, or religious, produces analogies to the form of Christ that are to be found strewn everywhere across the cultural landscape. Balthasar does not merely stipulate this; he shows it and suggests, through his readings of major intellectual figures, what the conditions for an encounter with divine glory might be outside Christian revelation proper. We will need to explore why for Balthasar Christian truth can seem so unique, and at the same time analogies to it so ubiquitous.

(2) A second reason that Balthasar is not readily called upon for theological insight in this area has less to do with Balthasar, I suspect, and more to do with the progression of theology of religions discourse. Theology of religions gets its original impetus from a desire on the part of many theologians to include non-Christians in the loving embrace of God's saving will. Balthasar's *Dare We Hope "That All Men Be Saved"?* is a text in this genre that argues that Christians have a duty to hope for the salvation of all human beings.[9] This is true of some Catholic theologians prior to the Second Vatican Council,[10] and even more after. This historical development is viewed by some theologians as the coming forth from a closed, Church-centered or "ecclesiocentric" view of divine grace, represented by the phrase *nulla salus extra ecclesiam* (no salvation outside the Church), to a more expansive notion of God's dealings with the world. Edward Schillebeeckx, for one, clearly sees the Council as a watershed in this regard.[11] This shift is then seen as a first step towards a greater openness on the part of Catholic doctrine. The second step can now seem a natural progression of this expansiveness. If in fact grace is universal, one might reason, then why assume that this grace presents itself preeminently in Christian revelation? Perhaps the different religions are co-equal expressions of a similar religious experience of the Infinite appropriate to different cultures. In other words, the momentum of development itself, in addition to a greater awareness of different cultures and religions, can appear to warrant a pluralist direction for theology of religions.[12] What I would label the "strict pluralist" position would argue that the experience of salvation receives a different cultural-symbolic realization in different religions and cultures, all of which point to the same ultimate reality which remains unknown save for different experiences of salvation. This position is attractive because it speaks to the contemporary desire for both openness to one's neighbors, and for humility with respect to one's own con-

victions. In this telling of the story, then, Balthasar's insistence on Christ as the savior "once and for all," and on Christ as the measure of truth, strikes a discordant note.

In fact, however, the pluralist position is not a necessary development from the desire for a greater affirmation of truth as it is found outside of Christianity. Indeed, it can be seen as an interruption from outside the process of theological reflection that preceded and found fruit in Vatican II's *Nostra Aetate*. In its essence, the pluralist position emerges from within a Kantian world of assumption where a differentiation between noumenal, unknowable reality and phenomenal, knowable reality holds sway. This Kantian interruption may take a strictly philosophical form, as in John Hick's landmark work, *An Interpretation of Religion: Human Responses to the Transcendent*,[13] or it may take a more theological form and apply these same categories, whether implicitly or explicitly, to Christology.[14] If the theological form is taken, Jesus can be viewed as a witness to God, and even as an incarnation of God, but Jesus is not the definitive, unsurpassable Incarnation of God. He is not God's ultimate self-interpretation for us. In either a philosophically or theologically rooted pluralism, God no longer reveals his own self-interpretation for the world, but instead remains a kind of infinite mystery gestured to and even experienced in this world, but not definitively revealed in singular events of salvation history. Once this distance between Jesus and God is opened up, it becomes possible, and perhaps plausible, to argue that experiences of salvation occur not only outside of the Christian Church, but apart from the grace of Christ. These non-Christian experiences of salvation are appropriate to their non-Western cultures and coalesce around a set of religious symbols, persons, and practices different from those of Christianity, but point to a similar goal of self-transcendence and human wholeness. Just as Kant assumed that there is a noumenal reality that appears in phenomenal reality, but is never known in-itself, so pluralists assume that the Infinite or Real is experienced in the world through the various religions, but is never known in-itself.[15] On this view, the various religions become pointers to a Reality that infinitely transcends all inner-worldly categories, and thus renders metaphysical and doctrinal differences relatively insignificant.

Whether or not a pluralist theology takes its direction explicitly from Kant, it will relativize Christian claims for Jesus' disclosure of divine reality and Christian claims regarding the universal saving efficacy of Jesus' Cross and Resurrection and, indeed, revelatory events more generally. This may occur through an appeal to the metaphorical, mythical, and symbolic character of religious and biblical language, the radical or absolute transcendence, and thus unknowability of God, and to the *apophatic* or negative theology tradition so important to Christianity. Balthasar would certainly recognize that symbolic language, divine transcendence, and apophatic theology have a fundamental and centrally important place in Christian thought. But he would also argue that the pluralist theologian misunderstands all of them because of a fundamental error: the pluralist argues as if Christian theological claims about the nature of Christ and the Trinity are claims rooted in human reason's always imperfect attempts to extend itself into the divine realm, rather than God's definitive hermeneutic or self-interpretation that reaches out to and for the world. Another way to think of Balthasar's point is to observe that for him Christian claims about God are impossible outside of the triangulation between revelation, the grace to grasp revelation as such, and the faith to trust in the form and authority of revelation.[16] Thus, in his view, Christians do not worship the unknown God, but can only worship the triune God because the divine life has freely opened itself to the world in Jesus Christ. Through the pattern of Christ's existence in time, God decisively interprets himself as absolutely sovereign, free, self-abandoning love. A second point is intimately related: God reveals himself in terms of self-abandoning love most profoundly in the saving event of the Cross and Resurrection of Jesus Christ. From Balthasar's point of view, the pluralist position implies that the salvation offered by Christ "once and for all" is really meant only for those living on Western continents, and, therefore, that this form of divine love is not meant for the East. Whatever its philosophical merits, Balthasar would see this as an untenable theological position. God's love is intended for all, as is the salvation he grants through Christ's Cross and Resurrection that gives the definitive form of that love to the world.[17]

If it is true that Balthasar is not a pluralist theologian, his thought nevertheless recognizes both an important insight of pluralist theologies and a crucial question that they raise. The insight: *a posteriori* examination of religious traditions alone can justify claims about those religions and about Christian uniqueness in relation to other religions.[18] For example, if Christians say that only their religion trusts in a God who takes on a human body and history, and scholars subsequently point to another religion that holds to both of these propositions, then the uniqueness of this Christian claim is forfeited. Of course, it is equally important to point out that the value a particular claim has within the Christian system and its relation to other parts of Christian belief and practice may thoroughly distinguish its meaning from that of an alternative religious tradition. So, a Hindu *avatar* might look like what Christians call the Incarnation, but upon more rigorous examination one might conclude otherwise. The question: what is the reason for and status of non-Christian religions in God's providential plan? Unless we are willing to say that all non-Christian religions are unfortunate dross—and neither Balthasar nor Vatican II are willing to say this—then reflection on the meaning of religions in God's providential design is unavoidable. Jacques Dupuis has been prescient in pushing this question to the forefront.[19] This insight and question will need to be addressed in relation to Balthasar's own work.

(3) A third reason we might surmise for Balthasar's relative neglect in this field is his high Christology. In short, if Balthasar's Christology holds, then Christ becomes the measure and fulfillment of all religious truth. If a theologian objects to the idea that Christ is the truth, and that he is the measure of all truth, then clearly Balthasar's position will hold no attraction.

Rosemary Radford Ruether's theology of religions is a clear example. She would reject Balthasar's position precisely because she rejects the development of Christological doctrine as itself the fertile soil that nourishes Christian anti-Semitism. Ruether finds Christian anti-Judaism inherently linked to messianic claims for Jesus in the wake of the resurrection. Christian belief in Jesus' resurrection and exaltation lead gradually, she argues, to the worship of Jesus as messiah and God. As patristic Christianity separates from Judaism,

Christians come to reject their "elder brothers" as "carnal" and as religiously obsolete because Jews fail to see Jesus as the fulfillment of their covenant with God. In Ruether's narrative, supercessionism becomes the prime motive for Christian anti-Judaism and later anti-Semitism. Ruether memorably claims that "anti-Judaism developed as the left hand of Christology."[20] This also means that she will view Trinitarian doctrine as a fundamentally non-Jewish imposition on revelation, as will John Hick.[21] All of this together leads her to reject absolute Christological claims; advancing what is essentially a pluralist position, she regards Christianity as the religion of a particular culture that should be in conversation with the religions of other cultures.[22] From this point of view, or any like it, Balthasar's Christocentric theology will appear hostile to inter-religious dialogue, and especially to Jewish-Christian dialogue. Yet Balthasar might question the pluralism of Ruether and Hick precisely on Jewish grounds. Insofar as Ruether and Hick recommend empirical or concrete reflection on religion, it is incumbent upon both to take seriously the forms of religious worship proper to Judaism. The Jewish community does not worship "as if" its Lord is the Lord of the universe, but sees itself as worshipping the One God who has graciously made a covenant with Israel. Indeed, this is the essence of the *Shema*. This God's sovereignty and uniqueness can suffer no relativization if it is to be represented as Jews worship. A pluralism that must attenuate Jewish monotheism no longer remains faithful to actual Jewish belief and practice, and so would not appear pluralistic.

Here it is appropriate to make more explicit another issue with pluralist theologies of religion, at least as they have appeared thus far. John Hick, Paul Knitter, Rosemary Radford Ruether, Hans Küng, and others have tended to focus their attention on the issue of salvation. This is perfectly understandable given that they are emerging from a context in which many Christians would have looked upon their non-Christian religious neighbors as outside of God's gracious design. After Vatican II, then, they want to provide theological reasons for understanding these religious neighbors as lying within God's saving grace. Yet this focus, I will suggest here, tends to marginalize other aspects of human religiosity that may have profound importance in actual non-Christian religions. For instance, Jewish covenant faithfulness in terms of Halakah and worship will tend to be obscured, while esoteric mystical traditions and efforts for social and political justice will be highlighted since they better conform to the author's notion of "salvation." This has the effect, however, of perhaps creating a new religion rather than opening a space for a dialogue of actual religions and religious people.

Of course Ruether and Balthasar share a desire to excavate the early Christian sources for contemporary thought. However, where Ruether finds in the development of doctrine an anti-Judaism that supports or facilitates Christian complicity in the *Shoah*, Balthasar discovers a very different tool for diagnosing the ills of modern Christianity vis-à-vis Judaism. Balthasar will argue that the Trinity is the Christian way of maintaining theological unity between the Old and New Covenant, Judaism and Christianity, against the true "hellenizers," Marcion and Valentinus. More important is that whatever the case is in the patristic period, modern thought rarely places its stress on divine transcendence, traditional Trinitarian theology, the divinity of Christ, or a traditional biblical hermeneutic. So these doctrines do little to explain the virulence of modern anti-Semitism or anti-Judaism.[23] Instead, Balthasar argues, the fundamental pathology of modern Christian theological discourse is Marcionism, which attempts to sever the God of the Old Covenant from the God of Jesus Christ, divine justice and Jewish law from divine love, Hebrew Scriptures from the Gospel, Israel from the Church. Marcionism, not authentic patristic theology, is "the first systematic form of theological anti-Semitism"[24] returning in modernity to deform Christian faith. Consequently, for Balthasar, Christian anti-Judaism has its roots not in Christian messianic claims, but in the view that Jews worship an unworthy God or in the view that Israel's preparation for the messiah can be replaced by other nations and national mythologies.

Thus, the anti-Marcionite task of this book relates directly to the connection between Judaism and Christianity. Perhaps surprisingly, however, Balthasar's emphasis on the continuity between Judaism and Christianity opens up all the material of the Old Covenant so as to relate this wealth to other religious, philosophical, and poetic works. Thus an anti-Marcionite position, in principle at least, gives Christianity a much broader and deeper potential for dialogue. On this view, high Christological and Trinitarian convictions are not necessarily hostile to Judaism or to non-Christian religions, but are doctrines that underscore theological continuity between the Old and New Covenants, Creation, Covenant, and Cross, and thus allow for a far more "thick" inter-religious discourse. Given the importance of Marcionism to the argument of this text, it warrants some special consideration at the outset.

B. Marcion and Modern Marcionism

WE SHOULD BEGIN OUR DISCUSSION OF MARCION with the disclaimer that all of what we know of Marcion comes from his early Christian opponents. Justin Martyr, Clement of Alexandria, Origen, Irenaeus, and Tertullian, especially Tertullian, wrote against Marcion's theological views. This means that a certain amount of caution will be necessary in presenting the following "Marcionism" as truly the doctrine of Marcion himself. Whatever its historical veracity, however, the following theological picture is what Balthasar works with when he finds different forms of Marcionism re-appearing in modern discourse.

Marcion of Pontus (d. AD 160), the son of a bishop, a shipping magnate, and perhaps a bishop himself, arrived in Rome from Sinope on the Black Sea in the 130s or early 140s desiring entrance into the Roman church. He reportedly made a substantial donation to the Church and was received into its fold. Yet by 144, he was returned his donation and sent packing. What happened in the intervening years to precipitate this break? What happened to inspire so many tracts against him—Tertullian alone dedicated five books *Adversus Marcionem*—from early Christian writers, those same tracts from which we ascertain whatever it is that we know of Marcion?

Like many modern writers, it seems that Marcion found the Old Testament vision of God completely incompatible with the New Testament depiction of Jesus and his Father. Depending on which account we take to be most accurate, Marcion either viewed the Old Testament God as evil and vindictive, or as merely just, in contrast to the New Testament's God of mercy. This God of mercy was unknown until Jesus emerged in the first century. I say Jesus "emerged" because Marcion evidently rejected the idea that Jesus was born in a human way. Marcion appeared to have viewed the Father of Jesus as a higher deity than the God of the Old Covenant. The Father sent Jesus to reveal his mercy and to redeem humanity from the world of matter, the God of creation, and the Law. Redemption, for Marcion, occurred through the Crucifixion, but not the resurrection. Marcion rejected the resurrection of the flesh. Moreover, this redemption would have been available to the impious of the Old Covenant (i.e., Cain, the Sodomites, and the Egyptians), and not to the pious (i.e., Moses, Noah, Abraham, etc.) who are tied too closely to matter and its creator to accept Christ's invitation. Marcion's desire to "expurgate" the Christian scriptures of all references to Judaism, to eliminate the Old Testament entirely from Christian belief and worship, and to reduce the New Testament to letters of Paul and parts of Luke (both also expurgated versions) is directly related to his dualistic view of the divine. If in fact the God of the Old Covenant and of Judaism is incompatible with the God of Jesus Christ, then it makes sense to eliminate the Old Testament and all references to it in the New Testament. And so he did.

Based on all the surviving sources and commentaries on his work, Marcion's doctrine seems to have been dualistic, and thus a repudiation of Jewish monotheism. His views also contradict mainstream Christian views of matter and of evil. Indeed, Tertullian thought that one of the main catalysts for Marcion's dualism was his hyper-concern with the problem of evil. Marcion's theory of an evil creator God seems to solve this problem. Evil is not the result of human free will, but rather the result of humanity's imprisonment in the material world, where the Creator also serves as warden. This dualism helps make sense of Marcion's objection to Jesus' actual human birth and the bodily resurrection: both doctrines were, for most early Christians, symbols of the fundamental goodness of creation and the material world. Marcion rejects this goodness. In addition, if Jesus were truly born of a woman, that woman would be the Jewish Miriam and would thoroughly inscribe Jesus in the history of Israel. This too would be objectionable from Marcion's point of view. The graphic on the following page should help visualize the basics of Marcion's outlook insofar as we are able to reconstruct it from our limited sources:

Marcionite Dualism

VS.

Old Covenant God / Yahweh	Father of Jesus (unknown prior to Jesus)
Creator	Redeemer / Jesus
Matter	Spirit
Justice	Mercy
Old Covenant	New Covenant
Law	Gospel
Jewish Worship	Christian Worship

Diagram Note: The categories on the left-hand side are opposed to those on the right. The categories in each column, running down from God to worship, are internally and positively related to one another. So, in the right-hand column, for instance, Jesus redeems the spirit and not the body, the New Covenant is the Covenant of mercy and not justice, and Christian worship ought to worship the Father and not the God of Israel.

Balthasar's vigorous anti-Marcionism is no doubt influenced by the heresiological tradition, particularly as interpreted by the powerful writings of his good friend, Henri de Lubac. De Lubac's writings against anti-Semitism and Nazism are still too little known, but all of the major themes we will find systematically treated in Balthasar's massive work, we find noted in de Lubac's letters and lectures from within Nazi-occupied France. According to de Lubac, the Hitler "virus" would crush "the human person (and, with him, the family), because, first of all, it denies the transcendent God."[25] De Lubac saw in this rejection of divine transcendence a "collective apostasy."[26] He finds himself consistently exposing and opposing the desire for a Gnostic and Marcionite separation of Jesus from Judaism, charity from justice, New Testament from Old.[27] His disgust at the hatred in so many central German and French writings is palpable: "It is repugnant to us to move about again in this bloody filth by rereading these blasphemous pamphelets."[28] De Lubac recognizes the "crisis" of the Old Testament, the Marcionite heritage as it returns in modernity, and the desire of many writers to eliminate the transcendence of God. In response, he writes, "No Christian must let himself go so far as to think that a movement of withdrawal with respect to the Old Testament would leave his faith intact.... We maintain the indissoluble bond between our two Testaments, always, in the final analysis, interpreting the Old by the New, but also always basing the New on the Old. In the light of Jesus we will be able to contemplate their 'harmony.'"[29]

Whether or not Balthasar ever read de Lubac's essay, his theology clearly represents a systematic working out of de Lubac's opposition to Marcionism. Indeed, for Balthasar, Marcion separates everything that Christianity must keep together in paradoxical union. As we have seen, Marcion's dualistic picture of the divine leads to other separations: New Covenant from Old, Christianity from its Jewish roots, the God of Justice from the God of Love, and matter from spirit. By contrast, Balthasar holds that Christianity proclaims one, triune God, who has one plan of salvation manifest through the unity of two covenants. The same God is both Creator and Redeemer, God of matter and spirit, justice and love. Balthasar certainly thinks that the Old Covenant reveals God as the Creator, but in contrast to Marcionism, he holds that this Creator is one with the Redeemer who frees Israel from slavery, and all humanity from sin, so as to live a truly liberated existence in right relation to God. Moreover, Balthasar reaches beyond a formal acceptance of Old Covenant revelation to demonstrate the significance of Old Covenant content to modern and contemporary thought. With de Lubac, and in contrast to the judgment of Adolf von Harnack, Balthasar argues that severing Christianity from its historical roots in Israel and the Old Covenant can only be a disaster for Christian theology and life. Balthasar strives to show that Marcionism has returned in modernity, and that its disastrous effects have already been felt.

Here, we must add a qualification and some specificity to the claim of Marcionite return. We can begin with a qualification. Balthasar's "Marcionism" is not limited to the second century variety. It would be odd to find an exact replica of Marcionism in modernity, just as it would be strange to accord fidelity only to those Christians who believed precisely as did second-century Christians in every detail. Presumably, if one can be a faithful Christian whose belief nevertheless differs somewhat from early Christians, one can be a faithful Marcionite whose beliefs similarly differ from ancient Marcionism. What is necessary is substantial overlap between ancient and modern views that would justify the ascription. Balthasar is aware of two key differences. First, ancient Marcionism will be a polytheistic system. Modern forms of Marcionite return will eliminate one of the gods but still juxtapose the Father of Jesus revealed in the New Testament to the depiction of God in the Old Testament. Second, modern forms of Marcionism will sometimes continue the matter-spirit opposition of ancient Marcionism but will frequently opt for the matter, earth, or chthonic part of the dualism, but again severed from the God of the Jews and the covenant context. This dualism can lead to idealism if it opts for the interiority or spirit dimension, to empiricism if it opts for the external world, or to a kind of retrieval of various Greek valorizations of the earth. In any case, what gets placed on the religious margins will be worship, law, and divine transcendence. In modernity, Balthasar argues, rejection of the Old Covenant and divine transcendence follows from modernity's distaste for external ("heteronomous") revelation and anything that appears to impose upon human autonomy. Thus, modern thinkers marginalize the Old Covenant and simultaneously eliminate divine transcendence and judgment. These cultural and theoretical moves serve a desire to find the measure of human existence from within the creaturely world rather than from a God who transcends, judges, and even enters that world. Marcionism, then, can sometimes be labeled "Prometheanism" by Balthasar. As Prometheus tries to steal fire from heaven, modern Marcionites claim divine glory for creation, nature, history, or the human species. In traditional terms, nature becomes conflated with salvation or grace. Immanent laws of creation / nature theoretically take the place of God's free, eventful relation with his people.

We can now specify five basic characteristics of Balthasar's "Marcionism": (1) marginalization or exclusion of Old Covenant revelation; (2) rejection or marginalization of juridical and judicial elements of religion; (3) conflation or confusion of creation and salvation; (4) human self-glorification or erasure of divine transcendence fundamental to Judaism and traditional Christianity; and (5) a tendency towards docetic forms of Christology.

One final note on Balthasar's "modern Marcionism." Balthasar observes two ways in which the five elements of Marcionism may come together. One version of Marcionism is the more obvious dualist variety that cuts off Old Covenant from New and holds them as fundamentally opposed to one another. Another version is evolutionary in that it holds revelation to be progressing from Old Covenant to New. This view could be orthodox, save that it views Old Covenant forms of revelation as obsolete once New Covenant revelation occurs. Some attempt may be made to salvage a bare minimum of material from the Old Covenant (i.e., the unity of God) but nothing having to do with the content of Israel's relation to God. The same progress can also render the New Covenant obsolete either in the present or the near future. For Balthasar, the common thread is the rejection of Old Covenant revelation, the formalizing, material emptying, and dis-incarnating of Christian belief, and the idolatry of human being. Finally, these different theoretical moves combine to empty out traditional Christian rationale for praise, or what we might call "doxological existence."

C. Theology of Religion: The Capacious Cross

"The Truth" for us is everything Christ was from his childhood to his death, and the eternal and infinite dimension of this truth was revealed in the Resurrection. Even the most humble of truths was redeemed by Christ, ... just like anyone at random from among us Christians. The

humblest truth, I say, has a share in the divinity of him who deigned to put on our nature—thus making us consortes ejus divinitatis [partakers of the divine nature].

Georges Bernanos, *Scandale de la vérité* (Paris: Gallimard, 1939), p. 57.[30]

THE ABOVE PASSAGE IS QUOTED BY BALTHASAR in his fascinating study of Bernanos, and it expresses with near perfection Balthasar's own theology of religions. Directly after he quotes this passage, Balthasar reminds the reader that this elevation of the human into the divine happens not by way of a law of nature, but only by "God in a deed of the most extraordinary freedom, and by virtue of his absolutely creative love, which makes an unfathomable choice and election coincide with God's wisdom."[31]

For Balthasar, the Cross and Resurrection are the central events of God's self-interpretation for the world. From this hermeneutic center, Jesus reaches back to the Father as the Alpha, the Beginning of all reality and forward to the Spirit as the world's Omega. In other words, through the Son's "unabbreviated human life from conception to death,"[32] a space opens up in God for all of human history and culture. While the Incarnation and Cross certainly represent God's judgment on the world's darkness and alienation, for Balthasar they show more than anything God's affirmation of the world in its very creaturely reality. Judgment, he thinks, always takes place for the sake of affirmation. Moreover, this "space" should not be thought of only along the vertical axis of the Cross; the horizontal axis, which represents history, is present as well, since the Son who becomes human, does so through the action of the Father and Spirit in continuity with the ongoing life of a historical people: Israel. Indeed, for Balthasar it is Israel that will carry the religious patterns of the world to the New Covenant to be taken up and granted space within eternity through the opening that is Christ's form. Right now this will all seem abstract and *a priori*, and is necessarily so in an introduction. What is clear, however, is that Balthasar believes that the many and varied aspirations for transcendence, expressed through the world's literature, philosophy, art, and religion, can be caught up, given their proper place, and included without violence within the pattern of redemption opened in the kenotic self-abandonment of God's Son.

Marcion and Prometheus is about the gathering and redemption of truths found throughout civilization to the glory of God's name. In this sense, this book is about right worship more than salvation, doxology more than soteriology. In this giving of glory, the Christian follows along the path of God's own affirmation of Being, of the divine work in creation. Indeed, for Balthasar, Christians are responsible for attention and care of the goods of Being wherever they may be found. This means that for him engagement with metaphysics is necessary for the Christian theologian. It is this engagement that will illuminate genuine analogies to divine glory from within philosophical, literary, artistic, and religious expressions that are pre- or extra-Christian. Moreover, these analogies will not be to any God whatsoever, but specifically to the God of the covenant, the God revealed as self-abandoning love in the Cross and Resurrection of Jesus Christ.

Chapter One

An Anti-Marcionite Theological Aesthetic

"It is the God of the Jews whom men's souls call God"
Tertullian *Against Marcion* I.X

We suggested in the introduction that Balthasar follows Henri de Lubac in seeking to write theology that illuminates its historical moment by the light of the gospel. Like many commentators, Balthasar seeks to grasp the underlying, or perhaps clandestine, intellectual streams that inform the historical moment that is modernity, or at least modern self-understanding as disclosed in its most prominent intellectual figures and movements. Much of the point of this chapter is to show that Balthasar's complex view of modernity is essential to his discussion of Judaism and other religions. One strand of the story he tells about modernity will be of paramount importance for us: the modern return and revitalization of Marcionism. As we have seen, Marcion argued that Christianity ought to rid itself of the Old Covenant, reject its God, and opt for portions of the New Covenant that oppose a God of mercy to a God of judgment, grace to law, redemption to creation. Thus, Marcion's vision would separate what Catholic tradition, in various and even paradoxical ways, has striven to hold together. Indeed, an observation of Balthasar's theological commitments reveals that Marcionism of any period is fundamentally opposed to his nearly Joycean vision of Catholicism: "Being Catholic means embracing everything, leaving nothing out."[33] As opposed to this inclusive and analogical embrace, Marcion would seem to think in terms of stark oppositions and stringent exclusions. Balthasar contends that Marcionite oppositions haunt modern theological and theologically accented discourse(s) and facilitate what he will call a Promethean or Titanic cultural moment. A brief sketch of how Balthasar believes this return of Marcionism takes place will help indicate some genealogical reasons for his insistence that Old Covenant revelation play a central role in Christian theology.

Balthasar finds that the basic assumptions of Marcionism—not to say exact replicas of ancient Marcionism—undergird important strains of modern thought that reject divine transcendence and judgment in favor of grace, but then turn grace into nature or nature into "supernature." In other words, the difference between creator and creature doctrinally articulated in the Catholic teaching on analogy (*analogia entis*), and founded in Scripture, disappears in most forms of modern thought in favor of what he calls "identity metaphysics." What Balthasar calls identity metaphysics takes many forms, but what they have in common is the dissolution of divine transcendence, enshrined in the biblical writings as God's glory and freedom, and the collapse of creation into redemption or the collapse of divine glory into human glory.

Such erasures of divine transcendence can, on the one hand, be considered atheistic or anti-Christian justifications of the secular moment; on the other hand, when secularism is given a Christian theological justification as the emptying (*kenosis*) of divine transcendence and the elimination of any difference between God and world on the one hand, Church and society on the other, they can just as easily be viewed as a form of Christian triumphalism. What is especially important to notice for our discussion is that the direct target of most forms of modern thought is the same as the target of Marcionism: the sovereign God of Old Covenant revelation, the God of the Jews, whom both ancient Marcionism and many influential forms of modern thought proclaim obsolete and unworthy of worship. Balthasar draws the connection by observing how many forms of modern thought follow the Marcionite practice of eliminating or marginalizing the Old Covenant, which in both cases—although more clearly in the modern than the ancient—facilitates the reduction, rationalization, or dissolution of divine transcendence into human self-glorification. This storming of the heavens, or alternatively a closing of reality off to the heavens, which he dubs Prometheanism, is latent in ancient Marcionism insofar as it works to eliminate the obviously transcendent and legislating Lord of the Old Covenant.[34] Modern forms of thought make the Prometheanism latent in ancient Marcionism prominent by juxtaposing the Old Testament God to a more domesticated or reductively immanent deity hospitable to Promethean visions of human autonomy.

But even more is at stake than the emergence of Promethean anti-Judaism. For Balthasar, Israel provides the eschatological New Covenant with a historical, religious, and theological context apart from which Jesus appears as a ghostly figure unconnected to history, culture, and religion. Like a vampire, he has no genuine form. Such an ethereal vision, Balthasar argues, runs counter to the emphasis of ecclesial tradition on Jesus as a real incarnate being who enters into the flow of history at a particular place and time and takes the traditions he is given into his own self-interpretation. Indeed, for Balthasar it is in this broad and deep solidarity with creation, history, and covenant that he becomes legible as a singular concrete figure who also bears universal significance. Running through Balthasar's work is the view that when Jesus' identity is extracted from its Jewish context, his form will be manipulated to suit whatever cultural predilections are to the fore; culture then comes to measure revelation rather than the other way around. Balthasar's focus on Jesus' relation to Israel serves to emphasize three points: a solidarity-in-relation between Christian revelation, culture, and history; the necessity of maintaining the legibility and normativity of Jesus' form (*Gestalt*); and the importance of opposing what he considers modern deformations of glory by placing the Old Testament,[35] and thus the biblical revelation that Christians share with Jews, front and center in his theology. For Balthasar, it is precisely Jesus' share in the traditions of Old Covenant faith that contrast so starkly with a Promethean view of human autonomy whose prime condition is the evacuation of Jesus' covenantal setting and historical particularity.

Perhaps even more provocatively, Balthasar argues that modern attempts to address Christian-Jewish relations have wrongly targeted central Christian doctrines such as the Trinity, Christology, and a canonical or ecclesial faith reading of Scripture as the central villains in an often disastrous history. Balthasar observes that modern theology often strives to sever its relations to Judaism and the Old Covenant while also either marginalizing or deeply transforming traditional forms of Christology, Christian biblical hermeneutics, and Trinitarian theology in a direction that runs contrary to divine personality, freedom, and sovereignty. A surprisingly contrarian conclusion follows: for Balthasar, if Marcion is the chief villain in modern anti-Judaism, then Trinitarian doctrine, biblical integrity, and a robust Christology are precisely not the culprits in Christian anti-Judaism, but instead the co-victims with Judaism of modern versions of anti-Judaism. Indeed, Balthasar argues that these central Christian doctrines, rightly understood, support a specifically Christian affirmation of Judaism, its role in salvation history, and its ongoing importance to Western culture. A further implication of this claim is that those doctrines often viewed as a "hellenizing" of Christ's simple message should instead be seen as genuine attempts to maintain the insights and practices of Jewish monotheistic religion within the life of the Church. This discussion should not indicate, however, that Balthasar replaces one simplistic opposition with another, now favoring Judaism over Hellenism. Instead, he thinks that what is at work is a complex negotiation between the form of revelation and the attempt to express this form in Greek cultural idioms, both philosophical and poetic.

We should observe that neither Balthasar's reading of the Patristic heritage vis-à-vis Hellenism nor his Promethean thesis are idiosyncratic. Alois Grillmeier, J.N.D. Kelly, Jaroslav Pelikan, and, more recently, Robert Louis Wilken argue much the same regarding early Christological and Trinitarian debates. In Grillmeier's view, for example, Christological and Trinitarian orthodoxy was largely a transformation or rejection of neo-platonic (or middle platonic) renditions of the Creator-creature relation by the light of Jewish monotheism and God's Incarnation in Christ. Orthodoxy, he contends, militates against any portrayal of God's relation to the world that cannot account for God's absolute involvement in the flesh of humanity and absolute divine transcendence or freedom simultaneously. Pelikan views Marcionism, not orthodox Christology, as a move away from Judaism toward "hellenization," whereas Trinitarian doctrine moves in the opposite direction.[36] Wilken calls for a definitive break with Adolf Harnack's "hellenization" thesis[37] and, like Grillmeier, sees the early development of doctrine as a development in constant conversation with Scripture. On the patristic end of things, then, well-known scholars would seem to endorse Balthasar's view that Christian doctrinal development was not a development away from Jewish monotheism, but a development of it such that Greek linguistic and philosophical categories had to be opened up to accommodate the new world of the biblical narrative and the divine freedom emanating from it.

If in a broad sense his reading of the early tradition finds a plurality of echoes in contemporary scholarship, so also does his concern regarding a modern Promethean (Marcionite, Gnostic) re-writing of Christian belief and practice. This concern finds cultural sympathizers as varied and prominent as Albert Camus, Eric Voegelin, Karl Löwith, Henri de Lubac, David

Walsh, and Cyril O'Regan. Each of these thinkers has noticed that an important modern view holds that secularism or secularization is not a simple removal of the divine from public discourse, but rather a will to take the divine into humanity itself, thus eliminating or vastly redefining divine transcendence.[38] The labels "Gnostic" and "Marcionite" are apt to be found in the writings of all of these thinkers as appropriate labels for significant strands of modern intellectual history.

For Balthasar, an ecclesial theology[39] can look to combat this Promethean, and also anti-Jewish, aspect of modern thought not by running away from central Christian doctrines, but by embracing them within their full biblical significance and historical development. Thus, Balthasar argues that it is the Triune God in his work for the sanctification or divinization of the world that holds together the covenantal monotheism learned from Israel with God's unprecedented openness to creation and human freedom found in Christ. In other words, it is the Christian doctrine of the Trinity, rooted in God's Incarnation, that carries forward Jewish monotheism in response to modern forms of Marcionism. He also shares with the philosophers and theologians named above the conviction that much modern thought envisions a humanity that views itself as radically autonomous and sovereign, in short, as divine. One particularly important corrective to this hubris, whether of ancient or modern provenance, is a good dose of the Old Covenant coupled with the realization that divine transcendence is not forfeited with the advent of the New Covenant.

In the process of identifying Balthasar's complex understanding of Marcionite Prometheanism as the most salient characteristic of modern religious thought, we will also find that on his reading both Marcionism and Prometheanism live off of Christianity as parasite to host, and in the process severely alter traditional interpretations of the Christian pattern of meaning or *Gestalt*. We will see in the first section of this chapter that because of the dangers he associates with both forms of thought, Balthasar believes necessary both a thorough re-presentation of the Christian form in opposition to Promethean and Marcionite de-formation, and a vigilant, ongoing Christian self-critique related to this deformation. The "hermeneutic response" section will then lay out the formal, hermeneutical characteristics of this response. In this section, I read Balthasar's theological aesthetic and ecclesial faith hermeneutic as a fundamentally anti-Marcionite interpretive strategy. I will foreground the re-presentation of the Christian form or

Gestalt. We will find an important element of Balthasar's anti-Marcionite theology in his holistic approach to Scripture, that is, his argument for the theological integrity of the biblical canon. Of course this discussion, given its formal character, cannot be conclusive because an argument for Old Covenant–New Covenant theological continuity will require an examination of Balthasar's reading of biblical content. Nevertheless, it is important to make clear Balthasar's theological presuppositions and how he relates these presuppositions to his cultural concerns. Balthasar gives a theological rationale, an aesthetic analogy, and a modern relevance to the integrity of the canon that represents a real contribution not only to ecclesial, but also to cultural self-understanding. We will underscore in this chapter the formal relationship of the Old Covenant to the New, the role of the Old Covenant in salvation history, and what we are calling the Old Covenant's "apophatic pedagogy," an instruction Balthasar believes modern thought forgets at its own peril.

Balthasar and the Genealogy of Modern Marcionism

IN THE SECOND AND THIRD CENTURIES, Marcion represented a severe threat to the perceived unity of God and God's plan that traditionally includes both Old and New Covenants. Tertullian, Irenaeus, and Clement would release all the arrows in their substantial quivers against this "menace" who "gnawed" at the gospels.[40] Balthasar renews not merely the substance of these second- and third-century concerns, but their vigor as well. He labels Marcionism a "demonic contrivance,"[41] associates it with Hitlerism,[42] and later makes this association a direct connection when he writes that Marcionism is "the first systematic form of theological anti-semitism."[43] By raising the specter of anti-Judaism, anti-semitism, and Hitlerism, Balthasar signals his view that Marcionism profoundly deforms the Christian faith and that the primary demon in modern anti-Judaism is not the ancient supersessionism of the Fathers of the Church—although they are clearly not without fault[44]—but a modern revival of an ancient heresy and its cultural displacement of traditional Christianity.

The Marcionite threat to ancient Christianity and its self-understanding is clear. Insofar as the Old Testament was regarded by many early Christians as authoritative scripture and part of their life of faith, it is understandable that they would see in Marcion a critic of their worship and practice. In addition, as a fledgling religion within the Roman Imperium, any sharp critique of Christianity's underpinnings that included the establishment of a distinct canon, and perhaps an alternative church, could be seen as endangering Christianity's very existence. Balthasar's more interesting and complex claim is that our time is, perhaps, not so different from that of early Christianity. Christians and non-Christians alike, he believes, have lost a sense for divine glory and for the Christian pattern of meaning, its attendant ethics, and the sort of logic that belongs to and supports Christian contemplation and action; in the context of such a hermeneutical vacuum, any worldview or ideology that looks something like Christianity can come to pass for it.[45] Indeed, he considers Marcionism a serious threat to Christianity in part because it resembles authentic Christianity more closely than do other and more fantastic heresies such as Valentinianism. For instance, Marcionism has an attractive modesty with respect to revelation that mimics Jewish and Christian rejection of elaborate theogonies found in Hesiod and theogonic / cosmogonic pairings found in a Valentinian text such as *The Gospel of Truth*, and other Gnostic texts such as *The Tripartite Tractate* and *The Hypostasis of the Archons*.[46] Moreover, like Christianity, Marcionism would appear to emphasize acts of charity, attend to the exoteric or plain-sense meaning of biblical passages rather than to hidden meanings available to an elite few, and link salvation to faith and grace rather than to esoteric knowledge.[47] Because of these similarities, and because of a modern return to something like the hermeneutical fluidity of the early Christian centuries, the way has been paved for the smuggling of Marcionism into the ecclesia under the guise of traditional Christianity or what purport to be legitimate interpretations of it. Thus the enemy, for Balthasar, is as likely to be found within the Church as without.[48]

For his part, Balthasar takes the side of Tertullian, the Alexandrians, and Irenaeus and argues that, appearances notwithstanding, Marcion's system impugns God's goodness as Creator and God's righteousness as Lawgiver, and thus would warrant a Christian identity hostile to Jewish belief and worship.[49] Indeed, in an exposé Balthasar obviously takes to heart, Tertullian had already labeled Marcion the "true Prometheus" in the second century.[50] In modernity, Balthasar believes, this situation only gets worse, and reviving the ancient exposé becomes more urgent when the latent Prometheanism in Marcionism identified by Tertullian becomes more explicit, and hence more powerfully hubristic; in its modern exacerbation, it more clearly opposes human autonomy to the transcendent freedom and sovereignty of Israel's God, and thus contests a Jewish and Christian spirituality of humble openness to the divine will.

The modern context, however, is complex, and Balthasar is never willing to paint all forms of thought with the same brush, even if in the end the theological verdict will be similar. This nuanced treatment is important to Balthasar not only because it makes for better argument, but also to better uncover the various avenues to a particular theological outcome and to gather some of the riches and insights that a particular discourse may promise, even if it cannot make good on the promise. Two forms of modern Marcionism become especially important in his work: anthropocentric and cosmocentric. In its anthropocentric form, Marcionism continues to reject the divine as judge or as legislating will and substitutes what Balthasar calls "autonomous freedom" for "theonomous freedom" on the ethico-political plane.[51] Balthasar thinks that modern aversion to the Old Covenant is not merely a reaction against the disturbing violence found, for instance, in the Book of Joshua, but is more nearly a rejection of any Transcendent that would seem to question absolute human autonomy. Of course this radical assertion of human autonomy has its own dangers. "Where an absolute Good has gone missing," Balthasar claims, "some relative value (the advantage of the party, the will-to-power) is posited as absolute, and ethics is trampled upon."[52] Thus, the elimination of the Old Covenant serves to eviscerate divine transcendence and freedom and to realize the Promethean thrust latent within ancient Marcionism.[53]

Ludwig Feuerbach's *The Essence of Christianity* presents a rather clear example of what Balthasar intends by a modern anthropocentric Marcionism that makes explicit the latent Prometheanism of its ancient parent. Feuerbach argues away divine transcendence as a human self-alienating projection of its own species-nature onto a remote deity. His atheism serves the purpose of reconciling humanity to its own deepest reality as a species, and thus taking back the divine nature for itself. So, for example, Feuerbach writes that God as "infinite spirit, in distinction from the finite, is therefore *nothing else* than the intelligence disengaged from the limits of individuality and corporeality."[54] Equally important to our discussion is that he relates this human self-reconciliation to a movement in religion from authoritarian and legalistic Jewish religion to Christian freedom and finally to genuine human autonomy in atheism. The paradoxical relation of transcendence and immanence evident in the Christian doctrine of Incarnation is placed on a systematic plot line that abandons the former for the latter. Transcendence becomes immanence without remainder.[55] Feuerbach's brand of humanism may be filled with good intentions; nonetheless, in the opposition he draws between the transcendent God of Judaism and Christianity on the one hand, and his own humanism on the other, the transcendent God must lose out and so must Christian worship. Balthasar argues that this kind of Prometheanism is profligate in modernity, and he thinks it turns out to be anything but a boon to humanity.

In Balthasar's discussion, a second, more earth-directed or "cosmocentric" form of Marcionism can be detected. This form of modern reversion to pre-Christian Greek thought, found for Balthasar in Romantic poets and philosophers, tends to envelop Christian revelation within a closed, fatalistic cosmos.[56] In this form of Marcionism, the dramatic interaction between divine and human freedom is lost in the stars or the cosmic gods or in the non-willing call of Being. There may still be some sort of horizontal transcendence of the human person in these systems, but no transcendence by grace to participation in eternal life and, certainly, no transcendent, free, creative, legislative, willing, loving, and divinizing God. The theological drama between the finite freedom of a creature and the infinite freedom of God the Creator will find itself reduced to various forms of inner-worldly tensions.[57] Just as for ancient Marcionism, in modern Marcionism the world of creation no longer opens up or sacramentally speaks of the ever-greater God. The difference is that for modern, pro-earth or pro-cosmic Marcionites, the banishment of the true high God from creation (the Father) opens the possibility of a new embrace of the world in purely Greco-Roman pagan terms rather than the traditional Jewish ones rejected by all types of Marcionism. While the poets and philosophers in this tradition eschew the idealism that Balthasar thinks of as *the* opponent of Christian realism,[58] nevertheless, like the idealists, they are incapable of gazing upon Creation and on all human beings as willed and gracious gifts of the Creator. Instead, Balthasar finds a reversal of the *spolatio Aegyptorum*[59]: "in the clear denial of Christian transcendence, the raiment of glory, which it reserves for the God of love and of the Cross, is removed from these and cast upon members of the universe, or of that *physis* which Heidegger called Being."[60] What makes this series of moves Marcionite, rather than simply Promethean, is the appropriation of the Christian trope of divine kenosis and the univocal opposition of this trope to the transcendent, electing, and willing divine of Israel which now loses out entirely. Indeed, on Balthasar's reading this kind of Marcionism can be just as dangerous as the former type in its attempts to revivify a mythical, "primordial Greek" religious pathos that has a violent, Dionysian center.[61]

Beyond their differences, what the two kinds of Marcionism we have outlined here have in common is their antipathy to Judaism and to the God revealed in the Old Covenant. To the extent that they have contaminated Christian discourse, both forms of Marcionism would have Christianity sever its roots in Torah, Covenant, and Prophets, in short, its roots in the Jewish faith. Prometheanism can in no way countenance a God who remains other than and judge of humanity, sovereign Lord of the cosmos, and Creator. At a minimum, then, the obviously transcendent God of the Old Covenant must be abandoned. What is perhaps surprising in all of this, however, is that Balthasar considers Prometheanism a post-Christian phenomenon. The "post-," here, indicates temporal succession, but, more importantly, it indicates that Prometheanism can only be born and survive as a parasite on and deformation of a Christian host.

Balthasar's view of this parasitic relation certainly connects with other versions of Christianity's relation to modern notions of autonomy and their historical development. Hegel and Max Weber, to pick the most obvious names, each speak to the idea of the world's "disenchantment" as grounded in the transcendence of Israel's God; Mircea Eliade has a similar view, and more recently Marcel Gauchet extends this discussion to a grand narrative of the end of religion. Balthasar, however, would not affirm the end-of-religion thesis, but instead puts forth his genealogy of modern Prometheanism and Marcionism to gain traction against what he considers unnecessary corruptions and enervations of Christian faith. Balthasar's genealogical diagnosis involves a three-part movement accompanied by three shifts in worldview brought on by the rise of Judaism and Christianity: (1) Disenchantment of the Cosmos; (2) Kenosis; and (3) the anthropologization of the Christian form, what Balthasar calls "post-Christian" thought. We will discuss these in order.

Disenchantment: From Myth to History[62]

ONE OF THE HISTORICAL EFFECTS (*wirkungsgeschichte*)[63] of God's revelation to Israel, Balthasar argues, is to break open a mythical, cosmocentric perception of the God-world relation.[64] The polytheism that relates gods to forces of nature and cosmos or depicts them in all-too-human visual guises begins to fall away once Yahweh and the God of the Covenant shows himself to be Lord of these forces and Lord of the heavens.[65] Yahweh's transcendent Lordship thus de-divinizes or demythologizes the cosmos, opening it up for a dramatic and dynamic relation of freedoms between Yahweh and Israel.[66] The cosmos is no longer *cosmos theion* (divine cosmos) enclosed by Fate, but the cosmos can still be used by Israel's God to express divine glory (*kabod*) and even provide a kind of sacrament of the dramatic interaction between divine and human freedom. In Augustinian terms, creation is not the end of Christian enjoyment, but that which usefully points to the Creator and reveals his presence. More specifically, Balthasar thinks the distance between the heavens and the earth manifests the ontological "distance" or difference between the creature and the Creator who can, because of this distance, enter into dialogue and dramatic interaction with the creature at his will.[67] Thus, Israel gives to the world a truly transcendent God, but in doing so subtracts divinity from the cosmos itself. The cosmos in no way circumscribes divinity or presents itself as divine. Yahweh speaks from the cloud; he is not to be confused with it.

It is precisely this opening up to divine transcendence that, Balthasar thinks, will be rejected by Romantic philosophers and poets to the detriment of traditional sacramental conceptions of nature and traditional understandings of God: nature because it can no longer be received as a purposeful gift willed and loved by its Creator; God because he loses the transcendence and freedom that would specify divine action as worthy of gratitude. Instead, Goethe, Rilke, and Heidegger, at least if we are referring to Balthasar's general and final verdict rather than his rich appreciation of each author, attempt to go behind this opening up of the cosmos to transcendence in the Old Covenant and to lock Yahweh within a kind of cosmic fate (*moira*) or make of him, and Jesus, members of a new pantheon. These attempts to digest biblical revelation and glory into a foreign system, however, are doomed to failure, Balthasar thinks, because after Christ the religion and gods of Greece always suffer under a suspicion that they are mere names for cosmic or psychological forces and because, for Christians, they are utterly unable to represent the sovereign glory of the biblical God and the Creator-creature difference that is necessary for all the kinds of wonder, contemplation, and glory that these same Romantic authors rightly wish to sustain.[68]

To the extent that modern thinkers locate in Israel's revelation a demythologization of the cosmos, Balthasar agrees with them. He also suggests, however, that this way of telling the story of Israel's religion is far too convenient a justification for modern secular culture and far too simplistic to capture the full significance of divine transcendence in the Old Covenant. For Balthasar, Old Covenant transcendence should not be reduced to a mere removal or subtraction exercise; instead, the elevation of the personal God above cosmic law accompanies and supports an eventful "downward" movement of God's word in the prophets on the one hand, and a dynamic opening up of future hope in messianism on the other. Balthasar believes that the descent of God's word (*dabar*) in the prophets, which he designates in dynamic terms as the "prophetic staircase," indicates God's desire to share the divine life with Israel, and through Israel all humanity, in an increasingly profound way.[69] On Balthasar's interpretation, it would seem that the prophetic staircase gets taken into a broader, apocalyptic opening up of heaven to earth, the Creator to the creature. On the one hand, then, the shift in worldview from myth to history can be characterized negatively as the exclusion of divinity from the cosmos in classical Weberian terms; on the other hand, however, this shift, if it is to represent the movement of the Old Covenant, also suggests a new sense of divine-human interaction and a deeper development of intimacy. The history of human freedom now becomes recognizable as an element of God's plan, a preparation and education towards a divinely given goal, namely, the world's share in God's own life.[70]

While such a covenantal view of history does rule out a form of secularism that proclaims absolute human autonomy, Israel's revelation nevertheless makes possible a relative form of the autonomy of nature and human culture. This is a central element of Balthasar's argument in his books on Karl Barth and Maximus the Confessor.[71] For Balthasar and for Henri de Lubac, nature and grace are not collapsible either from the side of nature or from the side of grace; yet neither are they opposed realities. Nature retains some kind of relative autonomy that contributes to the content of redemption brought to fruition in Christ. Israel's own covenant contributes to the New Covenant, in part, by disrupting a fatalistically enclosed cosmos and revealing a relation of freedoms between humanity and God, but precisely in this disruption, the world becomes *only* the world for the first time in history. Thus virulent secularism as "anti-theism" becomes a possibility as a perverted form of the Jewish sensibility for the world's relative autonomy. It is a properly covenantal relation of freedoms, and a sacramental view of the cosmos in relation to its creator, Balthasar thinks, that neither ancient myth nor modern cosmocentric and anthropocentric philosophies grasp.[72]

We should also notice here what Balthasar's reading of this shift means for his reading of Israel in relation to Promethean Marcionism. We noticed earlier that Feuerbach reads Israel as a positivistic, legalistic religion opposed to freedom. By contrast, Balthasar reads Israel as a divine pedagogy out of an inner-worldly and mythological fatalism and into a paradoxical relation of freedoms that finds its ultimate sanction and measure in the Incarnation. Through Israel, the world learns about freedom in its rightful, covenant context. Moreover, within this context, Israel's freedom does not involve them in titanic assertions of autonomy or acts of self-apotheosis. Israel is God's image, but unlike many "nations," it knows that it is not God.

Kenosis: From History to Realized Eschatology

THE SHIFT FROM HISTORY TO REALIZED ESCHATOLOGY emerges, on Balthasar's view, in the wake of the Incarnation, which for him includes the entire expanse of Christ's life, death, descent into hell, resurrection, exaltation, and even Eucharist. The Christ event marks an alteration in the meaning and structure of time as the true *eschaton*, that is, the Triune God, reveals itself in history. For Balthasar, the Trinity is the ultimate horizon, the "last thing," from which everything attains existence and towards which all things move. Through the pattern of Christ's revelation, this ultimate horizon makes an appearance that lends history its meaning, measure, and ethical norm. On this view, Christian revelation is akin to a mystery novel, where the end of the story (the *eschaton*) ties up loose ends and gives the rest of the story its coherence and meaning; with the end, everything falls into place in a way unforeseeable from within the story itself. Similarly, Christ's revelation gives meaning to all the strands and forms within Old Covenant history, and, on a larger canvas, to all of world history. Yet unlike the mystery novel, in Christian revelation the end erupts from within the middle of history and intensifies the dramatic energy and tension of the story. This is what Balthasar means by the movement into "theo-drama" proper, and this intensification also justifies his claim that while a Christian eschatology is a "realized" eschatology, it is also a relative eschatology. In other words, Christ's Incarnation does not end God's work in history or render everything that comes after a mere epilogue. Balthasar is thoroughly anti-triumphalist. What it does mean is that human existence in history is no longer moving in a simple linear way toward a future apocalypse, but is charged now with responding to the apocalypse or unveiling of Christ in the present. Every moment in history is now related directly to Christ's revelation of love as its inner significance.

If Balthasar believes that a reduction of Old Covenant revelation to disenchantment forms one leg of a Promethean and Marcionite distortion of Christian thought, he also believes that the Christian doctrine of kenosis plays host to another kind of distortion that again serves Promethean interests. Whereas the first distortion empties the world of the divine, the second collapses the ontological difference between the world, or at least human being in the world, and God. One way to put this, in Balthasar's terms, is that the Christian doctrine of kenosis, which represents a realized but relative eschatology, gets exchanged for either an unrealized absolute eschatology (Marxism) or a realized absolute eschatology (Hegel). The general pattern of these distortions can become clear through a brief juxtaposition of two ways in which the Christian story is told. The first is a generalized version of the traditional narrative, while the second represents a generalized version of a Promethean telling.

For Balthasar, the transcendent God of the Old Covenant seeks to instruct Israel in God's own ways so that this people can truly become a divine image in and for the world. The assumption in this traditional telling of the story is that human beings have sinned against God, and thus God's image is profoundly obscured in history (though not obliterated or lost). History has become a scene of self-seeking power rather than proper worship, righteousness, and compassion. God's pedagogy of Israel is to lead Israel towards genuine freedom from sin, communal righteousness, kindness, and humility, and into an ever-greater participation in God's own life. In this telling of the story, Christ comes to reconcile a sinful world to God. He must come "from above" so as to really unite creation *with God*, and must truly penetrate creation so that God is really united *with the world*. This traditional telling of the story does not end here. Rather, it continues through Christ's assumption of the sinful structures of the flesh (*Verbum-Caro*) in the Cross and the descent into hell, and through his Resurrection and exaltation. Resurrection and exaltation are important for they complete the cycle of the Son's coming from and returning to his unity with the Creator and transcendent God of the Old Covenant. They also demonstrate the inherent value of the individual to God, and prepare the way for the sending of the Spirit, Balthasar's expert witness, interpreter, and guide into the Truth that is Christ and into the relation of love between the Father and the Son. Finally, we should mention the Eucharist: for Balthasar the "incarnational curriculum," to invoke Mongrain's phrase, is not complete until his pouring out of himself continues in the Eucharistic celebration and life of the Church.

In Balthasar's interpretation of the modern Marcionite and Promethean version, it will be divine-human difference, rather than human sin, that is viewed as the offense to genuine human freedom or autonomy. Given this different axiological stress on autonomy, the Old Covenant God understood as external lawgiver comes to symbolize human self-alienation. The God of the Old Covenant is now perceived as the God who issues external commands and violates human autonomy. In addition, the original goodness of Creation, what Balthasar and Catholic tradition will envision in quasi-sacramental terms, is also called into question. Hegel, for instance, will not accept the fundamental goodness of creation, but instead views Creation itself as a form of divine self-alienation that can only become good teleologically.[73] If creation is understood as divine alienation, then it makes sense that "reconciliation" comes to signify that the divine, understood as transcendent Creator and judge, dies on the Cross in such a way that divine transcendence itself comes to an end. Notice that for this version of the story it is not so much human sin that requires reconciliation; instead, this view "corrects" the traditional Christian view that God and finite spirit are essentially different by envisioning a divine-human reconciliation of nature. We have also noticed some of this version of the story in Feuerbach's view of Judaism. For him, Jewish religion is dialectically opposed to the Incarnation, rather than a preparatory sketch or type of it. Atheism is understood in terms of human authenticity or the re-integration of human species-being.

At the end of the Christian story, we have equally severe differences. In the traditional version of the Christian story, resurrection and exaltation reunite the Son and Father as the one plan of salvation completes its circuit. In this second story, however, no transcendent God remains. In a kind of extreme patripassianism, the transcendent God of Scripture gives Himself without remainder into history, and history comes to full self-consciousness when it realizes humanity's own divine nature. Here, autonomy is radicalized to mean the freedom from a transcendent deity rather than a more traditional view of freedom as freedom *from* sin and *for* a communal and individual mission to the world by virtue of grace.

Of course this discussion of competing stories admits of a far more nuanced and complex discussion. But for our purpose, this simplified version should help clarify how an alternative anti-Judaic and anti-biblical reading of the Christian story, with a different axiology and thus a different rendition of the plot, can torque Christian identity in the direction of Prometheanism. We might also notice that to say a different "axiology" is to indicate a different ordering of praise and what one finds praiseworthy. The Promethean, in Balthasar's view, is not one who eschews social responsibility; indeed, "autonomy" in a modern sense indicates individual moral responsibility. But the Promethean will find praiseworthy the inner-historical construction of a kingdom regardless of whether or not coercion is necessary to that construction. This is what is meant by an unrealized absolute eschatology. Marxist eschatology seeks the building of the kingdom through an inner-historical event which has not yet occurred. But the kingdom is to be fully realized temporally. Of course the flip-side of this inner-historical kingdom-making is that the transcendent standards placed on autonomy will find themselves banished from the Republic like Plato's poor poets, but now without return. Balthasar sees in these inner-historical kingdom constructions, ironically enough, a reversion to messianic Judaism separated from any covenant context that would give messianism a transcendent norm. Peter Henrici finds in Balthasar's study of German thought a key expression of the axiological contrast we have been developing here: the "love of power" versus the "power of love."[74] Balthasar replays this contrast in *GL1* in terms of a glory defined by the lust for power and a glory defined by adoration and service.[75] From the standpoint of a love of power, the Prometheans may still speak of the Old Covenant and its religion as a dialectical preparation for the New Covenant, but this dialectic is only the presupposition for the overcoming of a God who would place transcendent limits on violent personal and national, and perhaps even ecclesiastical, ambitions.[76] By contrast, Balthasar, following Irenaeus, reads the Old Covenant as the work of the Father's two hands, the Son and the Spirit, as they educate and prepare Israel and the world to be formed by Christ's eschatological revelation.[77] Here, the people of God gains form in and through its readiness to receive its defining mission from God, a mission always intended to serve the world in non-coercive humility.

The differences between Christianity and Judaism, on the one hand, and Promethean forms of Marcionism on the other, are rather pronounced with regard to the different stories they tell, the different foci of praise that follow, and the different ethical stances that would result. Yet, Balthasar notices that Christianity's claims for the divinization of humanity by grace make possible these alternative Marcionite-Promethean interpretations that rationalize away the paradox of the Incarnation and allow divine glory to become humanity's own natural glory.[78] In other words, the Christian belief in divine-human intimacy provides a cultural pre-condition for Prometheanism, even if it can only come to fruition through an outright rebellion against the Christian God, in a gesture that de Lubac labels "anti-theism."[79]

Modern Loss of Glory: Anthropocentric and Cosmocentric

AS WE HAVE SEEN, the anthropocentric iteration of Marcionism draws into itself the disenchantment of the world executed by the Old Covenant and the extreme intimacy between God and creation revealed in God's kenosis, and then thoroughly and totally transforms these elements in order to claim divinity for humanity's very being.[80] Balthasar does considerable work in *GL5* to detail variations on modern resistance to what the Bible calls glory. He also resists the temptation to flatten the story, and instead gives a nuanced, at times equivocating, discussion of different figures and movements. Broadly speaking, Balthasar's main question in *GL4* and *GL5*, that is, in his volumes on metaphysics ancient and modern, is whether a particular form of thought permits the conditions for an encounter with divine glory—and thus for Christian doxology, action, and logic—or not. His judgments are complex because thinkers are complex and they may seem to present the Christian form precisely where they obscure it, or present aspects of it that get undermined by a counter-emphasis. Balthasar thinks that a discerning theological eye is capable of making judgments of more and less, as in more or less reflective of biblical glory, and need not limit judgment to Yes or No. This does not keep him from ringing in final verdicts, and in our brief account that is often all I can give, thus sacrificing much of his nuance.

Balthasar thinks that a variety of modern discourses, including Romantic poetry, rationalist ethics, German idealism and materialism, and some forms of phenomenology, frequently make the biblical form of glory subservient to forms of metaphysics hostile to Christian and Jewish faith. The cultural causes for these shifts are plural and complex, but Balthasar certainly includes the fourteenth-century breakdown of the Thomist synthesis, and the consequent severance between God's glory in creation and the human capacity to contemplate this glory as God's glory. Renaissance humanism, he argues, then attempts to re-conjure this lost connection, and rightly sought aid in a return to ancient sources, but also runs the danger of naturalizing the supernatural.[81] Science and its accidental metaphysical partners—atomism, materialism, and atheism—challenged traditional religious claims, as did the Reformation. Of course he also includes the subsequent fragmentation of religion and religious wars which hardly supported the centrality of Christian doctrines.[82]

In Balthasar's view, this cultural backdrop supports a darkening of divine glory in creation and a slow but definite suffocation of human transcendence. The turn in the Enlightenment to ethics as the site of religious truth is a great reduction of biblical glory ostensibly on behalf of human autonomy. Balthasar, of course, is not opposed to personal responsibility and freedom, and consistently opposes any scent of integralism. However, Enlightenment visions of autonomy often oppose "autonomous" religion not only to arbitrary authority, but also to objective and historical revelation viewed as "heteronomous" or as an imposition on free rationality. The overwhelming "more" of divine glory, experienced in creation and salvation history, now becomes subject to a rationalist measure, gradually becomes limited to a rational ethics, and loses its excessive and awesome character. Revelation will be stripped down,[83] negative theology will vanish,[84] and the Old Covenant will repeatedly suffer scorn as its undomesticated God must be brought to heel.[85] In different ways, both rationalist-ethical and Romantic thought dissolve divine glory into human or cosmic glory.[86] The Incarnation will soon be interpreted not as a singular event that occurs in one person at one time in history, but as a symbol of humanly constituted glory. The collapse between creation and redemption, which Balthasar also finds in Romantic theology,[87] could not be more glaring. To return to an earlier Balthasar image, Yahweh is truly "thrown on the scrapheap," that is, rationalized away or dissolved by an interpretation of the Incarnation that forfeits the resurrection and exaltation of Christ, the personal vitality and freedom of God, and, of course, divine mystery.

If we look to locate in Balthasar's work a historical figure who acts as a pivot where Marcionism and Prometheanism begin to merge and develop energy, it becomes clear that he follows the thesis of Henri de Lubac[88] in arguing for the twelfth-century Benedictine abbot and visionary, Joachim de Fiore.[89] Joachim saw revelation in terms of successive and progressive epochs, each epoch linked to (and not merely generically associated with) one divine person. The first epoch is that of the Father, and is linked to creation, Law, and justice; the second epoch is that of the Son, charity, and the sacramental-institutional church; the third epoch, which Joachim viewed as future, not present, would constitute the age of the Spirit, the end of hierarchical church order, and a new stage of human autonomy. On Balthasar's reading, Joachim's Enlightenment and post-Enlightenment interpreters seize on his heightened claims for human autonomy in the third age and then exaggerate those claims further by attributing the "radiance" of the incarnate word to "man himself."[90] Of particular importance to Balthasar is the support that Joachim's epochalism lends to schemas of revelation that would consign each previous stage of revelation to theological obsolescence in view of a newer stage of human development. This form of epochalism or progressivism will necessarily oppose later developments of autonomy to earlier stages of revelation. Thus the Old Covenant can be revelation at one stage of history, and also passé when juxtaposed to the New. Gotthold Lessing consciously takes on a version of Joachim's view in the eighteenth century as does Gianni Vattimo more recently.[91] While these authors, unlike Joachim, link their own time to the third epoch, they carry forward Joachim's developmental schema by placing divine judgment and transcendence in the past. Divinity becomes entirely immanent, while the revelation of the Old Covenant is viewed as definitively surpassed.

More important to Balthasar than Lessing will be Marx and Hegel, each of whom he sees as problem children of Marcion and Joachim. It might be wondered whether Joachim can stand as a genealogical reference point for both a pre-Incarnation messianism such as Marxism *and* a post-Incarnation pneumatocentric or Spirit-centered form of thought such as Hegel's. Marx is particularly likely to reject Joachimite paternity given that, in the relevant space of the Marxist system, the incarnation or apocalypse-revolution has not yet occurred, whereas for Joachim the Incarnation certainly has occurred. What Balthasar points out, however, is that insofar as Joachim's system comes to signify a movement of human autonomy beyond the stage of the Son, it helps to relativize the Incarnation itself and make it a preparatory stage akin to the Old Covenant. In Balthasar's view, this is to turn Christian hope back into a form of Jewish hope or eschatology that is unrealized and that, when severed from its theonomous context, will seek its absolute resolution in a coming period of history. It is in this way that he finds Marx to be Joachimite. It is important to recognize, however, that while Balthasar does think unrealized eschatology, especially of the Marxist variety, is dangerous, and that he does associate this eschatology with Judaism, he is also usually clear that what he is referring to is a kind of inner-historical absolute hope that avoids or abolishes its properly Jewish context, that is, its faith in Yahweh. Put simply, the issue is a form of secularized Judaism, not covenant Judaism.[92]

If Joachim provides a less than adequate, though plausible, paternity for Marx, it will be in part because he provides a far more plausible paternity for Hegel, the father Marx rejects, but not without carrying his genes. Hegel falls on the Gnostic side of the Incarnation that would iron out its paradoxes and conclude with a rational explanatory system that expels all divine mystery, and, by the end, divine personality and freedom.[93] The father-son relationship here is complex, and Cyril O'Regan has persuasively argued that Joachim does not provide the sole hermeneutic key to Hegel's system.[94] What Hegel and Joachim do however share, among other things, is a developmental scheme where the third and last stage, the stage of spirit, would juxtapose divine immanence to former periods of divine otherness and incarnational Christianity. O'Regan puts it this way: "Hegel, like Joachim, dismantles the *historia sacra / historia profana* distinction."[95] This reduction of difference to identity becomes more troubling when Hegel argues that the state can be understood as the Kingdom of God: "It is axiomatic in *LPH* [*Lectures on the History of Philosophy*] that the State has as much right to be identified with the Kingdom of God as the sphere of Church Christianity."[96] O'Regan would support De Lubac's genealogy, which Balthasar picks up for his own use, though in the process change its justification and argue that Joachim would need much in the way of supplementation to provide an adequate genealogical account of Hegelian thought.[97] Whatever the case genealogically, Balthasar finds in Hegel a realized absolute eschatology that Marx himself protested in the nineteenth century.

What comes to light, however, in this brief discussion of Balthasar's genealogy is that for Balthasar modern Marcionism in its anthropocentric iteration will frequently take on a developmental or evolutionary character perhaps implied, but never undertaken by Marcion himself. Whereas Marcion opted for a polytheistic dualism, modern, post-Christian thinkers such as Hegel and Marx replace his dualism with an evolutionary system of revelatory stages. The effect, however, is much the same: Old Testament revelation will be viewed as opposed to that of the New Testament, and divine transcendence will be opposed to divine immanence.

It is Balthasar's contention that Marcionite deformation reaches its acme in the systems of Hegel and Marx, each of whom, he argues, substitute an immanent and impersonal principle of history for the free, transcendent God of Christian tradition, oppose Old to New Covenant, and remove most of the conditions necessary for Christian praise and reverence. In *Mysterium Paschale*, Balthasar makes many of the connections we are pursuing here:

> ... *it should be observed that Luther's static dialectic between Law and Gospel (Old Testament and New), continues in a sense the ancient static dialectic of Gnosis, and of Marcion, while Hegel's early writings take us back, via Luther, to this primordially gnostic Anti-Judaism: the Cross, in the final analysis, is the "tearing apart" of Judaism— that Judaism which becomes, with the New Testament, itself a tearing force. It is no longer, then, the Cross of Jesus but a "dialectical situation" (with Marcion, located between the true God and the world-ruler) in which one can only suffer.*[98]

Leaving aside the complex question of Balthasar's association of Luther with Hegel and Marcion, this passage shows his central concern that the Marcionite drift of modern thought not only opposes Old to New Covenant, but also systematically reduces divine freedom and transcendence to inner-historical theoretical laws. Balthasar also shows an interest in the strategic misinterpretations of the Christian form performed by German Idealism:

> *But philosophical necessity binds God and his revelation, man, one to the other. Man is himself the manifest God, and therefore these titanic cathedrals must always lack what is decisive in Christianity, although they have absorbed all else from it: viz., that which is called in the Bible "glory." Being, God, is ultimately overcome. The Old Testament, which is the site of emergent glory, is rejected in favor of the Johannine final form of the New Testament, disassociated from Paul and the synoptics, in order to be able to reinterpret agape directly and freely in the direction of gnosis.*[99]

On his reading, the idealists turn a free divine-human dialogue into a tight and necessary dialectic, elevate knowledge above love, dismiss the glory of the Old Covenant, and eliminate the divine-human difference essential to biblical testimony and to a dialogue of freedoms. Hegel comes in for criticism precisely on these points:

> *In his insatiable and hateful polemic against the Old Testament, Hegel pursues the one element for which he has no use in his otherwise all-reconciling system: the sovereign and lordly elevation of God above the world, who acts, elects, and rejects in complete freedom of will.*[100]

Hegel's polemic, Balthasar observes, does not cease at the biblical door. Post-biblical Judaism too receives his condemnations. The Marcionite thrust of Hegelian thought severs Jewish legalistic abstractness from Christian concrete reconciling love. Thus, on Balthasar's reading, Hegel opposes love to law and traps divine mystery in a knowable system.

Balthasar thinks that Marx too substitutes for the personal promise of Yahweh "an abstract principle of hope that is empty, cheerless, and grounded on nothing but itself."[101] Marxism depersonalizes God's relation to the world, transforms Yahweh's transcendence into economic fatalism or into an abstract hope that is self-grounding, and substitutes an unrealized (absolute) eschatology for a realized (relative) eschatology that Balthasar finds in the New Testament. Neither the free, personal vitality of the Old Covenant God, nor genuine Incarnation is present in the Marxist system, both of which get sacrificed for a systematic view of historical development. If we can continue to speak at all of salvation in this context, we must admit that it derives from laws of development intrinsic to historical processes themselves, and not from "above" them.

We have established, then, that for Balthasar Prometheanism is fundamentally a post-Christian style of thought[102] that lives parasitically on its Christian host. It finds a natural habitat in Marcionite discourse and embeds itself there. But this sets up a profound challenge for Christian theology. If it is true that Prometheanism feeds off central elements of Christian faith, then it follows that the Church must practice constant vigilance against the transformation of divine transcendence and kenosis into human glory. Christianity must simultaneously refuse to degrade the goodness of the world and the real dignity of God's image and likeness. Indeed, Camus and Walsh, along with Tertullian,[103] each point out that what we are calling Promethean Marcionism is frequently a result of a felt alienation from this world and rebellion against its creator. Degrading the image of God or creation is no answer to Prometheanism. In this sense, Balthasar's relation to cosmocentric and anthropocentric Marcionism is asymmetrical. He finds much more to praise in the contemplative, receptive, and often thankful stance of the cosmocentric authors of modern Marcionism, such as Goethe, Rilke, and Hölderlin, and in Heidegger's emphasis on wonder, gratitude, and receptivity, than he ever will in anthropocentric iterations of Marcionism. In Balthasar's view, Christian theology must walk a razor's edge, always recognizing the *grandeur* and *miserere* (Pascal) of being human, and the non-divine, yet sacramental character of creation. We will see in our next section that Balthasar puts forth God's covenant with Israel as central to maintaining this frequently elusive balance.[104]

Two consequences of these modern developments, especially of the anthropocentric variety, stand out in Balthasar's analysis. The first is the loss of beauty as a transcendental characteristic of worldly being that serves as an analogy to divine glory.[105] We have said previously that Judaism removes the divine from the confines of creation, and thus leaves a world that is no longer, in itself, divine. For Balthasar this is no great gain unless the newly disclosed transcendent glory is still disclosed in the "clay" of creation that God can mold to reveal himself, through historical events, and through different forms of relationship between Israel and its God. Within a covenantal worldview, God still discloses his glory through the created order and in the various historical forms that mediate grace. By contrast, many modern philosophical and cultural movements will turn to the self and away from the created world as a site of divine disclosure, thus forfeiting any objective mediation of glory.[106] Alternatively, the cosmos can receive attention, and even gratitude, but ultimately as a closed realm that prohibits transcendent, in-breaking glory and thus the world's mediating testimony to something greater than itself.

If one consequence of modern Prometheanism is a loss of creation's ability to mediate divine glory, a second consequence, not unrelated to the first, is a movement towards secular utopianism. The two are related in the anthropocentric version of Marcionism through forms of secular utopianism that focus entirely on human history and disdain a contemplative stance vis-à-vis the world of nature. History now becomes the scene of a humanity bent on constructing the kingdom of God from its own resources in as coercive a manner as deemed necessary. Balthasar thinks that this movement, which he clearly associates with Marxism, goes behind the Incarnation to a distorted view of Jewish messianism that is separated from the Covenant norms of the Law and "liberated" for a horizontal transcendence that gives the future absolute value. Such utopianisms reject any transcendent judge beyond history's own outcome, and care little for individual lives. The messianic age is proclaimed as the future outgrowth of human historical forces rather than what God has done for creation out of love.

It is precisely the doctrine of the Incarnation, within a thoroughly Trinitarian horizon, that Balthasar thinks is the key to a Christian response to Promethean Marcionism. However, far from ignoring the legitimate cry of suffering that the protesting atheist sends out, Balthasar contests Promethean modernity in part by hearing its protests against human suffering, and showing Trinitarian theology as a unity of the transcendent and ethical divine on the one hand, and divine immanence and solidarity in human suffering on the other. That is, he seeks to restore the unity of divine justice and love by way of Trinitarian theology. His anti-Marcionite Trinitarian emphasis is clear in this passage on Ernst Bloch:

> *This is why Ernst Bloch's "Atheism in Christianity" (1968) is possible only by pressing into service the whole gnostic arsenal (Ophites, Marcion, Valentinus) against the Bible's indissoluble trinitarian union of old covenant and new. The new attempt shows once again that gnosis and atheism go together, and that they are in fact the alternative to Christian trinitarian theology. If one throws Yahweh on the scrapheap for the sake of a "principle of hope" and a "theology of the future," there will never be any possibility of making the transcendence with Jesus to a God who is still "a God to come."*[107]

It is Trinitarian theology, Balthasar believes, that can maintain the unity between Israel's revelation and Christianity, divine transcendence and divine immanence, and a genuine sense of hope. Balthasar will stress the passionate relation a God who gives up his "traditional privileges" bears to human suffering. Through Christ, God reveals divine glory as love:[108]

> *What is born of the Christian hope, deeper than all the pangs of the cosmos, is God himself: not the God of the ancient kabōd, which in his Heaven he cannot give up, but the God whose love for the world has made him "strip" himself of the form of his heavenly glory, so that he may find it once more with us.... this glory will never again be the inalienable kabōd of old, but the glory of the triune love that has appeared in him.*[109]

For Balthasar, divine love becomes the measure by which Christians must judge human action. Love and judgment are not revealed as opposed, but rather judgment is the form that divine love takes in the case of evil and sin. Christ's judgment will be an act of "subjection and forming anew," "judgment and division on the part of a love that is now 'exalted' and 'ruling.'"[110] The New Covenant maintains Yahweh's glory as "God's free personal vitality, the basis and fullness of which are disclosed in the trinitarian love."[111] No doubt Balthasar intends a surpassing of the God revealed at least in aspects of the Old Covenant, but there is likewise no doubt that he wants to stress God's transcendence, learned from the Old Covenant and maintained by the New, as a continuing block against Prometheanism. God remains judge.[112] Once thought rids itself of Yahweh, it also rids culture of a God who is not us.[113]

The Hermeneutics of Anti-Marcionism

THIS SECTION INVESTIGATES the formal, hermeneutical options Balthasar believes offer a strong first line of defense against Marcionism and its modern, anti-Jewish corruptions of Christian belief. I am particularly interested in demonstrating the link in his thought between a contemplative receptivity to the whole form of revelation, which engenders what he calls "true gnosis," and his anti-Marcionite project. Two hermeneutic elements of Balthasar's thought are of special importance here. The first has to do with Balthasar's view that theology never gets beyond faith, but rather is a process of seeking that comes to a more profound and holistic grasping of faith's inner meaning and its significance for the interpretation of all reality. This discussion will be brief since it is essentially a formal prolegomenon to our discussion of the second hermeneutical element, namely, Balthasar's analogy between encountering a beautiful form and encountering divine glory. Balthasar thinks that at this time in our cultural moment, it is important to think of revelation, both subjectively and objectively, in terms of an analogy to the human encounter with a beautiful form. The remainder of our chapter will take up what Balthasar believes this analogy entails and how this aesthetic analogy, joined to his view of the relation of *Vorstellung* and *Begriff* (representational thought to conceptual thought), provides hermeneutical support for his theological anti-Marcionism. Lastly, we will discuss the important role that Old Covenant revelation promises to play in any Christian confrontation with the kinds of modern ideological movements we discussed earlier. This discussion concerns what we are calling the Old Testament's "apophatic" function.

True *Gnosis* and the Unity of Revelatory Form

JOSEPH KOMONCHAK AND FERGUS KERR have both stressed the tendency of *ressourcement theologie*, as it broke from its neo-scholastic past, to emphasize not so much reasoning up to faith, but rather faith's hermeneutical function as the prime Christian interpreter of reality.[114] In order to distinguish Balthasar from Hegel, Kevin Mongrain has brought into play the distinction, so important to Hegel's philosophy of religion, between *Vorstellung* and *Begriff*. For Hegel, *Vorstellung* names representational, symbolic, or pictorial thought from the most rudimentary to the most sophisticated of senses. It can cover scriptural descriptions of the serpent, proclamations of divine justice, traditional Trinitarian doctrine, and the entire Christian narrative which, as we have seen, he views in progressivist terms. In Hegel's system, revelatory *Vorstellungen* are on their way to receive a conceptual, philosophical rendition that improves upon and makes obsolete much of their symbolic, positive, and thus finite, expression. Representation gets sublated into concept, and the conceptual needs of the Hegelian system regulate or "police" the symbolic world of revelation, that is, they remove from revelation any aspects that are merely representational and therefore limited. Philosophy, then, liberates the infinite content from the finite expression, maintains the infinite content of revelation, and gives it a new conceptual form and justification.[115]

Balthasar does not believe that altering the form of revelation maintains Christian content or identity. To the contrary, as we have begun to see, he believes that Hegelian trans-formation is also a de-formation in an anti-Jewish, Marcionite or Gnostic direction. Balthasar wants to contrast Hegel's tightly systematic movement from faith, understood in terms of narrative-symbolic and polyvalent language (*Vorstellung*), to knowledge, understood in terms of conceptual, univocal language, on the one hand, to what he considers a biblical and patristic view of Christian *pistis* (faith) and *gnosis* (knowledge) on the other. Balthasar has in mind especially John, Paul, Origen, and Clement of Alexandria when he presents faith and knowledge as ineluctably intertwined in a reciprocal relationship. This presentation springs, in part, from his agreement with Hegel that the only mystery in scripture is the mystery that is revealed. In other words, Christianity is a revealed religion, and thus cannot exclude knowledge. Thus, "faith" will include both the subjective disposition of humble receptivity and trust on the one hand, *and* response to an objective divinely revealed content on the other.[116] *Gnosis*, then, is not an abstraction that either departs from faith or comes only in the next life, but is inherent to the act of faith itself grasped as response to a personal Other. Faith depends upon God's self-revelation such that faith's true *gnosis* is always a departing from self into the God who desires to be known and desires to give joy.[117] For Balthasar, this reading suggests a Johannine riposte to Hegel and his progeny on a number of levels. First, Balthasar will argue that for John, love alone mediates *gnosis*,[118] that is, God's desire to share the divine life with creation is the purpose and only justification for the act of faith and the knowledge that comes with it; this means that for Balthasar, knowledge is justified by love, and not the other way around. Second, true *gnosis* requires receptivity to divine grace, a humble "pliancy" to God evident throughout the Old Covenant, and must never get beyond this fundamental disposition to a Promethean identity philosophy. Of equal importance is that for Balthasar this "pliancy" means that love and law are not opposed in either the Old or New Covenant. Law helps develop in sinful, self-centered humanity the kind of availability to God and others necessary for love.[119] It will become clear in the next chapter that Balthasar finds in Israel the basic model for this disposition, and that he directly opposes this kind of *gnosis* to Promethean forms of Marcionism in general, and to Hegel in particular. Third, Balthasar contends that faith requires the personal categories that we find in the biblical *Vorstellungen*, and these must not be reduced or resolved into "disincarnating" or abstract categories, whether these categories take the form of Catholic propositionalism, Hegelian *Begriffe*, or even a kind of "imageless inwardness" found in subjectivist streams of neo-Bultmannian thought.[120] Christian *gnosis* is not a movement away from the symbolic language of faith, but rather a grasp of its meaning and its interconnectedness so that *gnosis* passes beyond mere acceptance of authority or knowledge of individual pieces of Christian truth to a contemplation of the dynamic pattern (*Gestalt*) of revelation, and, finally, to the stage of personal expropriation for a mission of service. Thus, the goal of the genuinely Christian Gnostic is not to reach beyond faith to knowledge, but to attain a more profound and holistic grasp of the *Vorstellungen* of faith in their meaning, their interrelation, and their significance for self, community, and cosmos. In this sense, the Christian pattern of redemption will regulate conceptual articulation of faith and Christian identity.

Balthasar thinks that the form of revelation and its non-manipulative reception by the Christian community is a central condition for true *gnosis*. It is conceivable, however, that Marcion, if confronted with the claim that he manipulated the content of revelation by truncating the canonical story, might well reply that in the second century there in fact was no established canon. And so it was appropriate for him to make decisions about which books to include and exclude for Christian worship. While such a response is technically correct, it ignores a crucial point: if any texts carried canonical authority for early Christians, it was the Hebrew Scriptures, precisely the victim of Marcion's scissors.[121] Moreover, there is no doubt that by the eighteenth century the Christian canon was fully formed. Outright elimination of the Old Covenant, and the more subtle forms of modern Marcionite suppression or forgetting of key Old Covenant themes such as the personhood of God, divine election and transcendence, covenant, and law involves severing the form of revelation handed down by the Christian community for fourteen hundred years, wholesale revision of Christian worship, and, one would imagine, re-writing Christian creeds and prayers. Against what he sees as Marcionite distortions, Balthasar extols a theologically contemplative hermeneutic rooted in an analogy between an encounter with a beautiful form and an encounter with divine glory.

Balthasar's aesthetic retrieval has the express purpose of contesting what he perceives to be the modern theological and ecclesiastical reduction of Christian glory to a series of ethical rules and doctrinal propositions, neither of which has the power to captivate human beings or represent the believer's encounter with the God of Old Covenant and New. Balthasar argues that without the aesthetic dimension, that is, apart from the non-coercive and deeply personal attraction of the beautiful, ethical demands and truth claims come to rest on authority entirely external to the believing subject. In other words, Church teaching becomes a series of "mysteries" to be believed apart from a genuine encounter with divine glory. Exclude the beautiful from the good and true, he thinks, and the good loses its ability to compel, while the true becomes uninteresting for its abstractness. Soon, the exploration of evil and its depths becomes no less interesting than the good—perhaps even more so for its relative exoticism and putative mystery. In a passage directed toward twentieth-century events, Balthasar writes: "Man stands before the good and asks himself why it must be done and not rather its alternative, evil. For this, too, is a possibility, and even the more exciting one: Why not investigate Satan's depths?" [122]

Balthasar thinks that in the context of a distorted Christianity, it is not enough to attend to the *praeambula fidei* in order to move the atheist toward the possibility of Christian belief. What is necessary, in his view, is a rich presentation of the Christian form that, while not "anthropocentric," is both anthropologically significant and personally compelling. The idea here is not that faith is a series of disparate propositional truths unreachable by reason, disconnected from human existence, and thus accepted on authority alone, but rather that the dynamic form of God's self-revelation through Old and New Covenant, received in humble obedience, sheds unsurpassable light on the meaning of human being.[123] This is Balthasar's true *gnosis* again. Moreover, revelation cannot shed this light if it is reduced to propositions and ethical commands apart from an appeal to the interior life and the whole person. Such "extrinsicism" is futile, runs counter to the gentle persuasion of grace, and fails to represent the sacramental character of an encounter with the Incarnate Lord. Against such extrinsicism, and also subjectivism, Balthasar finds in his analogy to the encounter with beauty a way to unite the objective and subjective poles of revelation. In other words, he finds a way to depict the experience of divine glory as both originating from outside the self, as "objective," and as Augustine says, "more intimate to me than I am to myself."

The key to Balthasar's discovery is his contrast between revelation understood as a series of signs pointing to a remote content and his more nearly sacramental notion of beautiful form. Extrinsicism and subjectivism each see the "historical facts of revelation as pointers ... to something mysterious which lies behind them and which must be believed."[124] Whereas extrinsicist views of revelation are prone to ecclesiastical authoritarianism, subjectivist theologies tend to undervalue the content and authority of Scripture and threaten to become solipsistic. By contrast, to grasp revelation as form means to find its meaning within a spiritual work itself, not above or outside of it. Just as form always shapes content, the pattern or shape of revelation as a whole becomes essential to its proper interpretation. Form springs from and leads back to content. In aesthetic terms, "form" designates beauty in its actual appearance, so that the light of Being, or, in the case of Jesus, the light of divine Being, is not merely gestured to, but is discovered within the shape of revelation itself. The content (*Gehalt*) of revelation or of a beautiful entity is found through a reading or perceiving of its form, its form character being that which allows it to be "materially grasped."[125] In a Christian theology of revelation, "Visible form not only points to an invisible unfathomable mystery; form is the apparition of this mystery, and reveals it...."[126] We should notice here that revelation is specified for Balthasar as the revelation of mystery. Whereas earlier we showed that Balthasar, like Hegel, thinks that revelation and knowledge are part and parcel of faith, here we find that, in contrast to Hegel, Balthasar does not think that positive revelation and mystery, or cataphatic and apophatic theology, are opposed. To the contrary, to the extent that revelation is revelation of God's transcendence and freedom, it is precisely revelation that illuminates the ever-greater mystery of divine love, the visible Son who reveals the invisibility of the Father. In other words, positive revelation is so extravagant it points to the unknowing and non-seeing that always must accompany knowledge of God.

Balthasar's aesthetic analogy between revelation and the encounter with a beautiful form helps shed light on the Christian claim that revelation comes not from human subjectivity or creativity, but from God, yet appeals to human interiority at the deepest of levels. Just as an encounter with a work of art or an aspect of our natural environment emerges from outside the person, but can be deeply moving, so too divine revelation can come from a God who is not reducible to human subjectivity, yet evokes in the human person a profoundly personal response.[127] More specifically, Balthasar depicts Scripture as a sacramental form emerging through the interaction of divine and human freedom in covenant relation, centered on Christ, and arising as revelation through the Church's faith, not despite it.[128] Within such a narrative construal of revelation, God serves as the primary, but not sole, author, who can and does make more of faith than faith's testimony can see at any moment in time. The overall purpose and shape of revelation can never be foreseen by the believer who acts faithfully in the moment or by the author of a particular scriptural text who seeks to do the same. The object that we call scripture is then handed down through tradition as God's self-revelation capable of a variety of faithful readings.

Of equal relevance to our discussion is the "subjective" appropriation of revelation considered as form. Balthasar's aesthetic and sacramental view of Scripture prohibits an aggressive or manipulative mode of interpretation. Rather, revelation must be received as a whole, as it is given:

> *A finished work of art must be left as it is: we may not chisel away a bit more at a work of Michelangelo's, nor may we compose and add a couple of measures to a fugue of Bach's. In the same way, we must allow the form of God to be just as it is. By contemplating it, we can interpret its meaning unboundedly, but only provided we take our departure from God's manifest intention.*[129]

Balthasar takes his aesthetic analogy to preclude manipulation of the form of revelation prior to reception of it as it presents itself, for such manipulation creates either a different form altogether or an incoherent mess.[130] Instead, the reader of a play or observer of a work of art must confront the work in question with an alert receptivity to what is given in the work itself. The reader seeks to align her subjectivity with that of the work.[131] With respect to Scripture, "ecclesial faith" is this subjectivity. Ecclesial faith is the instrument or spirit through which Scripture emerges and the alert receptivity that characterizes the Christian encounter with revelation today.[132] When read from this standpoint, Scripture discloses the pattern and significance of God's unsurpassable revelation in Christ. It is the fittingness or the suitability of the whole form and the parts in relation to the center that gives us "revelation." Thus, faith is not a subjective superstructure topping off a more pristine revelation "in-itself." Rather, resurrection faith is both the condition for the Christian Bible emerging in the first place, and crucial to its ongoing interpretation.

It now becomes clear that Balthasar's hermeneutic analogy between aesthetic form and biblical revelation constitutes a potent rejoinder to Marcionite deformation. Christ's revelation, he contends, is "legible" only in light of the entire revelatory form, which includes the Old Covenant. The anti-Marcionism and anti-Gnosticism of his hermeneutic is evident here in two ways. First, Balthasar wants to emphasize Jesus' solidarity with human, fleshly existence. Thus, he writes,

> ... the God-Man, as a form in the midst of creation, cannot be an isolated entity without historical connections (Gnosticism, for instance, thought it could think of him in this way—as a sort of aerolith); rather, the God-Man must constitute a genuine composite form together with human history and must become comprehensible within this form: this is what Irenaeus argued against the Gnostics.[133]

Second, he wants to stress the connection between Jesus and a particular history, that is, the history of Israel. He is emphatic on this point: "Jesus constitutes one form with the history of the Old Testament."[134] To the "eyes of faith," the two testaments comprise "God's one revelation," one witness to their "higher center," the God-man.[135] Balthasar envisions God's election of Israel as a pedagogy that lifts them out of the "amorphous mass" of history into visibility.[136] The visibility of Israel's covenant grants to a sinful world a kind of education and preparation for God's eschatological self-interpretation in Christ. On this view, it is the role of the Old Covenant to carry the world of sin towards the world of participation in God's own life opened up by Christ. In other words, neither creation nor the Old Covenant are conceived by Balthasar as dialectically opposed to the New Covenant. Creation offers a presupposition for and, more so than for Barth, actual content that can mediate and help prepare for, grace. Beyond creation, the Old Covenant constitutes a path, nay, *the* path, into the freedom offered by Christ. For Balthasar, the apprehension of God's revelation in Christ requires God's covenant history with Israel.[137]

Seeing the Form: Against False *Gnosis*

BALTHASAR EXPLICITLY TIES HIS HERMENEUTICAL HOLISM to a rejection of Marcionism of either the "evolutionary-monist" or the classical dualist variety that we have discussed previously. Against Joachim, Lessing, and, more recently, Ernst Bloch, he dismisses distribution of the Trinitarian persons among separate periods of revelation as "arbitrary artifice."[138] The dangers represented by this "monistic view" are both cultural and ecclesial. Revelatory monism, he thinks, tends to identify the redemptive order with the people of God, reduce Christ to "merely one constituent element of the total process," and threatens to become an integralist vision of Church and political culture.[139] The underlying concern here is both idolatry and ideology: idolatry because of the identification between Church, culture, or human being and revelation / redemption; ideology because once this identification takes place, no basis for ecclesial or cultural self-criticism remains. Christ's Lordship is surpassed by the dissolution of God into the culture or the Church itself.

Balthasar rejects dualistic Marcionism with equal vehemence. Of course much of what he says about dualistic Marcionism can also be said about the monistic variety. Here, however, the emphasis is on a complete split between Judaism and Christianity rather than a progressive superceding of one by the other. Thus, he observes that a loss of contact with its Jewish roots causes the Church to "wither and become distorted into anti-semitism or Hitlerism."[140] Marcionite dualism is "diametrically opposed to the entire structure and form of revelation...."[141] As we earlier noticed his Trinitarian opposition to Ernst Bloch, we can now notice that it is the Trinitarian God who he again opposes to Marcionism: " ... one Trinitarian God is the Lord of history who makes his triunity known in an ever more eventful manner."[142] The unity of the divine plan of revelation through Old and New Covenants is grounded in the unity of the free, Triune God of covenant relation.

It follows from Balthasar's aesthetic analogy and from his theological hermeneutic that the meaning of God's revelation in Christ remains opaque apart from its context within Israel's covenant. Erase the Old Covenant, and we are left with a shattered form or with an oxymoron: illegible revelation. We would also be left with a savior who does not truly share in the concrete structures and tensions of creation, culture, and human fleshly existence. This last issue leads directly into Balthasar's view of modern historical criticism, for it is precisely the inability to integrate Jesus' historical, cultural existence with theological data that Balthasar wants to contest in another prong of his anti-Marcionite agenda.

This discussion is not designed as a general discourse on Balthasar's exegetical method, but only as an excavation of one more Marcionite, or at least quasi-Marcionite, site of deformation. This focus permits us a brief treatment. Historical criticism of the New Testament, especially insofar as it seeks the meaning of the biblical text outside of or behind that text, would appear to run counter to Balthasar's claims for the indissolubility of form and his view that only an ecclesial faith perspective can reveal the God disclosed through the Old and New Covenants. To an extent, this is an accurate impression. Balthasar believes that no neutral, purely historical reading of Scripture can reach its deepest significance. As he puts it, historians "cannot obtain any more meaning than it [the writing of history] is ready to deposit and invest in anticipation."[143] If the goal of biblical interpretation is ultimately the meaning of revelation, then any historical method that excludes either the resurrection or Jesus' mission from the Father is a severely limited resource. In other words, insofar as historical critics break up Scripture's form, they render discovery of its meaning impossible.[144]

Even if he does regard some types of that research as unhelpful or antithetical to an ecclesial faith reading of Scripture, however, Balthasar does not eschew modern biblical research. Rather, he takes that research seriously, and argues that form criticism shows "above all" that the various layers of composition and perspective are "colored by ecclesial faith."[145] Moreover, if Scripture arises through faith, then it is "faith alone" that "can guarantee the full objective (rational) knowledge of things as they really are."[146] This is a pregnant statement that bears review. Balthasar wants to recall his view that faith is both a humble response of trust *and* a humble response to what is revealed as it is revealed. In this hermeneutical principle, we can see the non-manipulative disposition of faith that Balthasar contrasts time and again to the Promethean stance of anthropocentric Marcionism. The contrast, however, is not between faith and reason, as we can see by his reference to "full objective (rational) knowledge."[147] Instead, the contrast he draws is between a proper disposition of receptivity to the form that appears and self-forgetfulness on the one hand, and an improper disposition that would manipulate the form of revelation for self-aggrandizement. For Balthasar, non-manipulative faith is shown by modern critical methods to be the subjective disposition appropriate to revelation. In this light, he can go further in his lauding of modern criticism:

> *The loosening up of the text by means of the critical method has in general brought with it invaluable theological gains since, with the heightened perspectivism that is its result, wholly new dimensions for*

the theological perception of the object are opened up in the drapery of Scripture's garment, as it were.[148]

Balthasar offers more and different praise for modern methods of biblical criticism, but the most relevant for us involves the possibility that modern attention to the historical Jesus might help fend off docetic Christology, a key element of Marcionite thought. He finds, however, that much modern Christology goes in precisely the opposite direction as it flees the doctrinally unfriendly results of historical criticism.

This is the story Balthasar tells in volume three of *Theo-Drama* as he prepares for the ascending part of his Christology. The gist of Balthasar's reflections is that the results of modern biblical scholarship must be integrated within Christology and faith rather than kept separate from it. Yet he reverses the order of priority found in many treatments today. He argues that the Jesus of history can only be apprehended from the perspective of the resurrection faith proclamation of the early Church. He again argues for the importance of unity and inclusivity:

> *If the Resurrection is excised, then not only certain things, but simply everything about Jesus' earthly life becomes incomprehensible. Or if we understand the risen Lord as merely the "Christ of faith," without an interior identity with the Jesus of history, then once again the whole form becomes incomprehensible.... Or if the trinitarian dimension is excluded from the objective form of revelation, then again everything becomes incomprehensible.*[149]

Balthasar contends that within a broad band of Protestant theological and philosophical reflection, this form suffers a crucial split between the historical Jesus and the Christ of faith. Resurrection, Ascension, and Second Coming will all be placed in a sealed-off category of faith, while Jesus' personality or personal impact on the believer is what is left as culturally and existentially worth retaining.

The problem for Balthasar does not lie so much with historical method as with its theological application. True, Balthasar poses challenging methodological questions to historical-critics if they believe that historical methods are adequate to the study of revelation. But the real difficulty lies in the fear that historical-criticism will undermine Scriptural veracity. Thus, various nineteenth-century thinkers strive to protect Christian belief from the conclusions reached by the critical method, especially conclusions related to Jesus' eschatological understanding. The unfortunate result of these defensive measures is that the details of Jesus' life, along with the details of Scripture, become mostly irrelevant to Christian faith and theology. An entire stream of Christology "abstracts from the historical particularities of Jesus' life"[150] to find some message or meaning that eludes the systematic uncertainty of historical research: whether it is Strauss, for whom the form (*Gestalt*) presented by the gospels must be penultimate, and must yield in Hegelian fashion to the higher idea of humanity's divinity;[151] Schleiermacher, who largely sidesteps historical criticism by focusing on an existential encounter between the person of Jesus and the believer;[152] Christian Weisse, for whom the "historical side of Jesus becomes a matter of indifference";[153] Rudolf Bultmann, who joins *kerygma* to existential faith, leaving behind the unknowable historical Jesus;[154] or Karl Barth, who views historical criticism as obsolete.[155] In all of these cases, Balthasar maintains, the mediation of exegesis, and with it the humanity of Christ as a particular human being, recede into the background of theological consideration. Results of protective maneuvers can be very different. While Barth and Bultmann return Protestantism to some version of orthodoxy, Strauss and Feuerbach read revelation as a mythical form giving pictorial expression to the philosophical-theological truth of humanity's divine species-nature. What does not differ is the tendency of these varied theologies towards docetic Christology. Balthasar does not hesitate to put the problem in Kierkegaardian terms. The theological danger of the dualism that arises between history and contemporaneity now comes "close to giving up altogether the fact of God's Incarnation: henceforth theology can be founded only on the sole absolute remaining to it, namely, faith's self-understanding."[156]

The subjectivism of this last point is clearly a worry for Balthasar. But he would not accuse Barth of subjectivism. What is more decisively at issue is the sacrifice or denial of the "time-bound" elements of Jesus' apocalyptic claims on the one hand,[157] or their transmutation into a "universal philosophico-theological truth"[158] on the other. In either case, the genuine Incarnation, as prepared for by Israel, will be lost to a kind of etherealization or disincarnation of Jesus' existence and meaning. For Balthasar, as we will see shortly, Israel prepares a model for the interaction between time and eternity, and in fact is that interaction in history.[159] Neither Jesus' real, historical self-understanding, nor the event character of revelation can be sacrificed. Such a "solution" would avoid reading the form in its covenant context where unrepeatable events open up the divine life through the two-sided drama between God and humanity learned first from the Old Covenant and deepened in the New.[160] For Balthasar, Jesus' solidarity with human creatureliness through his emergence from within Israel is essential to the reading of his form, and it is precisely this context that nineteenth century and much twentieth-century Christology downplays. To grasp the form of the covenant is to take seriously the dialogical and dynamic relation between infinite and finite freedom as this freedom concretely realizes itself. Instead, Jesus' humanity, while never before receiving such critical attention, nevertheless loses much of its significance for theological-doctrinal reflection. One loss leads to another. If his humanity is devalued for theological consideration, then the role of human freedom within the covenant relation will also be devalued, and thus the whole process gestures toward a kind of docetic Christology even as it inaugurates historical-critical studies. The danger—and Balthasar thinks it is a realized danger—is a pantheistic distortion of the covenant revelation that is intrinsically dramatic and dialogical.[161]

Israel's Apophatic Pedagogy

WE HAVE GRASPED THUS FAR that Balthasar's analysis of modern intellectual culture produces a picture that is broadly Marcionite and Promethean. Marcionism, he argues, supports Prometheanism by eliminating or marginalizing the transcendent God of Old Covenant glory, and thus facilitating various kinds of identity philosophy. It becomes more and more difficult for Western culture to perceive God's glory in creation and in humanity as the eventful, objective radiance that leads all things back to the Creator. Theoretical laws and principles become cold substitutes for this personal radiance, paradoxical religious language that suggests transcendence and immanence simultaneously becomes thoroughly rationalized, negative theology disappears, and biblical and post-biblical Judaism are often the objects of scorn.

It is in this context that Balthasar seeks to emphasize the importance of the Old Covenant for both ecclesial and cultural self-understanding. For Balthasar, this importance lies in Israel's pedagogical role in salvation history. The Old Covenant, he argues, serves as a pedagogue that, like any good teacher, offers both positive (*cataphatic*) and negative (*apophatic*) instruction. In the first volume of *Glory of the Lord*, Balthasar stresses its apophatic and demythologizing role in salvation history. Israel's covenant disrupts cyclical views of time,[162] mythical eschatologies, magical views of cultic ritual,[163] and human self-apotheosis, all of which are to be found in surrounding cultural myths.[164] What is crucial to recognize is that this negative pedagogy or demythologization does not occur through a simple "No," but instead through a positive relationship between God and Israel in its movement toward the world's healing and consummation by grace.[165]

It is this ongoing relationship that positively unveils the character of God and the meaning of human existence, and it is in contrast to this positive relationship and all that it entails that negative judgment on idolatry and anything that breaks with the requirements of this relationship will come to the fore.[166] Of particular importance to our discussion is what Balthasar calls the "realism" of the Old Covenant with respect to human nature. Contrary to the Prometheanism we have observed, Old Covenant revelation destroys mythological self-glorification without any corresponding impulse to self-destruction (or low self-esteem).[167] Israel relates God's standards of righteousness and compassion to its communal life and finds itself wanting both ontologically and existentially. Humanity is but ash, and, what's more, ash that sins. In Balthasar's words, Israel learns over time to view itself by the "standards that God applies to man in the world."[168] Moreover, through the visibility of Israel's covenant form as it coalesces into Scripture, the world gains a "sacrament" of God's standard and of time's relationship to eternity, that is, the relationship between human freedom and God.[169] Of course for Balthasar God's instruction, whether apophatic or cataphatic, does not end with the Old Testament. Instead, the realism of Israel's revelation brings the covenant towards the realism of a desolate, crucified Messiah who makes God's standard or measure visible, while simultaneously manifesting absolute divine freedom and therefore hiddenness. Christ reveals this hiddenness in an unsurpassable way.[170]

What needs to be extolled, especially in light of modern Prometheanism, is the sacramental realism of the Old Covenant. Old Covenant demythologization is not confined to the myths of old. Balthasar has in his sights the modern "anthropologization" of divine glory that we have discussed throughout this chapter.[171] Given what we have said thus far, it is possible to infer that Balthasar is arguing that modernity is oddly characterized by a return to a pre-biblical world that lacks the transcendent No to idolatry of the Sovereign Lord revealed in the Old Covenant. Balthasar is arguing that a remembrance of Old Covenant glory is necessary to demythologize modern religious thought just as it performed a similar demythologizing function for the ancient world. As we have seen, however, Balthasar thinks that modernity—whether in its defense against historical criticism or in its anthropological reduction of divine glory—can only occur as a post-Christian phenomenon that interprets divine kenosis apart from resurrection and exaltation. Whereas the "Greeks thought in terms of analogy ... Bruno and Shaftesbury [think] in terms of identity," he writes.[172] In this context, Balthasar appears to be arguing, the Old Covenant is not irrelevant to modern theology; indeed, it has never been more relevant in that after the New Covenant the cultural temptation will always be to confuse God and the world. Of course the Old Covenant is also not self-sufficient. What is truly necessary, for Balthasar, is an ecclesial faith reading of Scripture that envisions the unity of the entire plan of salvation from Old Covenant through the New Covenant with its higher unity in the person of Christ.

It is worth mentioning the further demythologization enacted through Israel's covenant, since it reveals again the biblical portrayal of humanity as a humble creature of God. Mythological scenarios of the afterlife also suffer God's negative judgment. Israel, for the most part, rejects these scenarios in favor of a steadfast trust in God without consolation. The covenant brings to the front of consciousness life's transitory nature apart from the resurrection of a suffering, crucified human being (and not a resurrected king, priest, or hero).[173] If Israel shows the world the nature and destiny of human existence, it also reveals God as free judge and passionate, suffering lover.[174] Giving Marcion his due, Balthasar writes:

But the dualists were right at least in this respect: in the tension, which amounts almost to self-contradiction, between the exaltedness of the free God and the humiliation of the loving God what opens up is the very interior space of the heart of divinity itself.[175]

This aspect of dualism points to the Trinitarian revelation prefigured in "the tragic history of God with his unfaithful people."[176] The Cross makes sense in the context of Yahweh's love crashing against the world's sin. It is also the context of God as free judge that must not be forgotten when thinking about the Cross. Divine judgment makes possible apprehension of the superabundance of grace offered through Christ's Cross and resurrection.

Or, rather, the "lifting" of divine wrath by way of the "Crucified One's" action on our behalf by which human alienation from the Father becomes transformed into the form of the Crucified One's uttermost love for the Father; this is God's "offer of love to the sinner, whereby he invites him to join in his reconciliation with the world."[177]

Israel's pedagogy is not conceived by Balthasar to be limited to negative theology or idolatry critique. Israel offers a "preliminary sketch," or a "five-staff line upon which Christ's melody can be written down for men to hear and understand."[178] Israel prepares the images—irreconcilable within the Old Testament—for the form to come. Covenant images retain their vitality because Israel's history is meant to comprise a total form of witness to God's Word with the New Testament. Various figures—such as the apocalyptic Son of Man, the different prophets, the suffering servant, as well as messianic figures—"fan out" and provide a poly-morphic context or "supernatural table of categories" that awaits its interpretation by that to which it witnesses, the Incarnation of the divine Word.[179] Christ's life, death, and resurrection gain their "legibility" through a complex relation of continuity and discontinuity with the Old Covenant, and through the Old Covenant to history and to human culture more broadly. On Balthasar's view, there is an essential rightness, a harmony between Old and New Covenants that at least in one sense reveals only a single covenant—but this rightness requires the full context of Jesus' incarnate life, death, and resurrection.

Conclusion

THIS CHAPTER HAS ESTABLISHED THAT MARCIONISM, and its attendant anti-Judaism, is a chief concern throughout Balthasar's work. Modern forms of Marcionism serve as subversive proxies for a Christian identity that has, in some respects, returned to the fluidity of its early centuries. As Marcionism slips in and takes over, the larger—and to Balthasar more holistic—pattern of Christian meaning fades from memory. If we allow our focus to fall on what Balthasar believes anthropocentric Marcionism has wrought, we can enumerate some of the basic transformations of the Christian form as he sees them. First, the God who creates, elects, and legislates comes to be viewed as unworthy of praise; second, divine glory becomes immanent without remainder in terms of the human species; third, divine glory takes on a purely inner-historical future reference that humanity is to construct for itself apart from a transcendent measure; fourth, Christian identity gets pulled in an anti-Judaic direction as Judaism is viewed as linked to the God who creates, elects, and legislates, a free and transcendent God non-reducible to human glory or projects. Especially in forms of anthropocentric Marcionism that take a Joachimite view of salvation history as proceeding along a vector away from divine transcendence to immanence and total human autonomy, this final stage will be juxtaposed to the earlier, more "Judaic" stages. Cosmocentric forms of Marcionism, while of some interest here in that there will be a shift of glory from God to cosmos, and thus another site of doxological reduction that leaves behind divine freedom, will also provide resources of contemplation, openness to reality in all its singularity and multiplicity, and even gratitude that can be taken up into Christian forms of thought. Of course both kinds of Marcionism are species of identity metaphysics for Balthasar, and thus both inevitably exclude the dialogical and inter-personal form of covenant relation that is, for Jews and Christians, a crucial condition for the possibility of prayer and worship, and, as we shall see later, for a mission of service. What the anthropocentric form of Marcionism eschews is the humility and "pliancy" of covenant-being in relation to the God of creation. Such a humble identity can be viewed by the Promethean only as a self-alienation to get beyond as divine attributes gradually accrue to human nature and designs. These designs, on Balthasar's reading, offer not redemption of creation viewed as gift, but rather an overcoming of an originally evil creation such that creation gets its sole meaning and significance from either future or present salvation. Otherwise put, the doctrine of creation gets subsumed into the doctrine of salvation.

After laying out Balthasar's diagnosis of the modern theological predicament, at least insofar as it relates to Marcionism and anti-Judaism, we then began to look at Balthasar's anti-Marcionism as fundamental to his theological options. Balthasar contests what he sees as an overly rationalistic and moralistic modern culture with a tremendous effort to rehabilitate the transcendental of the beautiful. It is only by recalling this transcendental, he thinks, that theology can find an analogy to the encounter with divine glory such that the objective and subjective aspects of faith receive their due. Against Promethean self-assertion, and the Marcionite opposition to the God of the Old Covenant that is its condition, Balthasar pits what he sees as the fundamentally biblical disposition toward divine glory: humble receptivity to the form of revelation as it gives itself. Just as in the encounter with a beautiful work of art, for instance, so in the encounter with biblical glory, to manipulate a form prior to understanding is to forego understanding for control. Balthasar contends that a contemplative beholding of divine glory and the form it takes opens the self to self-forgetfulness, joy, and a liberating mission of service.

The form that Balthasar beholds is a Trinitarian form that unites creation, covenant, and redemption without collapsing one into the other, and without ignoring the world's terrible suffering taken up into the Cross and the divine life itself. Balthasar's emphasis on the Trinity is directly related to his view of religious language as that of *Vorstellung* that is never reducible to *Begriff*. The paradoxes of Trinitarian doctrine and of the Incarnation should not be ironed out, he argues, through a dialectic rationalism that makes religious language univocal, de-personalizes the divine, and places salvation history in a tightly teleological system moving from transcendent divine to absolute human autonomy. For Balthasar, seeing the form of revelation leads to the admission that God remains transcendent judge in the New Covenant, deepens his covenant intimacy with humanity even beyond what he accomplishes in Moses, the prophets, and the suffering servant in the Old Covenant, and shows more definitively the measure of all human conduct in love.

Finally, we ended the chapter by emphasizing that Balthasar views the Old Covenant as of particular relevance to our contemporary moment. He believes that Old Covenant glory that critiques both idolatry and ideology is as necessary as ever to upset grandiose modern myths of human and cultural-political apotheosis. Balthasar thinks of this Old Covenant No to idolatry and ideology as apophatic or negative theology. This negation, however, is not based upon what human cognitive abilities are unable to grasp, but rather upon Israel's knowledge of who their God is and thus the excess of divine glory beyond the capacity of any creature to circumscribe. Biblical glory is excess that reveals mystery. It is this encounter with divine excess that reveals the creature as creature and leads to a realistic picture of the human person, a picture that the Promethean Marcionite seeks to distort. But this excess is also revealed as God's love for the creature created in his image, and the importance of this creature in God's plan of salvation. The next chapter will investigate in far greater detail Balthasar's reading of Israel's covenant as this reading performs its idol-clearing role and its positive preparation for the New Covenant.

Chapter Two

Against the Idols: Divine Encounter, Prophetic Covenant

Our first chapter set out to establish that Balthasar locates his theology, including his theology of Judaism, within a cultural analysis that interprets a main thrust of modern thought to be Marcionite and Promethean.[180] On this view, secularism is not conceived of as a mere rejection of God, but indeed as a proclamation, both soft and loud, that humanity itself is divine. We might say that Balthasar partially endorses Nietzsche's observation that the murder of God requires the self-deification of humanity. For Balthasar, moreover, this cultural movement is neither necessary nor indicative of progress. Instead, he suggests that Western cultural self-apotheosis symbolizes a post-Christian yearning for a mythology of the human person long since demythologized by the Old Covenant. What makes this yearning post-Christian is not chronology alone, but also its dependence on the universality of Christ's offer of grace. Whereas ancient mythology typically reserved glory for the powerful and spectacular man, Balthasar observes, Jewish and Christian scriptures often criticize the mighty, extol the humbly obedient, and thereby open glory to all human beings. It is the generalization of glory that the Promethean movements of modernity seize upon, while confining it to an innerworldly plane where praise and prayer become monological and, ultimately, self-referential.

Thus, for Balthasar, Prometheanism strikes at the heart of Christian faith. It arrays itself against any depiction of a transcendent divine who provides a measure for human behavior and for truth and will not suffer the threat to autonomy represented by the transcendent God of the Old Covenant. This God must be consigned to the distant past, a remnant of a time of unreason and superstition that the modern period has left behind. Prometheanism turns Marcionite; Marcionism supports the rise of Prometheus.

If for Balthasar some forms of secularism, or at least justifications of secularism, have this Promethean consequence, the turn to the secular also contains the genuine insight that the world exists as non-divine creature rather than divine cosmos. This realization sounds a note of progress in the development of human consciousness. Balthasar agrees with Max Weber[181] and more recently Marcel Gauchet[182] that Jewish and Christian faith in a transcendent divine serves to disenchant the world. In contrast to "secularism," the secular does not require worldly autonomy as an end in itself. Moreover, where "secularism" is a close cousin of nihilism, that is, the view that the transcendent place from which the values of the world emerge (e.g., the Christian God, the Platonic Forms) gets erased, the secular is the proper view that the world has a relative but real autonomy vis-à-vis the Creator.[183] For Balthasar, the world lies within God, provides signs and even "natural sacraments" of the divine, and finds itself shot-through with grace: thus the claim found in Balthasar and de Lubac that there is no "pure nature." [184] Yet Balthasar will also argue, against Barth, that creation is no mere presupposition for grace but has its own sphere, a kind of relatively independent order that cannot be deduced from the supernatural order. In attesting to God's transcendence, the Old Testament also points to the relative autonomy permitted creation. It is in the twofold context of modern secularism and Prometheanism on the one hand, and modernity's realization of relative cultural autonomy on the other, that Balthasar deems essential an emphasis on Old Covenant revelation and on the unity of the biblical canon.

The task of the present chapter is to address Balthasar's reading of Scripture with a view to understanding how his reading serves his anti-Marcionite and pro-Judaism purposes. More specifically, the central task of this chapter is to present Balthasar's argument from prophecy, that is, his rehabilitation of the patristic contention that the Old Covenant points to, foreshadows, and hides within itself the New Covenant that is its fulfillment. On Balthasar's reading, the argument from prophecy ties Christianity to the Jewish scriptures as the condition for properly apprehending the form of Christ, even as those same scriptures allow and promote a variety of emphases. It is important that throughout the following discussion of Balthasar's biblical exegesis, we will not depart from the modern genealogical contextualization provided in chapter one. Balthasar understands that his opposition to Marcionism and Prometheanism stands on sand unless he can make his case from a reading of Scripture.

The first section of chapter two is a discussion of Balthasar's hermeneutic emphasis on "encounter" in his text on Old Covenant glory, and how this emphasis serves his anti-Promethean agenda. I will argue that Balthasar's choice of this category helps him in his attempts to contest aspects of Hegelian Prometheanism that we discovered in our first chapter. Balthasar's opposition to Hegel brings into its orbit his opposition to Marcionism and Prometheanism, his concern for the theological significance of Jesus' human existence, and his desire to have a mediating, analogous discourse of creation that is non-deducible from biblical revelation.

This preliminary discussion then opens onto the stage of Israel's interaction with its God. For Balthasar, Old Covenant revelation provides both a preparation of forms that will be taken up and integrated by Christ, and an education of Israel, and through Israel the world, for the reception of God's definitive Word. The Old Covenant is both preparation and pedagogy for the Incarnation. Our discussion will emphasize the "incarnational logic"[185] of Balthasar's reading, to borrow a term from W.T. Dickens, and will also attend to the relations between the different forms of revelation that Balthasar considers important. In particular, we will examine the relation of theophany to covenant, covenant to the "prophetic staircase," and all three to the forms Israel gives to its experience in the post-exilic period, namely, apocalyptic, messianic, and sapiential literature. Indeed, it is in the discussion of the post-exilic period, the literary ground for much anti-semitism in modern critical biblical exegesis, that the modern contextualization of Balthasar's biblical reading proves most illuminating. This is not to say that Balthasar entirely transcends his environment. But as Dickens rightly points out, Balthasar does transcend that environment in remarkable measure. I hope to show that Balthasar's criticisms of post-exilic Israelite religion aim not primarily or only at post-biblical Judaism, but also at modern cultural and ecclesial movements. In a sense, Balthasar employs the prophetic corpus in just the right way: as Christian self-criticism.

What I want to suggest in this chapter is that at any given time Balthasar has at least three purposes to his reading of the Old Covenant: (1) to connect, yet distinguish, glory as revealed in the Old Covenant with glory as it is revealed in extra-biblical cultural forms, that is, to read the covenant as the fulfillment of those cultural forms; (2) to read the Old Covenant as deeply continuous with the New, and thus thwart the attempts of modern Marcionism to divide them; and (3) to read the Old Covenant in opposition to modern Prometheanism.

What I am arguing here helps amplify what Dickens says about Balthasar. Dickens reads Balthasar through the helpful lens of the Yale School, especially the work of Hans Frei. Frei argued that pre-modern readings of Scripture did not read the Bible with an eye to historical or scientific accuracy, but as a "realistic narrative" that interprets the meaning of human existence in relation to God's self-revelation in the Bible. The goal of community reading is then to place oneself within this narrative disclosure of divine identity, and have the community be interpreted—and by implication, measured—by it. Frei can certainly be of help in interpreting Balthasar. However, it is perhaps a different Yale School theologian, George Lindbeck, who is of greater assistance. Lindbeck is well-known for saying that pre-modern Bible readers found the world in the Bible rather than the Bible in the world. I am arguing here that Balthasar seeks not merely to recommend such a reading, but to enact it by showing how Scripture can interpret modern and contemporary cultural forms, and through this interpretation, help measure them as well. Central to this task is the annihilation of the idol of Promethean Marcionism.

Encounter with Glory

WITHOUT SENTIMENTALITY, Balthasar the patristic scholar proclaims the patristic argument from prophecy dead, slayed unceremoniously at the hands of modern critical scholarship. What's more, while this demise might be cause for mourning, Balthasar bids the old argument good riddance, and perceives in its passing an opening for a new and revised form of the *argumentum ex prophetia*.[186] Unlike the older argument, which tended to rely too flatly, he thinks, upon literary correspondences from the text of the Old Covenant to the New, Balthasar argues that the entire Old Covenant arises through encounters between Israel and its God. The formation of these encounters in an ongoing, dramatic narrative makes of the entire Old Covenant, or perhaps better, the Old Covenant as a whole, prophetic.[187] This is no innocuous claim. Against so much of modern thought that would either relativize the significance of the Old Covenant vis-à-vis pagan sources (Schleiermacher),[188] pick and choose individual motifs that cohere easily with a given picture of Christ (for instance, motifs of prophecy or ethics and not ritual or cult),[189] or exclude the Old Testament almost entirely (Lessing, Kant),[190] Balthasar claims that the central content of the Old Covenant is materially identical to the New Covenant—both proclaim salvation through judgment[191]—and that the Old Covenant provides revelatory forms that are essential to grasping the form of Christ.

Balthasar's fundamental intuition is always to broaden, not narrow, the range of biblical material that serves Christian faith and practice. Gerhard von Rad proves a worthy aid to this broadening enterprise, as von Rad shares Balthasar's desire for an integrative, non-evolutionary version of biblical revelation:

> *The Hexateuch in its present form arose by means of redactors who heard the peculiar testimony of faith of each document and considered it binding.... Only the one who does not look superficially at the Hexateuch but reads it with a knowledge of its deep dimension will arrive at true understanding. Such a one will know that revelations and religious experiences of many ages are speaking from it. For no stage in this work's long period of growth is really obsolete; something of each phase has been conserved and passed on as enduring until the Hexateuch attained its final form.*[192]

Von Rad was concerned to correct a widespread disregard for the final form of the biblical text and the faith that Israel confessed that was the *raison d'etre* of a scripture in the first place.[193] Von Rad brought about a focus on the Old Testament as testimony to faith, as rooted in and formed by *kerygma* and confession within Israel's community.[194] Barth's confessional influence, and a shared view that the final form of scripture is more significant to the community of faith than understanding the individual movements of its formation, informs the work of both von Rad and Balthasar. But equally important is von Rad's opposition to an evolutionary reading of the biblical text that would put some religious forms definitively behind as obsolete or passé. Von Rad's view that "no stage in this work's long period of growth is really obsolete"[195] joins Balthasar's view of Old Testament forms "fanning out"[196] to provide a "supernatural table of categories"[197] for redemption and interpretation in the New Covenant.

Central to the readings of von Rad and Balthasar is the view that Israel's scriptures emerge out of Israel's encounter with the genuinely transcendent God at any one moment. In other words, the reference point for revelation is not primarily the community or history, but instead the sovereign God of the covenant.[198] Given that all revelation concerns this God, it makes little sense to assume that earlier stages of witness have nothing to offer, or that revelation moves in entirely one direction away from its beginnings toward a dead ritualism, only to be restored in the New Covenant. This is not to say that qualitative judgments should not be made; Balthasar will certainly make them. Rather, it is to point out that for Balthasar, the many forms of Israel's witness to its encounters with YHWH do not get tossed aside, but rather get taken up, interpreted, and validated within the eschatological New Covenant.

Balthasar's decision to label the Old Covenant as a whole "prophetic" certainly indicates that no part of the Old Testament should be eliminated, but it also serves two further ends: first, to relativize the significance of individual prophets, and second, to give the covenant relation itself priority as the ineluctable setting and center for humanity's encounter with divine glory. It is God's ongoing, dynamic relation with Israel, *including* the individual prophets, that discloses the mystery of divine glory and provokes praise.[199] This means that Balthasar will dismiss any theology that opposes the prophets to the covenant, the Law, or the people, all of which take on a prophetic thrust within the realm of the covenant opened up by God's grace.[200] Balthasar will be able to find some remnant of this prophetic thrust even in those places where modern scholarship has denied it, namely in Israel's post-exilic forms. While the prophets retain a special status in Balthasar's work, the covenant stands as the condition for the possibility of prophecy in the first place. Thus prophecy should not be set in opposition to the covenant.

If Balthasar's emphasis on encounter suggests that he will side with von Rad against unilinear readings of the Old Covenant, it also suggests an opposition to particular starting points within systematic theology, an opposition that Balthasar at times makes explicit. Why "encounter" rather than "logic" or "truth" or "truths"? Certainly Balthasar's option for "encounter" reflects his concern for the objectivity of revelation's form, so important to his entire theological aesthetics.[201] Like Karl Rahner, Balthasar also wants to indicate his displeasure with neo-scholastic views of Christian mysteries or truths, where "mystery" designates not the personal encounter with the God of revelation, but a gnoseological deficit that will be overcome in the next life.[202] After quoting Sirach on the importance of "fear of the Lord" as not only the beginning, but also the "crown" and "full measure" of wisdom, Balthasar writes:

> *This is why it will not do to delimit the object of theology with the concept of mysteries, as if formally it consisted of "truths" that lie*

beyond the ken of the human mind and must therefore be believed, in order then to be understood in some measure as a "magnificent order, a higher heavenly world ... a masterpiece of God's many-splendoured wisdom." What is at stake here is not primarily truths, but the living God in his glory; he himself is all truth and he suffices.[203]

And even more pointedly: "what is essentially at stake is solely men and women's encounter with the divinity or glory of God."[204] For Balthasar, it is the identity of the transcendent divine subject that gives unity and coherence to Israel's varied encounters with YHWH.

Balthasar's emphasis on encounter, however, seeks to confront an adversary more pressing and more influential in modern thought than neo-scholasticism. German idealism and "identity metaphysics" remain a central, if obscure, adversary even in Balthasar's biblical commentary. As we have seen, in the volume directly preceding his treatment of Old Covenant glory, Balthasar argues that under the German idealist regime the Christian form suffers deformation in several ways: humanity becomes identified in some way with the divine, divine freedom and glory become subject to an immanent philosophical law, Old Covenant glory is excluded, the God of scripture is depersonalized, and conceptual articulation is exalted above *agapaic* love.[205] In addition, Balthasar calls attention to the impossibility of prayer and grace consequent upon an elimination of divine transcendence, and a replacement of faith or faith encounter with philosophical necessity.[206] Against this array of forces opposed to the divine Transcendent, Balthasar opens his Old Covenant volume with an appeal to the Marian archetype that is so fundamental to his entire corpus:

> *In a biblical sense, this means that, the deeper a creature is allowed to encounter God's glory, the more this creature will long to extol this glory as being exalted over itself and over all creation. Such is Mary in her Magnificat. The deeper a creature is allowed to penetrate into God's opened realm, the more it will understand grace to be grace. And the more deeply it attains to a real, cognizant understanding of God's divineness, the more clearly does it realize that God's love transcends all comprehension ... "to know the love that surpasses knowledge."*[207]

The encounter between Creator and creature evokes a paradoxical rule for Christian discourse that interprets and judges metaphysical systems: the more intimate the encounter with God, the more clearly God is known as Mystery. Through his phenomenology of biblical experience, Balthasar seeks to subvert the metaphysics of identity and theological anthropocentrism that he finds in great swaths of modern thought, which, ironically, end up dissolving the independence of the created order by identifying the world with God. Focus on the content and form of biblical writings forces the conclusion that divine glory resists reduction to the inner-worldly plane. The task of resistance becomes clear if we discuss in more detail Balthasar's reading of biblical encounter against what he finds in Hegelian thought.

Biblical Encounter versus Hegelian Prometheanism

BALTHASAR READS HEGELIAN THOUGHT, especially the earlier theological works, as anti-Jewish at a fundamental level. Hegel reduces divine transcendence to an inner worldly "structure of implication and explication," "tears the Bible down the middle," finds Judaism a "principle of opposition," names it a religion of "pure positivity," and views Israel as among the rejected.[208] Even without invective, Hegel's later works exhibit "a fundamental rejection of the biblical and theological reality: of the elevation of the God of Israel above every harmonizing reciprocity of complication and explication."[209] Along with divine transcendence, Hegel rejects the apophaticism that Balthasar considers so important to the biblical critique of idolatry.[210] Marcionism again supports Prometheanism. Yet both Balthasar and Hegel engaged in a phenomenology of sorts. The question becomes how they are different and what Balthasar's reading of the Old Covenant has to do with this difference.

The contrasts between what Balthasar takes to be the content of Hegel's thought and his own are clear: Balthasar is an anti-Marcionite thinker, who holds fast to divine transcendence and the unity of the biblical canon; Hegel is a Marcionite thinker who reduces the transcendent divine to the immanent secular, or, alternatively, reduces the world to God. Balthasar seeks to set his thought off from that of Hegel in three important ways relevant to our themes: first, Balthasar contests what Hegel argues is the proper object of theological thought; second, Balthasar argues that Hegel's phenomenology is actually a theology unconcerned with the historical aspect of Israel's life, and thus, Hegel offers only a theology from above; third, Balthasar reads Israel's narratives of encounter against Hegelian systematizing reason. The last point needs to be shown through our discussion of Balthasar's actual biblical reading. The first two can be addressed, albeit briefly, here.

1. For Hegel, the very object of theological and philosophical discourse, namely, "eternal truth," means that philosophy will formally surpass theological discourse in terms of adequation to its object. In other words, Hegel believes that theology and philosophy share the same discursive object, but the nature of that object as truth determines that a conceptual discourse such as philosophy surpasses a representational discourse such as theology. If theology provides, through both revelation and doctrinal-traditional articulation, the representational content—what Hegel calls "positivity"— philosophical discourse interprets, judges, re-forms, and formally surpasses this content.

Of course Balthasar agrees that theology seeks truth. But Balthasar believes that Hegel, in losing or evicting the *analogia entis*, simultaneously forfeits the ability to properly distinguish philosophical from theological discourse. Properly understood, Balthasar thinks, philosophical thought has Being for its object, and this reflection on Being can then become an analogous and mediating discourse for revelation. Theological discourse is to be determined not merely by the representational forms of its doctrines, or by a general search for truth, but by the content specific to the form of Christ, which centrally and normatively includes the material of both Old and New Covenants. Theology is to be determined by its content, and this content is not reducible to doctrinal symbols. Indeed, these symbols ought to send the community back to the scriptural testimony. When Hegel strategically conflates the objects of philosophical and theological discourse, he erases the analogous nature of philosophical reflection on God and seeks a univocal form of speech that suggests a loss of the Creator-creature difference essential to Israel's experience.[211] Balthasar wants to argue that doctrines receive their ground and justification insofar as they are faithful to the covenant encounter with Israel's God exhibited through Scripture across both covenants.

2. Balthasar thinks that Hegel's philosophical assimilation of Christianity excludes the "historical and positive" element for a philosophical interpretation of the dogmatic ideas. The tightly systematic nature of his thought

functions deductively to constrain and even transform revelatory content. The deductive nature of Hegel's thought tightens the system and closes the gap between creation and covenant. Balthasar's critique of Hegel on this point shines a light on aspects of his biblical reading and also on his criticisms of Karl Barth and Karl Rahner that we will need to address in later chapters, and so is sufficiently important to warrant a lengthier treatment here.

In his *Lectures on the Philosophy of Religion*, Hegel begins his discussion of the consummate religion, that is, Christianity, from a definition of the Trinity as "eternal reconciliation."[212] It is this definition that provides the formal and final cause for divine self-development and for Hegel's construal of salvation history. Reconciliation becomes a kind of master concept or symbol that determines the entire system. Indeed, Hegel deduces the doctrine of creation, understood by him as a divine fall, from the idea of reconciliation. If there is to be reconciliation, he reasons, there must first be alienation, an alienation that for Hegel is the very being of the finite world, also designated as the epoch of the Son or as the Son as finite alienation.[213] This alienation too is necessary based upon the definition of God as Trinity.

Hegel argues that if the doctrine of the Trinity, understood as reconciled otherness, is to match the full seriousness of its symbol, then it must take on real alienation by becoming other in the person of the Son understood as finite world. Given the idea of the Trinity as formal and final cause, God must become other as world, and other as alien. Notice that he deduces Creation entirely from the doctrine of salvation as reconciliation, and nature entirely from grace. For Hegel, creation is a necessary event given the definition of reconciliation ensconced in Trinitarian doctrine. We might note as well that when Hegel discusses the earthly Jesus, he is quite clear that his earthly life, though perhaps of historical interest, has little religious importance.[214] It is this deductive constraining of biblical and existential content that Balthasar has in mind when he argues that only the dogmatic elements of Christian revelation, and not the historical or positive, find their way into Hegel's philosophy. Despite appearances and his ostensible concerns for historical consciousness and religious content, Hegel's is essentially a theology from above.

Balthasar's attention to encounter, and to the religious forms to which Israel's encounters with YHWH give rise, means that content will stand paramount, and that no deductive logic will be permitted to circumscribe this content. As with Edward Schillebeeckx, so with Balthasar the category of encounter signifies a theology from below, that is, from within Israel's account of its own experience. The content of these accounts show, at the very least, that the Truth that is the object of theological discourse is the Truth of a personal, free, and transcendent God never reducible to human categories of thought. Indeed, Truth has to do more with being-in-relation than with conceptual articulation. Balthasar, as we will see, rejects the idea that the fundamental truth of divine transcendence vanishes with the onset of the New Covenant, with the Cross, or with any New Testament pericope, even if a deeper perspective on this transcendence is revealed in the New Covenant.

An important third issue remains: Balthasar's reading of Old Covenant glory as at least in part a reading against the identity metaphysics he associates with Hegel and others. This reading will be especially evident in Balthasar's treatment of the relation between theophany and covenant. First, however, we need to examine precisely what Balthasar believes the flow of revelation to be such that it can bring into its orbit the religious forms of mankind for the covenant to interpret.

The Central Plot and the Forms of Glory

IN HIS ESSAY "Balthasar and Eckhart: Theological Principles and Catholicity," Cyril O'Regan sheds needed light on Balthasar's hermeneutic of tradition by examining his equivocating discussion of Meister Eckhart in volume five of *Glory of the Lord*.[215] Balthasar, he argues, desires a rich, pluriform tradition that nevertheless maintains an underlying set of theological principles that lend the tradition its unity. Thus, pluriformity of both discursive genre and theological perspective can, depending largely on the particulars of the case, either foster creative tension or facilitate doctrinal entropy. Balthasar's biblical hermeneutic appears similarly equivocal. Wisdom literature supplies a necessary contemplative stance vis-à-vis creation but fails to reckon with divine judgment; apocalyptic literature opens up the vertical drama between heaven and earth but degenerates into a form of privileged knowledge (*gnosis*) that too neatly divides the world into the damned and the saved. Of course the purpose of this hermeneutic strategy differs from his hermeneutic of tradition. Whereas the latter strives for a certain Catholic theological inclusiveness, and thus a generous notion of tradition, his biblical hermeneutic already assumes the canonical legitimacy of all biblical books. Moreover, his biblical hermeneutic offers an apologetic designed to show the convergence of Old Covenant traditions on the New Covenant, and, simultaneously, the impossibility for an integration of these traditions apart from Christ.[216] Within this context, each and every Old Covenant form, i.e., prophecy, apocalyptic, wisdom literature, theophany, finds its measure and innermost goal in the form of Christ as the supreme expression of the divine will and word. Christ is the measure or standard in terms of the shape his life takes through its encounter and intimacy with the divine life. On Balthasar's view, the goal of revelation and salvation history is the infusion of creation with this divine life, that is to say, the union of archetype with image.[217] Jesus Christ attains a radical transparence to the divine and thus is the achievement of this radical intimacy without confusion between the divine and human. Yet while Christ is the unique fulfillment of the Old Covenant, he is not so unique that he lacks preparation or legibility.

On Balthasar's reading, Israel's many encounters with divine glory yield a great variety of revelatory forms that provide both a preparation for and a pedagogy into the Incarnation. As we have stressed, one form does not supplant another, but instead remains in suspension with its own unique offering to make to God's overarching plan of revelation. Balthasar does argue, however, that different forms of revelation reach different levels of profundity, which he differentiates by using the terms "abstract" and "concrete." Rather than polar opposites, "abstract" and "concrete" serve as endpoints on a continuum that moves from more or less abstract elements of Old Covenant revelation to more concrete elements of that same covenant, which, ultimately find their most concrete realization in the prologue to John's gospel.[218] Of great importance to our discussion is that Balthasar sees this criterion operative not only in the relation between the Old Covenant and New, but within the Old Covenant itself. Within the Old Covenant, pre- and extra-covenantal disclosure exhibit something of divine glory, but it is only in the covenant relation with Israel that God truly opens the "riches" of his life to his creatures. Thus, revelation converges toward the particularity of Israel's relationship to God, toward concretion. Yet this convergence also represents the most universally valid revelation of all. We can say that for Balthasar, the Old Testament's preparation of forms or images makes the form of Christ legible, while the Old Testament pedagogy shows Israel becoming "accustomed" to bearing God's Word in the world. This is the incarnational logic that Dickens finds in Balthasar's reading.

Balthasar believes with von Rad that, for Israel, soteriology holds a kind of noetic primacy over creation, that is to say, that Israel extrapolates from its experience of covenantal salvation to the God who is Lord of all creation. Yet if Brevard Childs is right to argue that von Rad subsumes creation within soteriology or covenant, then Balthasar refuses to follow down what he would consider an all too Hegelian and Barthian path. Creation, for Balthasar, brings its own goods into the covenant, where they find their proper transcendence and order. It is, then, for Balthasar the Lord of all creation who has entered into a special relationship with Israel. The intimacy of this relationship over time is what ushers forth a wealth of irreconcilable forms expressive of divine sovereignty, divine attributes, and their integration in one divine subject who nevertheless transcends them all.

More specifically, Balthasar envisions the Mosaic covenant as the center point toward which revelation tends and from which it radiates outward. This seemingly exclusive relationship, however, is both grounded in and propelled toward a wider universal purpose revealed in what Balthasar, after von Rad, labels "pre-history" and "primitive history." Pre-history designates the movement from Abraham forward, whereas primitive history begins with Adam and also carries a forward thrust. Like von Rad, Balthasar envisions the Old Covenant as an emergence out of mythical culture into a history with both purpose and direction. The use of the term "history" points to distinctions that Balthasar and von Rad draw between extra-biblical myths and the biblical creation stories. While the many distinctions are not directly relevant, attention to two of these helps underscore Balthasar's concern to read the biblical material against modern identity metaphysics.

Von Rad and Balthasar each believe that the Genesis stories assert a Creator-creature difference through a replacement of an emanationist or divine sacrifice account of creation by an account that emphasizes the divine word and will. According to Genesis, they argue, creation is an act of divine freedom, not divine necessity. Moreover, in contrast to Hegelian "ontotheology,"[219] the Genesis account involves no cosmogony rooted in divine alienation. Creation does not develop out of a divine being or from the alienation / fall of a divine being. Each of these contrasts drawn by Balthasar and von Rad provides support for the profound difference between Creator and creature held to by Christian and Jewish tradition. What is interesting here is the implication that Hegel and his followers engage in a remythologization project that has already been demythologized through the movement of Old

Covenant revelation itself. Of course neither Balthasar nor von Rad deny the presence of mythical images from surrounding cultures within Israel's testimony. They argue only that these images serve a much more modest form of discourse and become included and semantically transformed within Israel's specific story, rooted in their covenantal encounter with YHWH.

Balthasar's observations are designed to distinguish Israel's revelation from surrounding cultures, but they also carry an inclusive thrust important to his discussion of religions more broadly. The Abrahamic pre-history, he thinks, creates links to other religions and nations of the world by taking up descriptions of God found in surrounding religious traditions, for instance Elohim and El Shaddai, and integrating them as mythical anticipatory forms for YHWH, and also by linking Abraham to the surrounding religions / nations through a filial connection.[220] In this way, the pre-history of Israel exhibits a centripetal convergence of religions toward Israel's covenant and its special revelation. Primitive history can likewise be read as a movement of convergence toward salvation history, from Adam toward Abraham and on to Moses. Balthasar's reading sets the particular covenant within a universal context toward which salvation history also aims. The universal covenant with Noah and the universal list of peoples, he observes, "embeds Abraham and Israel in the context of the peoples of the whole world."[221] Even at the beginning of salvation history, Abraham is meant to be a blessing for all nations, thus making known a universal goal.[222] In contrast to the false universalism of Babel, however, Israel is gathered together and is "preparing the light in which the scattered world is to receive its definitive mid-point."[223] Balthasar is pointing out here that neither "convergence" nor "fulfillment" is a property of the New Covenant alone. The Old Covenant itself exhibits the magnetic power of the God of Israel that draws a great variety of religious and cultural forms into Israel's covenant to receive their fulfillment in relation to divine glory. Ancient Israel itself does not hesitate to make its own what it brings into the covenant from its cultural surroundings, and for Balthasar this means that Israel can later bequeath this cultural inheritance to the form of Christ. The universal, filial thrust of Balthasar's interpretation can only lend support to Christian language of a universal, human family united by Christ under the Parenthood of God. We can now turn to a more focused examination of specific revelatory forms and Balthasar's view of revelation's dynamic.

Theophany and Covenant

THEOPHANY AND COVENANT, for Balthasar, are two mutually supporting, if unequally profound, forms of divine disclosure that emerge through Israel's encounters with its God. One form does not dissolve the other, just as neither will be dissolved by the New Covenant. The transfiguration and resurrection appearances, and in a sense all of John's gospel, are theophanic. Indeed, the form that is biblical theophany, Balthasar contends, is perfectly suitable for revealing the "what" of God's *kabod* or glory: the wholly other, free and sovereign Lord. Physical or sensory manifestations of divine glory signal divine condescensions that alert Israel to the presence of the "absolute, spiritual, and invisible Mightiness."[224] Theophany reveals the Transcendent God who can accomplish his will.

Often spectacular, theophany can also mislead. Balthasar observes that theophany can confuse material manifestations of divine glory for the Creator himself. Ironically, theophanic revelation might morph into just the identity metaphysics that Balthasar wants to avoid. Working against this temptation, and in line with the *Shema* of Deuteronomy 6:4, Balthasar observes the paradoxical nature of the sense world manifestations of biblical theophany that would frustrate any attempt at logical harmonization. Contrasting images and sensory manifestations that Balthasar places under titles such as "dazzling darkness," "knowing and not knowing," "seeing and not seeing," "form and non-form," "abode and event," and a "dialectic of fire" point upward, so to speak, to the majesty and utter freedom of God to use created reality for his purposes. The dialectical form that the sensory disclosure of divine glory takes in Old Covenant revelation unveils, for Balthasar, the impossibility of a univocal ascription of attributes to God or their dissolution into a horizontal logic.[225] This is a remarkable point that bears emphasis. Rather than concede the movement from image to conceptual logic as the only reasonable interpretation of revelation *qua* revelation, Balthasar reads, against Hegel, that the paradoxical and pluriform character of revelation pronounces against such a reduction of content and simplification of theological language. Here lies the great paradox that we will find throughout Balthasar's work, namely, that theophany or divine appearance inspires theological apophaticism. As a form of revelation, theophany reveals the human inability to comprehend divine nature or circumscribe divine glory.

Just as crucially, however, Balthasar forswears an apophatic extremist position that would erase or ignore the Transcendent behind the various appearances, that is, choose the many over the One, and argues for a doctrine of analogy. Apophatic extremism, Balthasar argues, threatens to undermine the unity of the divine subject by viewing different theophanies as expressions of numerous individual divine entities or hypostases. Such a reading would preclude the integration of the different attributes in one divine subject and suggest a Gnostic interpretation of the biblical texts.[226] We can again note the irony: what begins as a kind of radical apophaticism would result in a form of absolute knowledge. Balthasar, then, respects neither Hegelian excision of divine mystery nor Kantian epistemic restrictions on theological discourse. Instead, he appeals to the analogy between personal human self-disclosure and divine revelation. Just as deeds and words reveal something about a person's "nature," and spring from an ungraspable center of freedom, so the infinite subject manifests something of its "unique being" through sensuous disclosures that point to an inner ungraspable depth. Balthasar also observes that divine appearance often shocks the one who encounters such an uncanny reality. The experience again is not without analogy. Theophanic shock serves the larger purpose of gaining attention, not unlike a parental or professorial stare as experienced by a child or student. Balthasar thinks that this shock is necessary to establish a kind of attentive listening, a fear combined with fascination where one is held fast by what one beholds. Different forms of manifestation give no warrant, he argues, for divine plurality; and given analogous human experience and Israel's own covenant testimony, neither do they warrant an absolute apophaticism or a negative view of divine mystery as that which is completely unknown. Instead, paradoxical theophanic manifestations rise and converge towards a vanishing point that is a unique center of freedom in the unique divine subject. The diversity of manifestations will find their material integration only in the New Covenant where divine mystery is not forfeit, but rather takes on a Christological premise.[227]

Divine sovereignty, manifest through theophanic forms of revelation, is also significant for what Balthasar considers a more profound form of revelation: the covenant relation itself. The obedience, fidelity, and righteousness that God demands of Israel requires belief in God's liberating power. Apart from such power, the covenant promises for liberation, land, descendants, etc. would be worthless. Yet for Balthasar, it is not theophany, but Israel's covenant relationship that yields an intimate knowledge of the divine character. If theophany reveals God's "what," the covenant relation makes manifest God's "who." Balthasar, then, simultaneously includes and relativizes the emphasis on theophany found in classic texts such as Rudolf Otto's *The Idea of the Holy*.[228] Otto's attention to the important moment that reveals the Wholly Other and the *mysterium tremendum et fascinans* is noted and cited by Balthasar in his treatment of biblical theophany. Yet Balthasar clearly privileges the more "prosaic"[229] relation through time over the theophanic event. The implication is twofold: first, apart from an emphasis on Israel's covenant, including its election, general "religion" categories cannot do biblical or Jewish and Christian faith justice; second, the covenant takes into itself the universally available religious form that is theophany. Covenant trust is grounded in God's display of liberating power in the Exodus. It is in the wake of this concrete set of events that Israel, through its mediator Moses, agrees to live in the sphere of grace opened up by God (see Exodus 24). Thus theophany and what it presents of God's Being supports covenant and what it reveals of God's character. Narrative, Balthasar believes, is the form most suitable to the presentation of character, and therefore of the covenant relationship, for narrative exhibits attributes as the manifestation of personal freedom within a particular context and over time. In short, narrative form and covenant grace join to specify the divine as good and just, merciful and trustworthy, and provide Israel its unique access to the identity and glory of God. Israel and God become the main characters in a developing plot that finds its dramatic dénouement in Christ.[230]

For Balthasar, then, Israel's scriptures already display a relation of analogy between creation and covenant. Within the covenant, immanent ethical values transcend themselves toward the unique divine "I" which reveals itself as both good and glorious. Balthasar discusses five divine attributes—*sedeqah* (righteousness), *mishpat* (justice), *chesed* (mercy), *emeth* (fidelity), and *shalom* (peace)—under the ambit of covenant grace. On his reading, the intra-mundane significance of each attribute is integrated and eminently elevated as it is appropriated for the one, absolute, and free subject. At this new ontological level, the divine attributes that explicate God's goodness also bring forth praise of divine glory so that an interpenetration or *perichoresis* becomes evident, especially in the psalms, between Goodness and Glory, the Good and the Beautiful. Balthasar's helpful summary is worth quoting at length:

> *This path [of Glory] was initially described as that of integration from an abstract-sensuous kabod to the concrete-personal kabod which was more and more understood as the total statement of those qualities of the covenant Lord which are revealed in the covenant event. This integration is not a dispersal, but a concentration of all that has been dispersed upon the unfathomably free and sovereign absolute "I" that opens up its own sphere of life for its human image in the covenant of grace. This "I" was as yet abstractly glorious (in power and holiness) in the dialectic, sensuous kabod, but it becomes concretely glorious through the fundamental concepts of the covenant reality: as grace, justice, fidelity, mercy and in Deuteronomy as the love that incomprehensibly chooses a people for itself.*[231]

The covenant reality transforms and integrates different created ethical values by opening them up to a transcendent referent. The immanent righteousness (*sedeqah*) of the created order, for example, undergoes a transformation when it confronts the "might of the transcendent *sedaka* of the Creator-God."[232] Thus divine transcendence reveals itself in free acts of salvation that "break through" "the order of the world"[233] and give rise to Israel's praise. In turn, this praise attests to the integration of the divine attributes in the one divine subject. What is also important to note is that Balthasar associates mercy with divine power and freedom. Mercy can overcome the justice that is inherent to the ethics of the world, and the further implication is that mercy and justice are related to each other not as polar opposites, but as mutually necessary goods.

This gracious self-disclosure afforded Israel as part of the covenant form carries with it related demands for behavior. Balthasar focuses not on the specific commandments that spell out right behavior, but on the more fundamental desire to accommodate human righteousness to divine righteousness. What matters, both in cultic practice and in the fundamental covenant disposition, is that "something is accepted as 'right' in God's sight, for he [the believer] must await his definitive being right as something that comes to him from heaven."[234] Such radical obedience requires that God is trustworthy, and is therefore grounded in the covenant relationship that from the beginning exhibits God's credibility and truth as truthfulness. *Sedeqah* means that one acknowledges God's righteousness by living in accordance with his commandments, which in turn brings about right human relationships.[235] The covenant, then, is the "space" within which it becomes possible for Israel to "incarnate" divine righteousness, among other divine attributes.

Like *sedek*, *mishpat's* location within the covenant elevates its significance above that of the intra-mundane meaning often given to justice: "to everyone their due." As a core element of its meaning, Balthasar argues, covenant justice includes compassion, especially for the poor.[236] Thus, to spread divine justice is to overturn the disordered order of the world and to care for the poor first. Inherent in this discussion is the recognition that "justice" so often stands for the rights of the powerful vis-à-vis the weak. In the covenant, this power relation suffers revision: God is the source of *mishpat*, which now bears an intimate and concrete relation to salvation. Out of compassion, God seeks to establish the right of the poor when that right has been violated, and he punishes all Israel when they adopt an immanent notion of justice in place of that established within the covenant. When the exile brings the entire nation low, the new situation permits divine compassion on the poor to include all of Israel: "Now *mishpat* is justice," Balthasar writes, "as the fruit of compassion, as grace."[237] Here he can highlight the unique status of the Servant of YHWH who becomes the "especial mediator of God's *mishpat* to the whole world."[238] The God of Israel, Balthasar argues throughout *GL6*, is both the powerful God of theophanic revelation and the faithful God of the covenant who deploys power on behalf of the poor in compassion and mercy (*chesed*). The covenant relation reveals a *circumincessio* of divine attributes such that righteousness can be mercifully granted on the basis of the Servant's act of vicarious obedience, and what appears God's just action towards Pharaoh is simultaneously mercy for Israel.

Here we can note that Balthasar's narrative treatment of the divine attributes offers a direct challenge to Hegel's systematic presuppositions. In his 1827 *Lectures on the Philosophy of Religion* (*LPR*), Hegel argues that the representational language of theology shows its weakness when it confronts the seeming irreducibility of divine attributes such that contraries remain contiguous without any reconciliation or resolution.[239] Divine justice and mercy sit uneasily side by side, waiting for a logical resolution that never comes. This claim presupposes what we indicated earlier, namely, that for Hegel theological and philosophical discourses have precisely the same object and that conceptual articulation is most adequate to that object. It is, of course, important to our interest in Marcionism that justice and mercy are the "opposites" that Hegel chooses as his examples. We have already seen that Balthasar rejects Hegel's discursive analysis. Balthasar also rejects the premise that different—not opposed—divine attributes should find a logical resolution or dissolution. His treatment of the divine attributes instead holds at its center divine personal freedom. A person does not contradict herself when she acts justly in some cases, mercifully in others. Far more than a conceptual logic, Balthasar indicates, a dramatic narrative can capably and concretely present this personal complexity and mystery. Within Israel's covenant, both love and justice point beyond the finite to the Transcendent God of mercy and righteousness.

Theological Anthropology

THE FIRST HALF OF THIS CHAPTER has addressed Israel's covenant primarily from the side of the divine. We have dwelt on the category of encounter, on spectacular displays of divine power, and on God's liberating mercy disclosed through YHWH's relation to Israel. Throughout we have been concerned to show how Balthasar's reading of Israel's covenant expresses positive content, and also his ongoing argument against Prometheanism and Marcionism. Balthasar reads Israel's testimony to theophany and covenant as revelations of a divine mystery of transcendent power and mercy that would frustrate any attempts at reduction to an inner-worldly dialectic. Within the covenant reality itself, justice and mercy coincide and interpenetrate in ways that lead to praise and gratitude. Narrative is not reducible to logic and justice is irreducible to mercy. Indeed, personal freedom in dialogue demands this complexity.

It is equally important to investigate Balthasar's reading of Old Covenant revelation from the human side. Here we will find that his discussion of Old Covenant theological anthropology largely parallels his discussion of divine disclosure as its subjective correlative. In other words, a movement from the formal and abstract to the concrete covenant can be discerned here as well. In this section, then, our discussion moves from a biblical consideration of the *imago dei*, to the "secular" drama of human autonomy in all its grandeur and misery, to the expropriation of Israel for divine service, to the height of divine disclosure in the drama of the prophetic staircase, and finally to the "empty time" of messianic, apocalyptic, and sapiential forms.

The "Abstract" Image

BALTHASAR'S ANTHROPOLOGICAL CONSIDERATIONS are "abstract" or formal in the same way that his discussion of theophanic revelation was abstract. Unlike reflection on the direct and concrete relationship between God and Israel in the covenant, this discussion takes the human as an image of God *per se*. It considers the nature of the human as a reflection of God outside their more important dramatic interaction.[240] The human image is meant to "attest" and "make present" the archetype and can be beautiful only insofar as it expresses the "splendour beyond all images."[241] Balthasar thinks that the relationship between image and archetype receives significant development from its first appearance in Genesis through the reflections found in Psalm 8 and in Sirach. Through their reflections on the image, the Genesis accounts stress human-divine relation in difference, humanity's reflection of God's sovereignty with respect to creation, the integrity of the human person as both body and spirit, and the presence of erotic love from the beginning.[242] Sirach takes up what Genesis offers but advances its reflections on the image beyond the role of governance to call forth praise, thereby exhorting what Psalm 8 accomplishes in fact.[243] Balthasar's "abstract" discussion begins with the liturgy of praise that will become the liturgy of obedience in the prophets and in the New Covenant. We can relate this view to our anti-Promethean context. If what makes human beings most human is the praise and obedience they offer to God, then the Prometheanism that has at its root a kind of anti-doxological animus, comes to seem, as Thomas Merton knew well,[244] a kind of anti-humanism only posing as humanism.

Balthasar's further anthropological reflections reveal the tensional drama inherent to being human, a view common to the patristic writers examined in de Lubac's treatment of tripartite anthropology.[245] Human nature finds itself stretched between two poles that can be described in at least four different ways: I and Thou, being and act, nature and grace, and Adam and Christ. All of these suspensions or tensions are related, and all presuppose a human *eros* for the other and for the divine. The "being-for-another" or I-Thou quality of the image provides a formal ground for the reception of divine revelation and reaches fulfillment in the New Testament spousal relationship between the Church and Christ.[246] The knowledge of the divine will given in our being finds its adequate revelation and response in Christ who thereby resolves the tension between being and act. "Badly tarnished" human nature also finds its ultimate meaning and fulfillment in the New Covenant, which will "gather up into itself the meaning of all suspended fragments of the image that is man."[247] The final suspension between Adam and Christ enfolds all of the others: Christ perfects the ancient form of the image from within and simultaneously exhibits the unity between human dominion over creation and pliancy to God that specifies this dominion as service.[248]

Autonomous Image and a Hidden God

THE FOUR ANTHROPOLOGICAL TENSIONS elucidate an anthropological framework, but for Balthasar the reality of human existence must be examined in action. This action, however, need not signify the central drama between God and Israel within the covenant. God permits his creatures a time of autonomy that stretches from David to Ecclesiastes. This realm of secular autonomy corresponds to a time of God's hiddenness, for Balthasar, but not to a time of divine inactivity[249]: "He [God] lets man explore the extremest possibilities of his freedom and yet he conducts events as a play of his manifold elections and directions."[250] The literature of Kings and Wisdom reveals divine glory in a more indirect or abstract manner than, for instance, found in the concrete, dramatic prophetic form. Balthasar contends that this period of Israel's history unfolds the story of paradise as it shows both the splendor and misery of human freedom.[251]

Balthasar reads these writings much like Greek culture might have read Homeric poetry. His emphasis falls on the ways in which different characters express various virtues and vices found in a worldly existence. David displays the virtues of friendship, magnanimity, and forbearance but also brings upon himself a curse when he murders Uriah. Solomon represents the overriding ambition for power that subjects even love to its *libido dominandi*. He marries Pharaoh's daughter in the interest of political alliance and establishes a standing professional army to subjugate the peoples conquered by David.[252] The Wisdom literature results from the advantages gained by the Royal Court and from Solomon's desire to remedy cultural deficiencies by establishing a professional class.[253]

Balthasar's treatment of Proverbs marks his most critical assessment of any element of the biblical literature. This discussion is of particular importance to us because his criticisms of Proverbs can shed light on his own view of covenant existence. In particular, Balthasar objects to Proverbs' backgrounding of the covenant and historical revelation, lingering Epicureanism, negative estimation of the poor, and easy linking of right behavior with success. Against Barth, however, Balthasar chooses to contextualize rather than reject this book's status as divine revelation. He thinks that from a Christian perspective, Proverbs represents an "anthropocentric philosophy with a religious backdrop, or an enlightened, liberal theology."[254] It concentrates on the human and human capacities in juxtaposition to the divine. Although its locus within the canon proscribes its theological erasure, Balthasar judges that it cannot compete with the historically grounded revelation that surrounds it. Essentially, Proverbs is concerned not with the glory and will of God, but with a religious rationale for its ethic of social and political aspiration. Such a form remains inner-worldly and has not really confronted the God of the Covenant, and certainly not the Cross.

We might add that Balthasar sees in all of this literature a kind of parallel to modern bourgeois culture with its professionalization, aspirations for power and success, and anthropocentrism that brings with it technological fetishism. Balthasar makes this position clear not only in his endorsement of Charles Peguy's positions on the modern techno-craze, but also in his text *The God Question and Modern Man*,[255] where the hiddenness of God in modernity becomes a major theme to be interpreted through the central Christian mystery of the Cross. As we continue to notice how each of Balthasar's scriptural reflections connect with his treatments of modernity outside the biblical text, we amplify the judgment of Dickens, namely, that Balthasar is retrieving a pre-modern biblical reading that sees the world and human beings always in relation to the divine actor. This is what I am envisioning as Balthasar's Catholic version of George Lindbeck's placing of the world in the Bible. Balthasar does not limit his biblical reading to the texts at hand but always has a bi-focal, to say the least, vision of culture and scripture. Scripture reads culture, just as culture provides material to be read.

Expropriation

THE COVENANT RELATION OPENS UP TO ISRAEL the nature and identity of its God. Concepts from the immanent plane of existence are elevated and related to the divine holiness, thus making them at once more beautiful and more weighty.[256] Within the covenant, then, God becomes the one who for no discernible reason "deigns to communicate himself to others ... permitting them to enter the sphere of his uniqueness and holiness."[257] To Israel, God is becoming more and more real, more concrete. But this revelation or invitation to enter the "sphere" of the divine also means that Israel is to become an expropriated people, that is, a people called beyond its own nature for a mission to the world. The covenant is a realm of salvation that is also the realm of deepest revelation. It is here that Israel is called to live beyond itself and to live by the commandments. For Balthasar, two biblical forms, the Levitical cult and the Deuteronomic Law, represent a deepening awareness of just what this expropriation implies.

Balthasar reads the tribe of Levi as a kind of second expropriation within Israel. This tribe is given to God by Israel, and by God to Aaron, for the sake of the cult. They become expiatory mediators charged with the task of staying the divine wrath.[258] Levi represents the poor man who is singled out and exposed and who must rely on God alone, embodying "in a privileged manner the covenant and the knowledge of God in the covenant."[259] This positive estimation of the Levitical priesthood provides Balthasar a way to tie cultic practice to divine grace and disclosure. Balthasar avails himself of this opportunity when he links post-exilic Levitical circles to a deeper expropriation of Israel exemplified in those "strange acts of transcendence," namely, the psalms. The psalms present a deeper calling into the divine life, a "rapture" that is demythologized to now signify a radical trust in God, even beyond death, rooted in God's intimate disclosure of his own identity.[260]

Deuteronomy too, Balthasar thinks, exhibits an expropriation within Israel's already expropriated existence. The author now places the people back at their origins, at Sinai, where they confront the prospect of meeting God face to face, but put forth Moses instead. As mediator, Moses is doubly expropriated: by Israel, who pushes him forward in its place, and by God who shows himself to Moses. Moses stands fast in the face of divine glory, and, consequently, he can communicate this glory to the people. Revelation deepens well beyond theophanic disclosure here and reveals the "true kernel" of glory as "absolute love."[261] For Deuteronomy, the mediator serves the covenant relation between God and Israel, who is called to respond to divine election in kind, that is, through a holistic love that springs from gratitude and includes the body. Concretely, this means obedience and a readiness to serve.[262] Balthasar argues that this response promises the integration of aesthetic justice or "rightness"—as in fitting response, attunement to God, appropriateness—and ethical justice or righteousness. Balthasar again makes the incarnational "pre-figuration" apparent in that Israel's desire to substitute Moses for itself allows the mediator to take on new importance in salvation history. God thus places the burden of the covenant on chosen mediators, those who will stand fast, speak for God, and communicate the divine glory to the people. It is this same mediator who must bear the sin of the people and die in their place. An obedience available to God's word on the one hand, and to the people's rejection on the other, "permits the covenant to be embodied substantially on earth."[263]

This incarnational pre-figuration deepens in the praise of Israel, where Balthasar finds the integration of human dispositions, including all those qualities that make up the ethical and the aesthetic, and the realization of God's word as scripture. Scripture is Israel's remembrance of God's great deeds on its behalf and on behalf of all creation in the past. To become such a true word of God, that is, to have the necessary mutuality that alone allows for such a glorification, Israel must become transparent to the divine word. Where transparency marks a realization of familiarity and intimacy with God through profound expropriation, the condition for transparency is humility. Balthasar does not hesitate to recall Augustine's notion of confession, itself rooted in the psalms: the public admission of sin and recalling of God's gracious ways.[264] It is precisely God's love that makes such an admission possible.[265] When Israel humbles itself in this way, it can become a conduit for God's word, which always includes Israel's words. Israel's doxological disposition is its perfection, a state of being that allows God to "make out of the word of answer a word of God himself" and therefore a word of revelation.[266] The suggestion is that liturgy offers a kind of consummation of covenant existence. More to the point of Old Covenant-New Covenant relation, Balthasar makes the rather stunning claim that insofar as this dialogue between Israel and God is shaped entirely by grace, "it is formally a trinitarian revelation, even before the Trinity is materially revealed in the new covenant."[267]

The unavoidable conclusion is that for Balthasar aspects of Old Covenant revelation are unsurpassable, especially with respect to the content of revelation. The New Testament, he claims, does not formally surpass the "correctness" (*justesse*) of the Old.[268] The anti-Marcionite subtext of von

Balthasar's reading should be patent; it is the one, Triune God who comes into view throughout the entire economy of Old and New Covenant. Israel itself has an incarnational thrust as it embodies or attempts to make real in the world God's attributes, God's word, and God's will. The incarnational pre-figuration that Balthasar finds in the Old Covenant itself becomes more evident through his discussion of the "prophetic staircase."

The Stairway of Obedience and Interruption

WHILE THE SINAI FOCUS of the Levitical priesthood and Deuteronomy signify for Balthasar profound instances of divine and human disclosure, it is through the covenant battle with sin, and in special mediators, that divine love and human response find their most fecund expression. This dramatic interaction shows most clearly the proper meaning of history or salvation history. The first section below addresses these issues. But the Old Covenant does not flow directly into the New upon the backs of these mediators. Rather, an interruption occurs in salvation history, and Israel experiences the dark night that is divine withdrawal. Somewhat ominously, especially for anyone concerned to argue that Balthasar has a positive view of post-biblical Judaism, Balthasar associates this dark night with movements of the Second Temple period. Balthasar has rightly drawn criticism for this discussion, but I will suggest that there is more here than meets the eye.

Salvation History—The "Stairway of Obedience"

ALTHOUGH THE PRIMITIVE- AND PRE-HISTORY OF ISRAEL manifest the divine attributes and their integration in divine glory through the covenant relationship, Balthasar maintains that it is only "history" that yields a truly concrete figuration of glory. In particular, divine glory gives its most "concrete" expression in response to sin.[269] Once Israel breaks the covenant, God shows his freedom to take on its requirements from both sides. Here, Balthasar introduces the trope of the "stairway of obedience":

> *Where man has utterly failed, the history of the covenant of God becomes a history of God with himself.... God wills to construct for himself a stairway in the men whom he has chosen, a stairway that is to lead him down into the god-less darkness. A stairway constructed of obedience.*[270]

The language here can be a bit confusing, if not confused. It is not clear why Balthasar speaks of "God with himself" when he wants to stress the free obedience or availability of the prophets to God's Word. In any event, human freedom remains a constitutive factor in revelation itself, even if that freedom is crucially specified as obedience. It is through the free mediation of those in whom God seeks to unfold his word (*dabar*) that the stairway leads toward full incarnation. Balthasar wants to stress that individuals such as religious founders like Moses and Abraham, or the prophets, exercise their freedom not through a capacity to command, through religious genius, or through an assertion of autonomy, but through a readiness to obey.[271] The Marian archetype again plays a key role in Balthasar's biblical reading. As we saw above, the theological significance of obedience for Balthasar increases in direct proportion to the profundity of divine involvement or intimacy. It serves to maintain the ontological difference between the divine and human natures, while marking a free union of wills: "Man serves God by making his will the servant vessel for the absolute will."[272] The emphasis on obedience, he argues, deters a "mysticism of absorption into the deity because the act whereby man transcends himself to enter the covenant realm which God has opened up always presupposes and displays the difference between the eternal God and man who passes away."[273] Through the motif of obedience, the ever greater difference between God and humanity becomes evident, but it does so from a position of divine-human intimacy, not the heteronomy rejected by Kant. Moreover, there is no divide between faith and works here. Faith shows itself as an active availability and trust. It is Abraham's obedience that allows the "history of revelation" to begin, and it is in the prophets that divine disclosure and Israel's response of praise converge most profoundly. The staircase expresses both God's love for his people and the praise-as-obedience that designates the correct human response to this love.

Balthasar's staircase trope also deepens his view of the Old Covenant as preparation and education. Phenomenological proximity to and movement toward the Incarnation at times becomes sufficiently radical to warrant the use of Chalcedonian two-nature or *perichoresis* language.[274] Humility and total, corporeal availability to God's Word combine to reveal God's openness to suffering within creation and thus bring to light new depths of divine love.[275] Of course judgment on those who would trade God's standard of justice for that of the world's remains stern. As well, the momentum of the divine *kabod* can wreak havoc on Israel precisely because it fails to treat the poor according to the divine will.[276] Jeremiah witnesses to this havoc and a new stage in salvation history when he offers only judgment and the hope that the God he knows will institute a new and eternal covenant. Balthasar reads Jeremiah as the end of Israel's intra-historical hope: the time for intra-historical salvation is past.[277]

The prophetic staircase also fills out the "abstract" anthropological tensions we considered earlier. Prophetic obedience intensifies the tensions proper to human existence in the world. The prophets are caught in a vice between solidarity with the transcendent God on the one hand and the people on the other. Jeremiah is "the first to experience a kind of supratemporal burden of the divine presence, of the actions and decisions of God";[278] Isaiah shares Israel's impurity and yet is given a mission to his people from God;[279] Ezekiel is entirely expropriated for his mission, and becomes a "personified word of God" for the people.[280] Yet he remains in solidarity with them as he enters "into its [Israel's] destiny of destruction" and shares their suffering.[281] All of the tensions are here: I and Thou—the prophet and Israel, the prophet and God; being and act—the prophet as human being-in-the-covenant who must act as prophet to the people of that covenant; nature and grace—the struggle to put human potential at the service of the divine word; Adam and Christ—solidarity with sin on the one hand, and the reflection of grace and judgment on the other. Each of these tensions is filled out through the personal presence of God and the presence of the people of Israel.

Like the other pre-figurations we have noticed, the "servant" represents for Balthasar both a moment in the flow of the Old Covenant toward the New and a form that bears its own unique analogy to Christ. In the wake of glory's departure, the servant consoles the people with an offer of salvation nearly devoid of judgment, "an unheard of admission of divine love."[282] Balthasar judges, however, that this salvation cannot be simply continuous with the ancient covenant, but must arise anew from the Source. More importantly, for Israel to partake in this new covenant, it must relativize the uniqueness of its own election. Their "boundaries are broken through," the promise now leading into an unforeseeable future.[283] Israel becomes a "model," "reduced in significance to serve a historical act of God that has its origin further away than Israel and a goal lying beyond Israel."[284] Thus, with the servant, Israel's role as a model for an offer of salvation larger than itself and set in the ontologically unique future makes itself known.

For Balthasar, the servant also gives the strongest pre-figuration of the Incarnation. He attains an intimacy with God "beyond everything in the Old Testament."[285] As opposed to the scenarios found in Jeremiah and Job, the servant offers no resistance or struggle with the divine subject. In contrast to Ezekiel, the divine-servant relationship is not a "lordly taking possession," but a "mystery of penetration": "the glory of God lies in the Servant, the glory of the Servant lies in God,"[286] an apt paraphrase of Irenaeus.[287] The servant suffers vicariously for the people and justifies those whose sins he bears. To achieve this, he had to become identical with his mission to console the people and prepare the way for the coming glory. Balthasar nevertheless judges that the Old Covenant lacks the "formative power" necessary to draw a complete picture of the Servant.[288] Yet the overlap with Christian faith is impressive, and before we enter caveats, we should focus on just where Balthasar's theology of glory has brought us.

Certainly for Balthasar it is in the prophets and in the Servant that we find Israel's most profound approximation to the revelation in Christ. However, there is no leap here. Rather, the prophets stand inside the same covenant as Israel in its entirety. The same covenantal grace that makes Deuteronomy a witness to divine glory as divine love, and makes the psalms witnesses to the glory of God throughout creation and in history, allows the prophets to reveal God's kenotic love for his people. Israel is expropriated throughout its history. The prophets are a deepening of this expropriation. With this focus on the covenantal context for all divine disclosure, Balthasar assures that not only is Israel's history crucial, but that Israel's free response to grace is constitutive of revelation itself. Israel as a people permits this revelation to take place through its obedience and in its praise.

Yet the prophets do represent a deepening disclosure of God. Collectively, they gather the form of the mediator who represents God to the people and suffers divine wrath in the people's stead. They incarnate God's word for the present time and show the depths of divine love through simultaneous solidarity with God and Israel. Here, in the prophetic commissions, salvation and revelation thoroughly intertwine. Divine self-abandonment opens up to the pain of the people's rejection in repeated attempts to save Israel from destruction and to turn them toward righteousness. It is precisely through this response to sin that God reveals the inner depths of divine glory as divine love.

Interruption and Continuity

THE GREATEST DIFFICULTY IN PRESENTING BALTHASAR as a pro-Jewish theologian, at least in his biblical theology, arises with his treatment of post-exilic or Second Temple Judaism. This period has been the *bête noir* of a long tradition of Protestant biblical theology stretching back to Julius Wellhausen (1844-1918). Jon Levenson has brought this bias against Second Temple Judaism to light,[289] and Dickens applies Levenson's critique to Balthasar, but then observes where Balthasar transcends the anti-Judaism of the many biblical critics he was reading. No treatment of Balthasar's theology of Judaism can afford to ignore Dickens' astute and astutely critical discussion or the insights of Levenson. Dickens is right to say that some of Balthasar's readings are "indefensible." I want to argue two points relative to Balthasar's reading of this period. First, Balthasar is in many instances reading directly against the tradition cited by Dickens and Levenson. In fact, he wants to show a great deal of continuity between Sinai and post-exilic Judaism, even if this continuity shows evidence of stress. Second, I want to read Balthasar as in some sense Lindbeckian, that is, as not only proposing that the world be found in Scripture, but as actually enacting such a reading in very pointed ways. The target of Balthasar's critical comments with respect to post-exilic Judaism, I suggest here, is often not post-biblical Judaism or the supposed "works righteousness" of this Judaism, which he explicitly denies, but rather Christian and Western civilization as it develops from the late middle ages through its modern Promethean manifestations. Balthasar's targets are two: the Church itself and modern Prometheanism.

There can be little doubt that in relation to Balthasar's assessment of the "staircase of obedience," his estimation of the post-exilic literature is negative. Balthasar repeats the division between Israel and Judaism known since Wellhausen (but as we shall see, rejects the content of this division). Thus the post-exilic literature represents a "twilight of glory" where the covenant code that proclaimed the "eternal in the transitory" is "sealed up."[290] While each kind of post-exilic literature participates in the preparation of forms for the coming covenant in Christ, in relation to Israel's salvation history, the post-exilic literature lies a whole "level down."[291] Balthasar here alludes to Luther and treats these post-exilic theologies under the rubric of "*theologia gloriae*," a title that carries at least a threefold negative significance for him: the attempt to force the presence of glory and salvation, placement of divine judgment in the past to artificially proclaim salvation at hand, and placement of human constructs in the way of divine glory's genuine disclosure. Yet Balthasar believes the messianic, apocalyptic, and sapiential forms of this period play a crucial role in mediating the coming form of salvation. Balthasar puts this more strongly: "Without messianism, apocalyptic and wisdom theology, there would be no New Testament: all three are indispensable mediators, because they permit the historical form of Israel to become transcendent in three directions."[292] If Balthasar thinks that these mediations *at times* obstruct God's realization of the covenant, "the same is true precisely within Christianity too."[293] While each form will receive a transformation in light of Christ, there is no way, Balthasar claims, to connect the New Covenant in Christ with the glory of the Old Covenant and Israel apart from the post-exilic forms. Briefly put: there is no way to Christian glory but through Judaism.

We can briefly tally the positives and negatives that Balthasar sees in the different forms of the theology of glory: Messianism provides the notion of a special figure sent by God to bring salvation but limits its vision of salvation to the "purely temporal future."[294] Daniel's apocalyptic vision discloses the vertical drama absent in messianism and also provides the son of man imagery to be taken up in the New Covenant.[295] But apocalyptic reduces great biblical figures to moral exemplars, shades into a kind of Gnostic mysticism and world pessimism, and takes an anthropocentric tack. Worst of all, apocalyptic reserves salvation for the few while the multitudes are condemned to suffer in Hell, a perversion, Balthasar thinks, of Israel's doctrine of election and one that the Church itself fails to avoid.[296]

The Wisdom writings discover Sophia as a mediating agent between their own religion and surrounding worldviews, thus opening the way for genuine Christian mission. In addition, Ben Sirach supplies a vision of God whose transcendence is such that it allows for a radically immanent relation to the created world.[297] Old Testament Sophia finds a home in the Johannine prologue as God's act of "going forth from himself."[298] Nevertheless, Balthasar thinks that Wisdom literature makes two significant errors. Influenced by apocalyptic, the Wisdom writers came to believe that Israel alone will be saved while all "Egyptians" will be cast into darkness. Equally erroneous, he asserts, is the view that Israel has seen the last of divine judgment and need only praise God in all his works, seeing his glory all around.[299] Balthasar uses strong words here. The lack of divine judgment regarding

Israel in the wisdom literature "means that they too [the authors] stand in the 'long twilight,' and the glory that they praise remains ethereal and bloodless.... they belong to a bourgeois age...."[300]

Balthasar would appear to follow much of German biblical scholarship in positing a severe break between Israel and "Judaism." Yet Balthasar also offers an impressive critique of essential elements in this story. Because we have reached such an important point in our argument, we will need to quote Balthasar at greater length than we have previously. Indeed, Balthasar simply does not believe that the absence of new events of revelation means that somehow Israel was without the word of God as a living event in their lives:

> ... even in a present deprived of glory, there must have remained such strong impulses from the historical period, such strong witnesses of the kabod of Yahweh, that these could be experienced as fully valid substitutes for what was missing. And de facto, the event-character of two factors in Israel's religion retained their power even in the period when events were few; the event of the word of God and the event of the blood of man and beast.[301]

Writing in direct contrast to the Wellhausen line on post-exilic Israel, Balthasar argues that:

> ... the period of Judaism is said to be the period in which the verbal form of the Bible received its definitive fixed written shape ... while on the other hand the living word, which had always been spoken out of historical situations, became an absolutely posited "law" which solidified ahistorically. But although this account of things does reflect aspects of what was a very ambiguous period, the whole phenomenon of the "word of God" or even of the "Torah" cannot in the least be so described, for God's word never ceased to be a speech event in Israel.[302]

Balthasar is able to draw important points of theological continuity between Israel and Judaism and a positive estimation of Torah interpretation, ritual, holiness laws, and even sacrifice. As Dickens points out, Balthasar is able to transcend much of the biblical theology of the nineteenth century and his own time in just this way.[303] Within Israel's covenant context, Balthasar argues, the word of God continues to have an event character in its canonical form of "Torah." The sermon as interpretation of Torah and the enactment of the holiness laws make the divine word present and incarnate and thus permit a "living relationship to the ancient words."[304] The exclusivism associated with Josianic or Deuteronomic reform movements should not be construed as an "arrogant consciousness of election," but as an attempt to "continue faithfully the ancient forms."[305] Likewise, Torah observance discloses the "will to remain in the covenant relationship to YHWH at any price and to show him [YHWH] the harmony between word and answer by means of the Torah itself."[306] When viewed in the light of a doctrine of imminent expectation, Jewish Torah observance is not static, self-righteous, or perfunctory. Rather, it expresses a dynamic trust in YHWH and a will to maintain the significance of historical events in the present.[307]

Balthasar equally refrains from an entirely negative reading of Israel's cultic sacrifices. Israel's sacrificial offerings represent a "persevering action" that seeks to retain hope in the midst of an "empty time,"[308] exhibit the total and corporeal commitment of Israel to the will of God, and disclose the freedom and sovereignty of God over creation as both a giver of life and as a righteous judge who stands for the oppressed. We should be clear that Balthasar is somewhat critical of the cultic sacrifices, as Dickens points out. But we should be equally clear that no current Jewish clamor for resuming the Temple sacrifices exists. In criticizing this practice, Balthasar does no more than agree with the predominant Jewish sensibility by the second century and certainly today. Balthasar's view sounds much like that of the contemporary Jewish philosopher Michael Wyschogrod, who does not wish to see sacrifice resumed, but nevertheless believes that the end of cultic sacrifice does indicate a loss, namely, of a sense of Israel's full, corporeal commitment to the covenant as the people of God.[309] For Balthasar, moreover, cultic sacrifice recalls for Israel the Passover as an "act of substitution carried out by God himself, whereby he wins Israel for himself as his first born...."[310] In other words, Balthasar suggests that Israel's sacrifice has a positive role to play in the interpretation of redemption itself.[311] Balthasar's reading of the post-exilic period puts the Wellhausian line under great stress.

Our second major point was that Balthasar has a goal in mind with his reading of Old Covenant glory that is not confined to biblical scholarship. I want to make explicit here what has been suggested through our brief discussion of his treatment of the post-exilic period, namely, that Balthasar enacts what George Lindbeck recommends: he reads the world in reference to the biblical account. This does not mean, however, that the biblical account is allowed to construct the objects of interpretation garnered from extra-biblical sources. They are to be interpreted and measured as forms in their own right. In other words, Balthasar maintains the relative autonomy of the created world in a way that Lindbeck may not. More specifically, I want to argue that Balthasar has in mind both Christian ecclesial culture and modern Western culture when he reads the biblical stories.[312] Several hints can be found to suggest this. First, we can recall a point of organization. Balthasar might reasonably have placed his material discussion of biblical glory, found in volumes six and seven of his theological aesthetics, immediately after his formal treatment of glory in volume one. This would be an obvious order. That he chose not to is significant and should caution against reading his biblical theology as separate from his narrative of modern Prometheanism. Instead, the formal volume and the biblical volumes might be said to wrap his cultural genealogy in volumes four and five, lending those cultural works their proper theological context, interpretation, and judgment. Second, the presence of anachronistic terminology such as "bourgeois," "Gnostic," and "anthropocentric" in the midst of a biblical discussion should tip us off to a target other than biblical or even post-biblical Judaism. Early in his discussion of post-exilic Judaism, Balthasar gives us another clue:

> *If here the three dimensions in which Judaism developed its theology of glory are presented under the title of "Theologia gloriae," this is done bearing in mind the further meaning that this phrase has acquired in more recent Christian theology: it is a theology that has somehow put the nights and terrors of the judgment behind itself, without integrating them in depth.*[313]

Balthasar's concern is the loss of divine transcendence and divine judgment in modern theology and religious thought. Thus, what ought to be a theology of glory often becomes instead a philosophy of beauty as the divine gets domesticated. As we have seen, he is not arguing that post-biblical Judaism is devoid of a relation to divine glory.[314]

A more pointed reason for seeing in Balthasar's discussion an intra-ecclesial critique is that each criticism Balthasar allows in his biblical discussion of post-exilic Israel finds its counterpart in his criticisms of either historical Christian existence or modern cultural movements. We can begin with his designation of the post-exilic period as an "empty time." It might be supposed that after Christ such a time cannot happen, glory cannot go hiding, but for Balthasar this is painfully not the case. Neither the Church nor Western culture is immune to a loss, forgetfulness, usurpation, or even outright rejection of divine glory. While examples abound, especially in his *The God Question and Modern Man*,[315] the following passage from *GL5* is particularly apt for our purposes:

> *The late Middle Ages is a time of darkness like few others; the social order is in ruins, war and plague prevail, secular and ecclesiastical facades are collapsing, the face of the visible Church is disfigured beyond recognition, especially through the great schism; and the radiance of the heavenly Jerusalem no longer breaks through the clouds to illumine God's earthly realm.*[316]

While on Balthasar's reading the late middle ages is a particularly dark or empty time, it is hardly the only one. Balthasar believes much of modern thought—though not as much as supposed by Martin Heidegger—has lost any feel for the presence or event of divine glory as God's "earthly realm" serves to mediate it. The loss of creation's mediating role in modern metaphysics means that divine revelation and creation will at some point be collapsed, as they are in the identity metaphysics that we have discussed. Thus biblical glory, the glory of the transcendent God, finds little room to make itself known as anything other than categories drawn up by human thought.

According to Balthasar, out of the "empty time" of Israel's post-exilic existence springs a desire for a purely temporal, innerworldly version of salvation. Balthasar's concern, however, is not primarily with the troubles and faults of ancient Israel, or even of post-biblical Judaism, but, as we have seen, with the modern results of innerworldly messianisms. Balthasar rejects any erasure of a transcendent norm that announces itself both through Israel's covenant and in Jesus Christ. Messianism apart from the transcendent norm of the Old Covenant, on the one hand, or the Incarnation on the other, leads for Balthasar to some of the greatest Promethean tragedies of the twentieth century. Note that his target is not religious Israel or post-biblical Judaism, but rather the secularization of Jewish messianism in Western and Christian culture.

Balthasar's account of apocalyptic indicates that it provides the vertical dimension lost on messianism, but then greatly diminishes the importance of the world and the historical dimension of revelation so important to messianic religion. Otherwise put, messianism without apocalyptic is Marxist, whereas apocalyptic without messianism is Hegelian. Neither accounts substantially for the figure of Christ who, as Lindbeck so neatly argues, joins the historical particularity and eschatological singularity inherent to messianism with the universality of the Incarnation.³¹⁷ In addition, apocalyptic too often indulges in a kind of soteriological parsimony and Gnostic *hubris* that determines the saved from the damned prior to the *eschaton*. Along with this issue, Balthasar cites "world pessimism" and anthropocentrism as tendencies associated with some versions of apocalyptic, though certainly not all. Of course, Balthasar's critique of modern anthropocentrism is a staple of his thought. In *Love Alone Is Credible*, this critique forms the second major way in which biblical glory finds itself reduced in the direction of an identity metaphysics; in *GL5*, the same critique consumes the greater portion of his text (as we have discussed in the previous chapter). If anything, Balthasar's criticisms of Church soteriological parsimony are as evident as his criticisms of modern anthropocentrism. He notes that the error of dividing the saved from the damned is one that the Church has not entirely avoided and writes what was a controversial essay arguing that Christians have a duty to hope for universal salvation. Perhaps more interesting, however, are his critical comments on Dante in this regard, and his laudatory treatment of the French poet, Charles Peguy, after noting Peguy's disgust with any teaching that might consign human beings to eternal torment. Balthasar's sympathies are entirely with Peguy's position, even if he wants to keep the "Origenist" doctrine of *apokatastasis* at arm's length. Certainly Balthasar believes that apocalyptic of a certain kind, mainly that found in Daniel and Revelation, offers essential content for Christian faith. What he rejects in apocalyptic is what he believes is a rejection of the goodness of the world and of the possibility for its redemption, neither of which he finds at issue in post-biblical Judaism, but both of which he finds at issue in Christianity. Indeed, Balthasar will argue that Christianity's relation with Judaism is essential to Christianity precisely if it is not to become a disincarnate ethereal mysticism without regard for its neighbor. Balthasar's view of the relation between post-biblical Judaism and Christianity will be the main topic of our next chapter.

Conclusion

BALTHASAR'S PHENOMENOLOGY OF DOXOLOGICAL ENCOUNTER, that is, of the encounter with, reception of, and response to divine glory, manifests itself in a variety of discursive forms. All of these forms, however, remain rooted in the covenantal dynamic of divine glory, seeking to fill its created image and radiate through Israel into the world. I argued here that

Balthasar's phenomenology of encounter as a biblical datum serves his anti-Promethean agenda precisely by showing that biblical encounter never indicates the supposition that human glory and divine glory are equivalent. To the contrary, the glory of the image lies in its humble receptivity to divine glory and, Balthasar argues, to the extent that the encounter is a genuine one, it will reveal divine glory as Mystery. Biblical encounter leads not to identity metaphysics or "false gnosis," but to praise, obedience, and service, all of which direct Christian identity away from Prometheanism.

If Balthasar's focus on biblical encounter points away from Prometheanism, his phenomenology of glory similarly contests a Marcionite view of the covenants. We saw this formally in chapter one, and here I have argued that for Balthasar God's Word desires to make itself incarnate throughout the Old Covenant in manifold, but not contradictory, ways. Thus, Balthasar rejects simple juxtapositions of Law, ritual, and cult to grace, spirit, and prophecy. Under his reading, each form becomes a distinct mediation of divine glory, and all of them will find their place around the incarnate glory of the New Covenant. In Balthasar's view, neither divine transcendence nor the covenant context for revelation, which includes Torah, cult, prophecy, apocalyptic, and wisdom, are lost in the New Covenant. Instead, he seeks to show how each form finds its full realization and glorification as they give themselves over to the measure of Christ.

In agreement with Dickens, I also observed that some of these *alethic* or revelatory forms are more problematic for Balthasar than others. Certainly Messianism, apocalyptic, and wisdom, in short, the post-exilic literature prompt some of Balthasar's sharper criticisms. Nevertheless, it becomes clear through a close examination of his texts (a) that Balthasar thinks of post-exilic Judaism as an essential mediation of the New Covenant by way of opening up the vertical-apocalyptic, futural-messianic, and contemplative-wisdom dimensions of glory and (b) that Balthasar's criticisms of these forms are not directed at Judaism *per se*, but at imbalanced readings of scripture that have proven detrimental to Judaism, Christianity, and to Western culture generally. Like Origen, yet in a fashion appropriate to his own time, Balthasar envisions both the Incarnation, and also Judaism's own covenant, as a critical measure of the secularized messianisms and the Gnostic Prometheanisms of his own age. Whether going forward to Christ, or backward to Moses, the Promethean hermeneutic of revelation fails on the merits.

Chapter Three

Balthasar and the Encounter with Post-Biblical Judaism

Our second chapter focused on Balthasar's reading of the Old Covenant as both ideology and idolatry critique on the one hand, and as a preparation for Christ on the other. These two functions are related for Balthasar because a clearing of false images is necessary if the true image is to make itself visible. As we have seen, however, this negative or apophatic pedagogy does not exhaust Israel's teaching mission. Israel provides the forms of revelation that lend a historical context for the apprehension of the eschatological revelation in Christ. As pedagogue, Israel bears a mission from God for all humanity:

> ... the history of Israel is indeed a school, not only for Christians, but for mankind as a whole, preparing them for the religion of Christ. It is the introduction ordained by God himself to the most intransigent of faiths, which falls like a meteor from heaven. Man must begin with his own thoughts on religion, with what is rather crudely called "natural religion" and there is not a single idea, not a single thought in the religion of Israel—down to and including the most unique among them, such as the covenant, the kingdom, prophecy—which cannot be paralleled from a religious or sociological point of view; and, whether a priori or a posteriori, they can all of them be shown to be part of a universal religious phenomenon. But at the same time they always have a unique colour, and can be seen for what they are, God's signature in history.[318]

We will investigate what Balthasar believes to be the proper Christian view of Judaism's relation to non-Christian religions in the next chapter. Here, our purpose is to underscore that for Balthasar one requires an Old Covenant education to rightly apprehend the form of Christ.

The misapprehensions of this form for which Balthasar shows greatest concern are those which emanate from Promethean worldviews and substitute human glory for divine glory. Balthasar argues that a contemplative reading of the Old Covenant and the New gives the lie to the idea that Christianity ought to be about the Marcionite excision of Old Covenant revelation or the dissolution of divine transcendence. His reading suggests instead that an encounter with divine glory reveals at once the radical intimacy God desires to have with his creatures and the ever-greater difference between the Creator and the creature. Mary's Magnificat provides a phenomenological centerpiece for Balthasar's argument, but Mary is Jewish and her experience is part and parcel of the prophetic encounter with God, not divorced from it.

The first two sections of the present chapter seek to get beneath Balthasar's reading of specific biblical texts to the "kenotic substructure" of his thought. Christian thought on post-biblical Judaism will be rooted in Christian thinking about the relation of continuity and discontinuity between the two covenants. This is certainly the case for Balthasar. In these first two sections I will argue that he grounds both continuity and discontinuity in the idea of divine kenosis. This is a dangerous move and Balthasar is aware of it. By placing kenosis at the heart of his theology not only of redemption, but of creation and covenant as well, Balthasar risks becoming precisely the Promethean he most despises. I can address this issue here only in brief and as it pertains to Balthasar's reading of the relation between the Old and New Covenants. Yet even within this limited treatment, we can see how Balthasar's kenotic theology positions itself against contemporary uses of "kenosis" often deployed in such a way as to disassociate Christianity from Judaism.

The third section of this chapter focuses on issues directly related to Israel's post-biblical religious significance. Balthasar's book on Martin Buber was his first major treatment of these issues, and his views remain consistent, though not undeveloped, through his discussions in *Spouse of the Word*[319] and *Theo-Drama*. He focuses in all three accounts on Paul's discussion in Romans 9–11, and a significant part of what Balthasar wants to do is to recommend that Christians focus their discussion of Judaism in these texts rather than more tendentious sounding Johannine texts. We will ask whether for Balthasar salvation is open to Judaism even as it rejects Christian messianic and incarnational claims for Christ, whether Jews remain the people of God, and whether, for him, Judaism retains a divinely given mission in the world. While positions as such are not as interesting as how one arrives at them, these questions nevertheless point to a verdict on Balthasar's theology as either pro- or anti-Jewish. Given our claim that he offers what Rosemary Ruether worries is impossible, namely, a high Christology joined to a pro-Jewish theology, his answers to these questions take on even more weight in our overall scheme.

The fourth and final section of this chapter places questions of Jewish-Christian relation once again within a modern problematic. Even if his answer to all the above questions is yes, we must ask what difference Judaism's rejection of the Incarnation makes. If Judaism and Christianity ought to have been one people of God, then it is reasonable to believe that negative consequences accrue from the split. Balthasar believes this is the case both for the religions themselves and for Western culture at large.

Kenotic Continuity: Encounter and Recapitulation

BALTHASAR ARGUES THAT GOD'S SELF-REVELATION emerges into the light of history through the mediation of the people Israel. Their story lends the world a model of the relation between divine and creaturely freedom available for contemplation.[320] Israel's story, Balthasar contends, is also one that develops towards the definitive eschatological revelation in Christ, the two covenants comprising one revelation: "Because the Old and New Testaments, together, constitute God's one revelation, the Old Testament possesses the same 'rightness' or truth as the New: here there is identity, not analogy."[321] Scripture has, for Balthasar, a "single and indivisible content: salvation through judgment."[322] Such a claim is not surprising after we have discussed his rendition of the "prophetic staircase." Even those post-exilic texts that form the *bête noir* of an older Protestant exegesis, in Balthasar's work provide links necessary to the apprehension of Christ's eschatological form. For Balthasar, the light of the Old Covenant is God's light, "and, therefore, not essentially different from the light that will become incarnate in human nature."[323] What I want to stress here is that for Balthasar the continuity between the covenants has a deeper theological basis than a philosophical or abstract monotheism on the one hand, or a superficial exegesis on the other, might suggest. This continuity lies in God's desire to give himself to creation, that is, in a divine *eros* that issues in divine kenosis and descent, which, in turn, makes possible Israel's varied encounters with divine freedom.[324] Because God is one, and because this God is the same One who desires in both

Old and New Covenants to share the divine life with humanity, a high degree of continuity between the covenants is to be expected.

Balthasar conscripts the kenosis language of Philippians 2 for his theology of creation and for the Old Covenant as well, but he does so with the significant concern that identity philosophies of various stripes will take in Christian kenosis language and transform it into an inner-worldly law of historical and even divine development thoroughly available to human reason.[325] Yet Balthasar does not want to ignore the profound insights made available through an extension of the "kenosis" term. After all, if the God who out of love gives up his form is the same God as the God of Israel and the God of creation, then it stands to reason that kenosis is always a possibility, and perhaps a divine desire. Balthasar's solution is to carefully modulate, based upon revelation, what sort of self-emptying he means in each instance and to ground God's kenosis in history through analogies—only analogies, but analogies nonetheless—with the inner Trinitarian life. For Balthasar, the possibilities of historical existence themselves lie within the positive and vital life of the Trinitarian persons.

Thus kenosis in creation and in the Old Covenant bears an analogous rather than univocal relation to that of the New Covenant. Contrary to Hegel, Balthasar does not indicate that the kenosis of creation is a bifurcation of God such that creation itself is in some sense divine, even if divine as alienated finitude.[326] Instead, for Balthasar the kenosis of creation is a divine "giving up" of freedom for the sake of created human freedom made in God's image. The divine kenosis of creation permits humanity its share of freedom and rule. Indeed, it is precisely this act of divine self-limitation that provides a theological presupposition for the human encounter with God. Only because God "lets be"[327] in this way can a true negotiation between divine and human freedom occur. Yet it is equally important to distinguish this self-emptying from that of the New Covenant. Certainly creation offers nothing of the depth of divine kenosis where God takes on finitude, a body, and even death.

Old Covenant kenosis does deepen God's self-emptying beyond what one sees in creation. Balthasar argues that Israel becomes a "model" of the interaction of finite and infinite freedom.[328] God forms a special relationship with Israel, a relationship of promise and fulfillment to which God binds his Word repeatedly. It is this more profound divine self-binding in covenant relation that fosters Israel's encounters with its God, permits new insights into God's character and nature, and forges the prophetic staircase that reveals its incarnational logic. God grants Israel his word (*dabar*) for Israel to carry as a blessing for the nations. Of course Balthasar will want to observe discontinuity even here, and the extreme kenosis of Christ will for him be the mark of New Covenant singularity. We will address the issue of discontinuity between the covenants soon enough. Here we can observe that for Balthasar kenosis provides for deep theological continuity between the Old and New Covenants and that this continuity is rooted in the Trinitarian relations. Balthasar brings this all together:

> ... *the mystery of God's redemptive kenosis ... consists in the identification of the divine Logos with the man Jesus, an event that is itself in continuity with the antecedent kenosis of the Word of God in his covenant with Israel. (The latter continues the covenant with mankind as a whole, which is itself based on the prior creation of creatures endowed with freedom).*[329]

True, the Trinitarian form of kenosis will become fully evident only in the New Covenant, but for Balthasar it is already apparent in the Old Covenant that kenosis is the "property" of the second person of the Trinity, the Word of God, and with this extension of the "kenosis" term Balthasar is able to find Christ hidden in the Old Covenant. This, then, is the key anti-Marcionite point: the Old and New Covenants cannot be separated because it is the one God of kenotic love revealed in both. Neither can creation and redemption be separated, for it is the one God of kenotic love revealed in the creation of the *imago dei* and in Christ the Redeemer. Thus, God's kenotic *eros* undergirds his encounters with the world in Creation, Covenant, and Christ's redemptive crucifixion, including his Eucharistic pouring out.[330]

For Balthasar, then, divine *eros* spurs *kenosis*, and *kenosis* in its different permutations grounds the possibility for human-divine encounter across the Covenants. Balthasar's term for the continuity of these covenantal encounters will be the Irenaean one of "recapitulation." In a passage that neatly ties together the themes of *kenosis*, encounter, and recapitulation, Balthasar writes that recapitulation is "the encounter to the point of identification, of the Israel who has been made ready and the God of the Covenant who descends to Israel."[331] Recapitulation signifies a fulfillment from "beneath" and "within," where "beneath" refers not merely to Jesus' human nature, but also to his emergence from the daughter of Zion:

> *Had Jesus not truly come from beneath (from the depths, from the interior of the filia Sion), then he would not truly have come from above. Had he not borne the whole history of Israel (and therein of the world) with God in himself, then he could not have been the final word of the history of God with Israel (and therein with the world).*[332]

Balthasar once again articulates here his view that Israel mediates Christ's redemption of the world's religious forms, a salvation that occurs only through judgment. Also important to point out is that for Balthasar Jesus' immersion within the context of God's people is not an accidental supplement to the main story. Rather, it is intrinsically necessary to salvation history in at least three ways: for the justice of divine judgment, for the visibility of the total revelatory form, and for the credibility of the call to discipleship. The credibility of Jesus' call hinges on the continuing presence of the covenantal context so that what Jesus requires does not come out of the blue as an arbitrary demand. Instead, the demands he makes on his disciples continue the demands of God on his people as they are "expropriated" for divine service in the battle against sin and evil. It is the context of the covenant that helps verify and authenticate the standards and even the call to suffering that Jesus issues.[333]

"Recapitulation" for Balthasar comes to mean that Christ is the concretion of the Covenant from both sides of the relation, the human-Israelite and the divine. He is, in N.T. Wright's phrase, the "climax" of the covenant.[334] Two distinct types of recapitulation are apparent in Balthasar's usage. The first, which we can label "historical" recapitulation, corresponds to Balthasar's explicit use of the category in *GL7* and refers to the reinvigoration of prophetic salvation history after the "empty time" of the post-exilic period. For Balthasar, this means that salvation historical time gains eternal validity through its embrace by the eschatological New Covenant.[335] From the New Covenant side, it is the baptism, infancy, and temptation narratives that express this kind of recapitulation and carry forward the Old Covenant. With John the Baptist, Balthasar contends, salvation history suddenly "jerks into motion again."[336] The baptism of Jesus recapitulates the Old Testament proclamation of judgment in both its prophetic and legal forms and thus calls forward "the whole situation of God as partner in the covenant."[337] The purpose of this baptism is the forgiveness of sins and the penitent's conversion called for by the prophet. Jesus stands in for Israel, who obeys the Word of God that comes through the prophet and enacts his solidarity "with all who confess their guilt and dive into the waters of judgment and salvation."³³⁸ Mary embodies Israel as the daughter of Zion, and eschatologically surpasses the birth from a barren woman through her virginal conception.³³⁹ Mary as the image of the Church "stands beside the Baptist who is the real symbol that surpasses the prophecy of the Old Covenant, and indeed all of salvation history."³⁴⁰ And as redeemed, "Zion / Mary is already in anticipation the pure essence of the Church that is to come...."³⁴¹ In the context of the temptation sequence, Jesus offers an absolute obedience that brings the "staircase of the prophetic obedience" to ground, thus closing all distance between the "mediator" and the "Word."³⁴² It becomes clear that for Balthasar what is important about the Jewishness of Jesus has everything to do with the theological context that his Jewish heritage makes possible. And this context is the pluriform covenant between Israel and Yahweh.

"Theological recapitulation" encompasses its historical counterpart as eschatology encompasses history; more specifically, "theological recapitulation" refers to the re-presentation of divine glory in and through the life of Jesus of Nazareth. Balthasar argues in *GL7* that Jesus recapitulates the power and sovereign freedom of the divine on the one hand, and the divine attributes that specify this power as good and beautiful on the other. But for this recapitulation to take place, Jesus must also express the covenantal disposition required of Israel. This recapitulation occurs, he thinks, through the interaction between Jesus' formal claim to authority on one side, and his poverty and self-abandonment on the other.

Balthasar agues that the relation between Jesus' claim to authority and his poverty and self-abandonment recalls the relation of the divine attributes to the formal theophanic disclosures of the Old Covenant. Jesus' claim to authority recapitulates the divine *kabod* or *doxa* that serves to shock a person into a state of attention, whereas his poverty and self-abandonment give this authoritative claim its content. According to Balthasar, Jesus' authority is manifest within the New Testament in his subordination of the Law and the sabbath to his interpretation, in his judgment of various individuals for the sake of forgiveness and salvation, and in the Johannine "I am" sayings. Balthasar claims that it is primarily the quality of his power that is new, a power evident in his *cardiognosis*, healings, forgiveness of sins, and especially in his exorcisms.³⁴³ Yet Jesus does not point to himself; instead, the basis of Jesus' knowledge and authority, according to Balthasar, lies in his transparency to God, the same transparency required of Israel so that their words can become words of revelation. Jesus can be the truth for John, Balthasar believes, only because he looks to the Father and receives the truth from him in the Spirit.

Other pericopes, Balthasar shows, place the attributes of God in the Old Covenant on Jesus. Drawing on Mark 12:14, "Master, we know that you are true," Balthasar links Jesus' honesty and dependability to the *emeth* of Yahweh that forms the basis of covenant relation and trust. Different gospel texts add to "truthfulness" the attributes of "holiness" and "righteousness," and fill out with narrative "Paul's idea that in Jesus the righteousness of God is present and accessible to us."[344] When applied to Christ by Paul, Balthasar argues, these attributes "overlap one another in the same way as the attributes of God in the old covenant."[345] Just as the "I of Yahweh gave itself concrete utterance in each of the great divine attributes, and thus concretized his glory," so Jesus' "I am" sayings in John reflect back to Jesus and point to a uniquely intimate relationship with the divine.[346] Jesus presents the infinitely concrete and unique I, the divine disclosed with unsurpassable and inexhaustible depth. Given the dialogical form of relationship between Jesus and God throughout the Gospels, however, the attributes of Jesus and his intimacy with Yahweh require a Trinitarian solution.[347]

Two attributes revealed over the narrative flow of Jesus' mission specify Jesus' authority as both good and in solidarity with the poor. Divine *kenosis* forms the backdrop for a mission that determines Jesus' existence as poverty and self-abandonment for others. He embodies not only divine disclosure, but also Israel's—and thus, all of humanity's—proper response to that disclosure. In other words, he reveals the true nature of Israel's faith as total availability to God. Balthasar suggests that it is perfect spiritual poverty that leads to a perfect and active obedience that alone can incarnate God's righteousness and love in this world. Moreover, and from the other side, it is also Jesus' kenotic humanity that recalls the divine virtues of *mishpat* and *chesed*. The poverty of Jesus configures itself as solidarity with the poor and thus carries forward the righteousness of God disclosed in the Old Covenant. Self-abandonment contextualizes and deepens "poverty" by raising it to the properly theological plane where the Son freely takes to himself the world's sin and God's wrath, and thereby reconciles the world to God.[348] It is Christ's self-abandonment that institutes salvation with the entire world (*shalom*) and establishes God's forgiving and compassionate love (*chesed*) for all.

In Christ's self-abandonment, Balthasar thinks New Covenant glory moves beyond the parameters of Old Covenant disclosure. This is where the exorbitance of Christ's mission and God's love become evident, and where the uniqueness of the Christian vision becomes apparent: "What is specifically Christian begins at the point where necessity, justice, and the thought of balanced settlement cease."[349] Through the total gift of himself, Jesus expresses the radical nature of divine love for the world through God's will to save, *chesed* in and through *shalom*. The theme of self-abandonment marks Jesus' entire existence from Incarnation through resurrection and even Eucharist, with its ground in the Trinitarian circulation of love between Father, Son, and Holy Spirit. As such, for Balthasar it designates a move beyond all prior mythological, philosophical, and even Old Covenant glory.[350]

Kenosis and Discontinuity

WE HAVE SEEN NOW that Balthasar argues for a fundamental continuity between the Old and New covenants: "... the moments of new fulfillment are always at the same time a recapitulation."[351] We have also argued that this continuity is rooted for him in an analogical extension of the *kenosis* trope from Philippians 2 to describe creation and the Old Covenant itself. Yet for Balthasar the motif of recapitulation ultimately proves inadequate to express the dialectical relation of the covenants: "The paths that led from the old covenant demanded an intersection which they were unable to reach by themselves; mere recapitulation of what had already been was insufficient for this."[352] What is of interest here is that just as *kenosis* provides for theological continuity, it also provides for Balthasar the key break in that continuity and the advent of a new and newly profound relation to God. The depth of *kenosis* in the New Covenant is the way in which New Covenant revelation will surpass that of Old Covenant revelation. Yet in surpassing the Old Covenant, the New Covenant does not fail to take into itself the content of the Old Covenant and the divine transcendence announced there. In other words, Balthasar rejects any notion that the new Covenant repudiates divine transcendence or judgment. Indeed, Christ's *kenosis* provides new ground for a judgment that comes from within.

It is worth a moment to reflect on the anti-Promethean character of Balthasar's view of *kenosis* as opposed to a more nearly Promethean view of the same trope. How, one might ask, can *kenosis* language be usurped for Promethean ideology? In fact, the Philippians hymn is directed precisely to the community as a warning against hubris. We need not go all the way back to Hegel for our example this time as more recent thinkers prove willing inheritors of his legacy. Thomas Altizer and Gianni Vattimo are two recent thinkers who embrace a kind of contemporary version of Hegelianism for theological ends. My purpose here is not to give an overview of their thought, but only to set Balthasar's work in a larger context and to show that the idea of *kenosis* can be interpreted in ways that sever Old and New Covenants and ways that maintain a kind of difference-in-unity. Balthasar's theology is of the latter kind; Altizer's and Vattimo's are of the former.

For Altizer and Vattimo,[353] *kenosis* indicates the end or dissolution of divine transcendence into the immanent historical plane and the realization on the part of humanity of its own divinity. This realization requires for both authors not only a movement beyond the Old Covenant, but a repudiation of the God of Israel as reducible in some way or another to a transcendent and violent deity. Thus, for Altizer and Vattimo, the *kenosis* of Christ marks a radical departure from and refutation of the Old Covenant at both the theological and anthropological levels. Theologically, the divine as revealed in Christ is a god who is no longer transcendent; anthropologically, biblical virtues like obedience and faithfulness must either fade away or be reconfigured in terms of autonomy. In fact, it would seem that theology becomes anthropology without remainder. The Promethean and Marcionite characteristics of these moves are clear. The Old Covenant and divine transcendence with it both suffer exile from the territory of the true and the good.

While Balthasar will certainly argue that New Covenant *kenosis* opens up a new relation to the divine, he maintains that this new relation is nevertheless in continuity with elements of the Old Covenant and that the same God is revealed in both covenants. Moreover, Balthasar argues that *kenosis* indicates that humanity *en Christoi* shares in the reception of a mission from the Father to redeem the world. *Kenosis* neither forfeits divine transcendence nor eliminates biblical obedience and fidelity, but it does configure transcendence and glory definitively as God's love. In contrast to Altizer and Vattimo, then, Balthasar does not read *kenosis* as a rejection of the

Old Covenant, divine transcendence, or obedience to the Father. He rejects the covenantal dualism of Vattimo and Altizer for an analogous relation of unity-in-difference. We now must attend to the content of this difference.

For Balthasar, there are three essential markers of difference between the disclosure of glory in the Old and New Covenants: first is the radical humility and humiliation of glory in the New Covenant; second is the kind of perception of glory that becomes possible in relation to such a "hidden" revelation; third is the nature of "mission" as it must be rethought on the basis of Christ's kenotic existence.[354] We will consider the first two together since faith's ability to "see" glory is directly related to the nature of glory as it appears.

For Balthasar, Christ's death most profoundly and definitively reveals God's glory as self-squandering love.[355] It is in this death that New Covenant glory surpasses Old Covenant glory. In the Cross, Balthasar writes, glory is:

> ... not the God of the ancient kabod, which in his Heaven he cannot give up, but the God whose love for the world has made him strip himself of the form of his heavenly glory, so that he may find it once more with us: naturally, this glory will never again be the inalienable kabod of old, but the glory of the triune love that has appeared in him, the love that has revealed its true omnipotence in the powerlessness of the Cross and that will never go back to a lesser, cheaper form of glory.[356]

The contrast here is between restrained and unrestrained self-giving. Paradoxically, Balthasar thinks, Old Covenant restraint can manifest itself in theophanic, spectacular shows of power: the booming voice from a cloud, the unexhausted burning bush, the split of a sea, the terrible and terrifying plagues, the victorious army. Throughout the Old Covenant, though, God rarely appears as one who makes himself vulnerable. Even in the depths of the Servant, it seems it is more the human person who becomes vulnerable on behalf of the word of God to which he is beholden.

For Balthasar, at the center of difference lies the hidden, but thoroughly unrestrained self-giving of New Covenant *doxa* that corrects the gnoseological hubris of Old Testament wisdom and apocalyptic, and expresses "the fundamental character" of New Testament glory.[357] The Son's divine *kenosis*—and Balthasar leaves no doubt that the divine Son is the subject of *kenosis*[358]—grounds this paradoxically clandestine revelation. Balthasar argues that *kenosis* designates not merely the moment of the Incarnation, but the entire incarnate life and death of Jesus.[359] In this sense, the Cross and the descent to hell are the goals of glory as it seeks to share in the deepest despair of human suffering. Cyril O'Regan gets at the radical transformation in glory that this reading entails: "Covering both the incarnate and crucified Christ, *kenosis* accounts for the shattering subversion of the expectation of one schooled in mythic or even OT glory. In Christ glory is hidden."[360] We might add to this "philosophical glory," for Balthasar argues that the *kenosis* of the Son also surpasses the philosophical conception of the self-diffusive Good and its exitus-reditus metaphysics, for no cyclical limits apply to the divine self-giving hidden in Christ.[361] It is this utter lack of restraint on divine love joined to humility that for Balthasar provides an unparalleled measure and judgment of inner worldly beauty.[362] If the Old Covenant critiques idolatry through command, Torah, and divine transcendent freedom, the New Covenant judges that same idolatry through the paradoxically cruciform *doxa* of the messiah. Glory is revealed as a love that is unanticipated and beyond all anticipation; precisely because it is so exorbitant, it can be neither captured nor controlled.

If *kenosis* specifies the form of New Testament revelation as hiddenness, then the perception of this revelation must admit a correlative alteration of non-biblical, and to a degree Old Testament, forms of perception. A vision of hidden glory must be described differently than a vision of theophanic glory. Thus, faith as "vision" must be qualified as a kind of "non-seeing seeing," an act of trust and risk whereby the believer surrenders to the divine glory revealed as love.[363] Now clearly Old Covenant revelation suffers no control over the divine. Old Covenant faith is a trusting obedience, but an obedience that has great signs as its evidence, not a crucified messiah wherein glory and love appear submerged in darkness; yet in this darkness—and not despite it—Balthasar finds the salvific love in and through death that is New Covenant glory.

A third and final point of Old Testament-New Testament demarcation focuses on Jesus as the temporal expression and narrative exegesis of the Son's eternal mission from the Father. Glory reveals itself here not in epiphanic or "lyrical" moments, but through Jesus' fidelity to a mission with which he wholly identifies. Jesus' mission reveals the Trinitarian life and vitality and specifies the imitation of Christ as existence devoted to the Father's will over the course of an entire existence.[364] *Kenosis*, in this sense, never relinquishes the value that the Old Covenant places on divine transcendence. It serves to open that transcendent reality up to the creature. This opening up or Trinitarian reading is for Balthasar absolutely essential to a proper interpretation of the crucifixion.[365] Only on the basis of the free selflessness of the divine persons can the Cross remain within the "love of the Father who gives up (Jn 3.16) and the love of the Son who places himself at his disposal...."[366] The Son does not want to bring to the Father the world's rejection of divine love, but only wants to enact his mission from the Father. For Balthasar, it is "men themselves in their darkness" who "burden the Son, the 'Lamb of God' ... with the unimaginable load of the entire world's No to divine love."[367] Apart from a Trinitarian context where the Son acts in freedom, a theological interpretation of the crucifixion would conjure a sadistic image of a Father god demanding expiation via human sacrifice. It is because he opposes such sadism that Balthasar stresses that Jesus "willed out of love to experience only the judicial character [of the Passion] ... so that he might be in *kenosis* merely a free space for the collision of the sin of the world."[368] God the Father does not make a demand; rather, Jesus wills to lay down his life for his friends and the world. Salvation takes place through the exchange that occurs on the Cross whereby Jesus takes to himself the unfreedom that results from sin and gives to humanity a new share in the freedom of the covenant.[369] Well beyond what is available through Old Covenant revelation, in Christ the divine life opens itself to the extremes of human suffering and thus takes on an absolute concreteness for the sake of the world. Jesus becomes the absolutely concrete universal, the revelation of God's openness to creation and creation's penetration by the indwelling Trinity.

One final point is important here regarding our anti-Marcionite thesis. Balthasar does not shy away from the biblical motif of the "wrath of God." While he rejects any notion that wrath is inherent to the divine nature *in se*, or that the Son receives wrath as a punishment, he does argue that the Son freely takes to himself the wrath of God deserved by the world for its sin. Divine wrath, according to Balthasar, is an aspect of God's love seeking to convert the sinner to covenant righteousness.[370] Jesus himself expresses anger many times, and if we are to see Jesus in light of Abraham Heschel's notion that the prophet expresses the divine pathos,[371] then Jesus also can be seen to express God's own anger at resistance to the mission of the Son.[372] But ultimately Jesus is the one to take God's wrath to himself for our sakes:

> Can we seriously say that God unloaded his wrath upon the Man who wrestled with his destiny on the Mount of Olives and was subsequently crucified? Indeed we must. Even in life, Jesus had been the revealer of the whole pathos of God—of his love and his indignation at man's scorning of this love—and now he has to bear the ultimate consequence of his more than prophetic mediation.[373]

Balthasar thinks that neither divine transcendence nor divine judgment are expunged on the way from the Old Covenant to the New. Yet both transcendence and judgment are configured and contextualized by the mission of the Son to make all people friends of God.

Post-Biblical Israel: Israel's Redemption

BALTHASAR'S REFLECTIONS ON JUDAISM span his post-war writings from his 1957 text on Martin Buber through his essays in *Spouse of the Word* and his trilogy. At this stage, I want to investigate his theological reading of post-biblical Judaism. Without ignoring other New Testament pericopes, Balthasar consciously centers his discussion of Judaism's relation to Christianity in Paul's letter to the Romans, especially chapters 9–11.[374] Indeed, he believes that had Christians more frequently attended to what Paul says there, much historical heartache might have been avoided. For Balthasar, the historical split between Judaism and the Church produces warped self-understandings for both and yields disastrous effects in Western culture. We should also note that Balthasar's decision to stress Pauline writings flies in the face of the vilification of Paul found in Martin Buber's *Two Types of Faith*, and, more recently, Michael Wyschogrod.[375] Balthasar is hardly unaware of Buber's arguments.[376]

Just as Balthasar refuses to simply follow contemporary exegetes in his reading of the post-exilic writings, he also departs from tendentious readings of Paul as a proto-idealist or a pseudo-mystic unconcerned with the realities of the present world.[377] Rather, Balthasar gives us a different image of the Apostle: Paul is one who is sent by God into an eschatological drama within which he needs to address the status of God's people as one who himself stands within the drama, not outside of it.[378] This status must take account of Jewish acceptance of Jesus as the long awaited messiah, Jewish rejection of Jesus as messiah, and gentile acceptance of Jesus' saving mission and resurrection. Balthasar argues that Paul reads these issues in a thoroughly Jewish context—and not as a Hellenistic metaphysician who has left his Judaism behind for armchair speculation—and for Paul, he thinks, this means a context of divine sovereignty and Abrahamic faith.[379]

Balthasar argues that for Paul, the radical freedom of God indicates that neither wrath nor mercy function as a simple calculus of human cause and divine effect, as if human efficient causality could manipulate grace. Indeed, he makes the subtle and important observation that divine rejection and divine mercy are equally a response to human guilt.[380] Paul, he thinks, is arguing in Romans both that Israel is culpable for its refusal of the messiah *and* that God's rejection of Israel—a qualified rejection, we will see—is not a mere consequence of Israel's guilt.[381] Balthasar believes that Paul's rationale for God's rejection of Israel is to be found in the mystery of God's plan for salvation history rather than at the level of ethical behavior. Paul envisions a complex movement at work in history whereby Israel is rejected *so that* gentiles may be grafted into the holy root that is the covenant relation with God.[382] Yet in God's plan Israel's prior reception of the promise is predicated upon and a function of the eventual opening of the promise to all peoples. Israel's reception of the promise remains grounded in God's plan for salvation as it is opened to all people in Christ.[383]

Balthasar observes that to make his case, Paul roots much of his argument in a re-reading of Israel's history, including the faith of Abraham, in light of his emphasis on faith. Thus the distinction that Paul draws in Romans 4 and again in Romans 9 between Israel after the Spirit (*kata pneuma*) and Israel after the flesh (*kata sarka*) does not emerge in the first century as a division between Christians and Jews, but for Paul and Balthasar runs through the center of salvation history from Abraham forward. Balthasar reads "Israel of the spirit" to mean those Israelites who depend upon faith and trust in God rather than physical descent for a special covenant relationship with God. Paul discovers this contrast in several stories from the Old Covenant and now reads *pneuma* versus *sarx* as a central motif of salvation history. Throughout the stories that Paul chooses, God shows the freedom to offer grace against the "rules" of culture, lineage, and even nature itself.[384] On this view, what makes Abraham a true patriarch is not his physical ancestry alone, but his radical trust in a free and surprising God, the same God who is now doing something new in Christ. For Balthasar, it is spiritual Israel that now finds its place in the Church, but, he is quick to note, "spiritual Israel" certainly does not exclude corporeal Israel.[385]

Balthasar argues that the temptation Israel faces—and one to which the Church is not immune—is the temptation to find within itself rather than in the "whyless love"[386] of God the means or reasons for its election.[387] In our previous chapter we noted that Balthasar reads a dialectic of particularity and universality from the story of Abraham's call itself. Abraham is called to be the father of a particular people, yet this same people is to be a blessing on the nations. We can now add that for Balthasar the "efficacy" of this universal mission demands that Israel surrender the idea that redemption lies in becoming a member of a nation or ethnic group. The surrender to a larger redemptive purpose that Balthasar believes lies at the center of all theological mission, including that of Christ, individual Christians, and the Church, is what Judaism cannot accept, and so its universal mission will lack its full effect.[388] Israel's culpability remains real, Balthasar thinks, because they do have the option of resting their election completely in trust and obedience; but this culpability remains subordinate with respect to God's larger plan of salvation history in which Israel is "cut off" to allow gentiles in.[389] What does this imply for Israel's salvation? For their continued mission or purpose in history? For the Church's relation to Judaism?

Balthasar's reflections on Israel's salvation return us to the relation between God's sovereignty and human action. Staying with Paul, Balthasar argues that God's "destruction" or rejection of the people must be read in the Old Testament context where God threatens such destruction, but ultimately remains "faithful because he cannot deny himself."[390] God remains faithful to Israel even through Israel's lack of faith. The destruction of Israel thus remains subordinate to Israel's election, and any notion that Israel's guilt requires damnation would be contrary to the meaning of the Cross.[391] In the end, all Israel will be saved.[392] Reflecting on Israel's culpability in light of Peter's speech in Acts 3, Balthasar writes,

> *Peter's sense of solidarity with the Jews is such that he can address them in a way that is inconceivable and almost offensive to Christian ears.... The speech does not merely excuse the crucifixion and death of Jesus—Peter, who denied Jesus, knew how the risen Christ had behaved to him and goes further; he sets the grace and the necessity of Christ's death, which had been announced so far back, so much above its unknowing instruments that it altogether outweighs their action.*[393]

The synoptic gospels present a more difficult challenge for Balthasar. He notes in particular the contrast drawn by Jesus in Matthew 8:11 between the gentile centurion, who depends upon faith, and the Israelites who depend upon lineage and will thus be cast out into the dark, a place of wailing and gnashing of teeth.[394] Nevertheless, Balthasar believes that Matthew 23:39, "for I promise, you shall not see me any more until you say: Blessings on him who comes in the name of the Lord," suggests the possibility for all Israel to attain salvation in the eschatological future. For Balthasar, Israel's ultimate election is beyond question, the whole of Israel finally being reinstated by the one Savior of all whose love transcends divine wrath.[395] Balthasar goes further than this. He connects his reflections on Israel to Paul's profound sense that Christ was "made sin" for the world's salvation, a phrase that functions centrally in Balthasar's theo-dramatic soteriology.[396] If Israel's blindness functions to permit gentiles into the plan of salvation, then Israel's suffering of this blindness resembles and participates in the suffering of the innocent Messiah for the world's salvation. Balthasar makes his point strongly: "And so anyone who strikes Israel strikes the Messiah, who, as God's suffering servant, gathers up in himself all the afflictions of God's servant Israel."[397] Israel as the suffering servant suffers for others. Thus Israel, now in the person of Christ, still bears a redemptive significance in history.

Balthasar thus seeks to go beyond the position of Karl Barth, certainly one of his major influences. Barth argues that Israel represents God's wrath and the Church represents God's grace, both of which find their focal point in Christ crucified and both of which are therefore witnesses to Christ.[398] Judgment and salvation, the material center of both covenants, find their most efficacious form in the Crucifixion of Christ. However, where Barth leaves it at that, Balthasar adds a crucial parenthetical statement: "Here we must surely add the converse, namely, that the Messianic salvific suffering is present in a hidden way in the judgment and suffering of Israel."[399] Israel itself would seem to undergo, at least in the figure of the Suffering Servant and its prophetic witness, a kind of kenotic suffering for the nations. Balthasar also corrects what he considers a far too simple contrast between the Jewish "malefactor" who turns away from the Cross and the representative of the Church who turns toward Christ. Since both Israel and the Church require God's grace, he observes, each can be represented by a malefactor and by a faithful disciple.[400]

At least one concrete consequence of Balthasar's view is the end to a Christian mission to the Jews. For Balthasar such a mission would suggest that the Jews are no longer God's people, and on the basis of Romans 9:4, where Paul asserts that Israel retains its privileges of "sonship, glory, the covenant, the law, worship, the promises and the patriarchs," Balthasar believes this suggestion utterly misguided. Israel remains for him God's chosen people.[401] In his book on Buber and throughout his work, Balthasar rejects the notion that Christianity's relation to Jews should be conceived as akin to the Church's relation to other Christian groups. The separate versions of Christianity, he thinks, are different branches that all need re-engrafting into the holy root which is Israel:

> *Above all, the problem of unity should not be formulated as though Israel were a people to be evangelized by mission of a rather special kind, and as though Israel were further from the Church than Christian sects. The sects are branches which have been separated and which should be re-engrafted—but Israel is the "holy root" (Rom. 11:16).*[402]

Balthasar thus rejects Christian missions to the Jews here, and argues that while Jews and Christians cannot be said to comprise two separate peoples of God—for in the end there is only one people of God—historically speaking he thinks that the two people may be considered complementary. Certainly the Church will in the end be complete itself and can be called the "new Israel," but, he argues, this vision is not fulfilled until the Elect have been gathered from the "four winds, from the uttermost parts of the earth" (Mk. 13:27) ... which means, above all, Israel gathered together and brought home."[403] Balthasar is worth quoting at length here:

> *Individual conversions may be very fruitful; but the whole meaning and sense of the continued existence of Israel simply cannot be that Israel should be absorbed into the Church by multiplying them. Israel has a destiny as a people. And once Christians have opened their eyes to that fact they then will not merely think of the individual Jews in Israel, but think in terms of a better understanding and convergence between the two separated halves of the people of God.*[404]

For Balthasar the destiny of the Church and that of Israel are inextricably intertwined. The Church remains rooted in the promise and faith of spiritual Israel on the one hand, and in Jewish flesh and blood through Christ on the other. Like Jesus, the Church must have its roots "both in Abraham and in heaven."[405] Israel's deepest hope has been fulfilled in Christ, even if for a while Israel does not see this fulfillment.[406] Israel's continued hope in the promise is justified by the fact that Christians too still hope for this promise to be fulfilled in the eschatological future, a future wherein God makes the reconciliation of the world fully manifest. Not only will the hope of Christians and Jews be realized, but redemption in Jesus Christ will be shared (Romans 11:25–29).[407]

It is worth pausing for a moment to recall that Balthasar is writing his book on Martin Buber two to three years before the Second Vatican Council and seven to eight years prior to the document, *Nostra Aetate*. He is arguing in 1957 that Christians ought to cease their missions to the Jews, that salvation remains for Israel in the eschatological future, that in some way Israel retains a mission after Christ, and that Christians and Jews share a final hope and final consummation. In response to a direct plea from Buber that Christians find some hope for Israel within their thought, Balthasar gives a resoundingly affirmative response. Arguing that for Jews the first and second coming of Christ will coincide,[408] Balthasar writes: "After as before, therefore, there is hope for Israel; and what is more, not hope in any ordinary sense, applicable to anyone, but its own special hope: the restitution and fulfillment of everything which its God, its prophets had always promised."[409] It is an open question whether theologians have yet to catch up to some of his more profound insights on Jewish-Christian relation.[410]

The title of this section, "Israel's Redemption," then, can be taken in two ways. On the one hand, we can stress that for Balthasar Israel will be rejoined with gentiles to form the one, eschatological ecclesia. On the other hand, "Israel's redemption" can also signify that Israel itself forms a community that brings a model of the redeemed life and even redemption itself to the world. As a model of the redeemed life, Israel critiques idolatrous religion, adheres to and worships the One God, and seeks to incarnate that God's righteousness and love in a world for which it often suffers. Israel offers redemption to the world by bringing forth from its womb, as it were, the Incarnation of God's Word such that Israel's covenant relation opens up to all creation.

A Lonely Dialogue: Christianity and Judaism in the Context of Prometheanism

BALTHASAR'S DECEPTIVELY BRIEF BOOK on Martin Buber carries with it a certain sadness. Though not captured in the English title, the German *Einsame Zwiesprache* (solitary or lonely dialogue) sounds a note of futility, as if Balthasar wonders whether any genuine conversation remains possible above the din of history.[411] Commenting on the nature of past Christian discourse on Judaism, Balthasar sharply criticizes Christians who enter into discussions with Jews in a spirit of condescension.[412] What is needed, he thinks, is a genuine dialogue which is neither disrespectful nor overly circumspect.[413] Buber himself opens up the possibility for such a dialogue with his somewhat tendentious *Two Types of Faith*. In that book, Buber argues that while Jesus is a good if all too idealistic rabbi, Paul abandons Judaism and Jewish culture for a rather sanguine metaphysical view of world history.[414] The implication is that Christians who follow Paul abandon Christ or vice-versa. Either way, Buber places a wedge through the heart of Christianity. Balthasar does not limit his discussion of Buber—or Judaism for that matter—to a treatment of Buber's thesis. But like Buber, he thinks that genuine dialogue means entering into real areas of difficulty, and this includes areas of theological and cultural concern.

If Judaism and Christianity are meant to be one people of God, then it must matter that they are instead separate, and for a Christian theologian, it must matter that Judaism rejects the Incarnation. Balthasar believes there are serious consequences for both, and he lays them out on a broad intellectual canvas. For Judaism, separation means the loss of a transcendent, eschatological judgment on inner-historical utopianism; for Christianity, separation leads to a sacrifice of concern for the concrete issues facing the world and a descent into massive infidelity. We will discuss his critical reading of post-Christian Judaism first and then turn to the consequences that accrue to Christianity whenever it chooses to sever branch from root.

Balthasar argues in several places that Christianity must avoid both a monistic and dualistic view of salvation history. We discussed some of this in our first chapter. The monistic view underestimates the newness and eschatological definitiveness of Christ's Incarnation, and thus presents a thoroughly historicized messianic dynamism headed toward a would-be temporal utopia. In Balthasar's understanding, this view carries the danger of integralism.[415] In *Theo-Drama*, and in an essay on Liberation Theology[416], Balthasar contends that a dualistic view of salvation history holds the Incarnation as so radically new it separates Christianity from Judaism entirely and loses itself in a miasma of mystical nonchalance vis-à-vis the world. The first lacks a transcendent criterion, the second any history to be judged. Balthasar believes that the monistic view is characteristic of Marxist and neo-Marxist movements influenced by a modern, secularized Judaism. Within these views, hope is reduced to the purely intra-historical plane. Balthasar agrees with Karl Löwith's thesis that Marxism is a secularization of Judaeo-Christian eschatology and argues that Judaism contributes to this development by joining a theologically warranted secularization process to the unwarranted rejection of the Incarnation. This needs some explanation.

We have treated Balthasar's view that Israel's worship of a truly free and transcendent deity served to make the cosmos, for the first time, a genuine creature, and to triumph over the cosmological *fatum* within which the gods, as personifications of cosmic forces, would find their places.[417] In other words, Israel introduces secularism into Western consciousness. Balthasar believes that this is inherently a good thing because it opens up the possibility of genuine human responsibility for the world in relation to a truly free God. This goodness is conditional, however, on whether this new consciousness accepts its proper locus within a Christian incarnational context, that is, so long as secular autonomous reason places itself at the service of the God who has kenotically granted this freedom and remains its ground, and not in service of a purely secular and autonomous version of the Kingdom. What Balthasar fears is an identity philosophy that provides no transcendent criterion for the kingdoms of this world, but instead baptizes them as if they were the eschatological kingdom. Perhaps surprisingly, he argues that Jewish rejection of the Incarnation means that Western culture is left with a world devoid of God that nevertheless longs for God. Judaism in particular feels this longing, and, Balthasar thinks, is prone to attempt to make the relatively "abstract" command and promise of Yahweh incarnate in the present. Balthasar thinks that this desire will often befriend titanic or Promethean attempts to construct the kingdom by way of technological means. Thus he associates modern, secularized Judaism with the titanic: the usurpation of divine action and purpose in history by human calculating reason. In brief: idolatry critique *sans* Incarnation turns into idolatry. Marx is Balthasar's persistent example:

> *Marxist anti-theism organizes and channels all the pagan, diffuse anti-Christian atheism and gives it a shape, a plan, a striking force. It may do this by interpreting the Messianic expectation as a dialectic that presses forward with iron necessity; or it may take the "watching and waiting" that is built on a concrete faith in Yahweh's promise, substituting for it an abstract principle of hope that is empty, cheerless and grounded on nothing but itself.*[418]

Balthasar reads Marxism in its most virulent forms as a kind of secularized Judaism.[419] We have previously seen that Balthasar thinks Marxism is an offspring of a more distant "Jewish" deformation of Christian thought that he finds in the work of Joachim de Fiore. It is in this secular political context that Balthasar's most troubling comment should be read:

> *There is a secular tradition that the Antichrist will be a Jew; this may be more than crude anti-Semitism: it may be a genuine theological deduction, for Israel alone, among all the nations, is the abiding bearer of an absolute hope that is identical with its existence. Such a hope, consistently followed through and lived out side by side with the rejection of Christ, must seek to offer a countervision of world history.*[420]

Balthasar believes the Jewish people to have been given a special and absolute mission to the world. The rejection of the Incarnation, however, means for Balthasar that Judaism retains its absolute hope as a messianic people, but that in modernity this absolute hope loses the context of a transcendent criterion, whether that of Christ's Incarnation or the transcendent covenant partner, Yahweh. Judaism, he thinks, is susceptible to an atheistic titanism that takes its dynamic force from some genuine piece of Jewish revelation but refuses to suffer the insult of a divine judge.[421] As disturbing as Balthasar's passage above is, it can be read as a plea for Jews to become more deeply Jewish, that is, to embrace their God and their prophets rather than the prophets of secular power. The enemy for Balthasar is neither religious Judaism nor faithful Christianity, but both when they substitute an inner-worldly force or law for a transcendent norm.

With that said, however, we do need to question the relation Balthasar draws between Joachim and Judaism. Joachim is no doubt employed in the service of the dissolution of divine transcendence in Christian thought, and I argue elsewhere that in Thomas Altizer and Gianni Vattimo, among others, his vision is employed for just this purpose.[422] Balthasar draws the connection with Judaism on the basis of Henri de Lubac's observation that Joachim's three-stage progressive Trinitarian theology makes of the New Testament a second Old Testament in light of the Third Age. In other words, just as the Age of the Son displaces the Age of the Father for Joachim, so the Age of the Spirit displaces the Age of the Son. In Balthasar's view, this means that the Age of the Son becomes incapable of providing an absolute or eschatological measure for revelation, for history, and even for political power. The Cross somehow becomes de-centered and displaced. While this may all be true of what happens when Joachim is commandeered in a cultural landscape that holds transcendence in deep suspicion, our question is whether or not an association with Judaism is warranted. Here, Balthasar seems to have made an inner-Christian issue into a Jewish issue. To put it precisely, we can say that Joachim's theology of the Spirit is a post-incarnational rather than pre-incarnational theology: whereas Judaism denies the Incarnation itself, Joachim denies only the finality or absoluteness of the Incarnation in relation to the Spirit. Regardless of Joachim's possible Jewish cultural background, his position is not a Jewish one at all. To associate it with Judaism in any theological sense is misleading.

With respect to Judaism itself, we should also note that Balthasar's criticisms are not directed against Jewish worship, its adherence to Halakah, or Torah. His concern in *Theo-Drama* is with what he believes is the identification of the political with the religious as it occurs in modernity and insofar as secularized Judaism contributes to this identification through an unrealized eschatology. Insofar as Judaism conceives of its land as a religious inheritance, for instance, there is an identification of the political with the theological that Christianity cannot accept for itself. In this sense, Balthasar interprets the promises of the Old Covenant as fulfilled in Christ in line with much earlier Christian tradition. But he notes that the spiritual-incarnational interpretation of Israel's earlier history is not anti-Jewish; indeed, such interpretation is part of Israel's own vitality as a tradition as it took up ancient promises and symbols and interpreted them anew. Moreover, it was common practice in first-century Judaism to interpret its symbols in a variety of ways. The holiness of the Essene community becomes the "Temple"; the Song of Songs comes to represent God's love for his people.

Of course, Christian experience plays a role here as well. Balthasar believes that in the long wake of the Crusades, Christians ought to be extremely wary of associating God's kingdom with a particular land. The problem is not simply that the Crusades did not work out well, but with the very idea that we can *realize* God's Kingdom in a particular world order rather than see in the Incarnation God's own realized measure for any kingdom. The danger is always that worldly kingdoms root themselves not in the glorious weakness of divine kenotic love, or even in the power of the Spirit, but in human power and coercion. Balthasar thinks that such a view is both dangerous and contrary to Christian faith. He also believes that the unrealized eschatology inherent to a secularized Judaism is particularly susceptible to this utopian temptation.

Jewish rejection of the Incarnation, Balthasar thinks, also has consequences for the religion of Judaism. He argues that in rejecting the Incarnation, Jewish theological anthropology becomes powerless to integrate the spiritual and material realities of existence without collapsing them into one another. He raises this issue in typically provocative fashion:

> *However, most things remain in a state of flux; but it is a different flux from the "pagan" one, which alternated between the kosmos theion and man. Judaism hovers in an openness that is unfulfilled. In what sense is the Jew a person? Certainly, the great ones, chosen from among the people to be its prophets and leaders are persons. But what of the individuals of the nation? They are not persons in the New Testament sense. In what way, for the Jew, is the sexual, in its orientation toward the species, transcended in the direction of the personal? The Jew regards the "Song of Songs" as a nuptial hymn celebrating Yahweh's union with his people, but does this also actually become a physical union?*[423]

We will address the relationship between Israel and the "nations" in our next chapter. Here, it is important to make absolutely clear that Balthasar regards Jewish individuals as persons with full human dignity. A person in "the New Testament sense" or what Balthasar elsewhere calls a "theological person" is a technical term that designates a person enraptured by a mission *en Christoi*. Balthasar argues that the reception of a Christological mission for the world elevates the individual beyond the mere numerical dialectic between individual and species; an ecclesially mediated mission *en Christoi* endows the individual with a new body caught up in a purpose that gains significance even beyond death due to Christ's Incarnation and Resurrection. In foregoing the union-in-difference of the Incarnation, he thinks, Judaism becomes unable to join the non-Incarnate Word of commandment and promise, which the "wise of Israel live by pondering and interpreting,"[424] to the desire for this Incarnation in genuine flesh-and-blood humanity. This primary tension gives rise to others. If Israel can read the Song of Songs as a spiritual union of Yahweh and his people, one must ask whether this union can ever become real or whether, going in the other direction, the sexual can attain a truly transcendent significance. Apart from the Incarnation, Balthasar contends, a body-soul dualism is likely to emerge when various heterodox mysticisms seek to storm heaven rather than await divine descent. He associates these dualisms with Cabbala and Hasidism, and notes that Buber, who had similar concerns, strove to eliminate such dualisms from the Hasidic tradition. For Balthasar, however, this attempt threatens to compound the problem by identifying the spiritual with the material and succumbing to a utopian monism. In the end, this is another way in which immanence trumps a transcendent measure.

Because most of this book has been and is about what happens when Christians forego their Jewish roots, we can be fairly brief in our discussion here. While Balthasar thinks that Christians at times will slip into a monistic view of salvation history, as is the case with Joachim and his followers (and he thinks with some liberation theology), he clearly believes the more usual danger is a soteriological dualism that pits Old Covenant against New Covenant revelation. We should note that the lines between a monist and dualist view are not to be drawn thickly. A progressivist revelation scheme such as Joachim's can give rise to an antipathy for the Old Covenant, as it does in Lessing, Vattimo, and Altizer. Soteriological monism then becomes soteriological dualism. Balthasar is willing to accept the idea that a continued Jewish mission in history may have to do with Judaism's care for existence in the present world: marriage and family, political institutions, etc. And he argues that a Marcionite Christianity will tend to leave these concerns behind. In Balthasar's terms, Christianity must not sacrifice history for eschatology.[425] Balthasar's response to this criticism occurs in *Theo-Drama* and is twofold: on the one hand, he deploys the Jewish criticism against Christian philosophers and theologians who do, he thinks, slacken the tensions inherent to Christian existence in the world; on the other hand, he gives an alternative interpretation of Christian faith that mandates engagement with the world in all its dimensions. What we can say here is that Balthasar accepts the basic point: when Christianity separates itself from its holy root, it fails to take sufficient account of the needs inherent to the world.[426]

Certainly a Christian failure to concern itself with the needs of the human family would be serious enough on its own to warrant notice. Christianity's failure in the twentieth century, however, is more spectacular. Balthasar observes that a Christianity severed from Judaism threatens to degenerate "into Gnosticism, Marcionism or some form of Hitlerism."[427] In this case, it is precisely the anti-Jewish element that must be cut out of the Christian organism lest the "anti-Christ" incubate from within Christianity's own body.[428] As Balthasar puts it himself, "There can be no Christianity which is not, *a priori* and inwardly, related in a deeply sympathetic manner to the 'holy tree,' as the branch is related to the root."[429] Insofar as Christianity denies this relation, it denies what it is, falls back into some form of pre-Christian mythology, forfeits divine judgment and transcendence, and commits apostasy of the worst kind. Put simply: Christianity severed from Judaism is not Christianity.

Conclusion

SINCE BALTHASAR'S BOOK IN 1957 the dialogue between Judaism and Christianity has become far less lonely. Theologians, commissions, and committees have gathered, thought, and written on the issues that Balthasar passionately took on in the wake of twentieth-century catastrophe. It is an open question, however, whether anyone has better comprehended the issues at stake for Christian and Jewish faith and Western culture. Balthasar simply tends to work with a bigger intellectual canvas than most. This does not mean that he always makes for pleasant reading or that he is always right. He takes over ideas from Karl Löwith without sufficient critical acumen and at times lets his rhetoric run beyond sound judgment. Yet even in his rhetorically rough comments, Balthasar does call to mind some of the evils truly associated with modern secular intellectual and political systems when they divorce themselves from the transcendent framework of the covenant or the Incarnation of Christ. Autonomy run amok becomes slavery; justice apart from love becomes injustice.

Balthasar's Christian theology of Judaism is thoroughly Christian. That is to say, he refuses to compromise Trinitarian doctrine, Christ's divinity, or the resurrection that is its presupposition. Nevertheless, he strongly revises and harshly criticizes a long tradition of Christian supercessionism. For Balthasar, the Jews are God's people and God remains faithful to his people. Peter knows the need of all human beings, Jew and gentile, for forgiveness and so can hardly hold Jews to a higher standard than Christ held him; likewise, Paul, the persecutor of Christians prior to conversion, can hardly judge his people condemned. In hotter moments, this was Christian judgment; but in moments of deeper reflection on the meaning of the Cross, Balthasar, Paul, and Peter see that Israel's hope for entrance into the eschatological kingdom remains real. Nor does Balthasar support a Christian mission to the Jews. Certainly dialogue is a good thing, and if individual Jews find their way into the Church, that is all to the good; but Balthasar believes that Judaism itself has a mission in history. He is not sure what to name that mission from a Christian point of view. He surmises that it may have to do with care for the world of culture, politics, and social life, and that Israel's post-biblical mission will continue to be a preparation for Christ, an idolatry critique and an exposure to the truly transcendent God, assuming that Judaism does not give in to modern secularizing tendencies and political distortions. Working from the symbol of the Servant, Balthasar suggests that Judaism's sufferings may also have redemptive significance for the nations, especially as Israel's sufferings are taken up into the paschal mystery itself.

Balthasar does of course have a kind of soft supercessionism, what we might call a formal rather than material supercessionism. He argues that the content or matter of the two covenants is the same. Broadly speaking, this content is rendered as salvation through judgment. Moreover, Christ does not trample or destroy the Old Covenant, but fulfills it; he recapitulates the relationship between God and his people Israel and opens up that covenant relation to all humanity. Jesus requires the same sort of faithfulness and availability to God's word demanded by the prophets and Israel's covenant more generally. Jesus incarnates God's divine attributes in the world as Israel strove to do. But even beyond this, it is God's kenotic love in Creation, Covenant, and New Covenant that unites revelation. In a sense, then, Balthasar anticipates George Lindbeck's nice formulation regarding the Old Covenant and the New. Reaching beyond a type–anti-type or promise-fulfillment model,

Lindbeck suggests substance and form as a way to conceive of the relation between the covenants. Balthasar certainly wants to remind Christians that the Old Covenant provides far more substance for Christian anthropology and theology than Christians have been intent on remembering.[430]

Formally, however, the Incarnation and the Trinitarian relations of transcendence and immanence read off of the profound *kenosis* of the Son do for Balthasar make for a greater concreteness of divine glory in the New Covenant. This revelation is definitive and eschatological; as such, it is able to redeem history and grant Israel's covenant significance in eternity. Moreover, even the discontinuity between Old and New covenant glory does not sever connections to the covenant context that allows it to be read at all. In other words, Christ's submersion in the depths of Israel's history permits the contours of Christian revelation to emerge into visibility through comparison and contrast with this earlier revelation. It is through this unity that the difference can be perceived in its right dimensions and proportions.

The judgment, both historical and theological, then, that Balthasar makes is that Marcionism, and not Christian supercessionism, is the truest form of theological anti-Judaism. Of course he strongly opposes a simple replacement or "strong supercessionism," meaning that Christians replace Jews as God's people. Balthasar thinks it naïve to argue for a dissolution of the Jewish people into the Church in historical time. This view then leads him also to oppose a Christian mission to the Jews. The Church of Jews and Gentiles is both a historical reality insofar as Christianity's earliest members were Jewish, but is more accurately perceived as an eschatological mystery as God will find his own way to reunite root and branch(es) in the end. Marcionism is, in his view, the more prevalent danger in modernity, and the danger that continually threatens to make the form of Christ illegible and to remove Christian anthropology from its fundamentally dialogical and covenantal setting. It is Marcionism that Balthasar sees at the root of Christian anti-semitism in modernity, and he seeks to remedy this issue by arguing for a deep and abiding theological continuity between the Old Covenant and New Covenant, a continuity grounded in the One God of passionate kenotic love, and a spirituality of humble receptivity to the divine Word joined to readiness to act on that Word in the world.

Finally, it is the case for Balthasar that Christianity needs Judaism to be itself. And he does not mean simply Jewish texts, but the living people of God. He argues that apart from a genuine and ongoing dialogue with the

Jewish people, Christianity itself is always threatened by a temptation to an ethereal mysticism divorced from historical reality; Christianity without Judaism forgets that it is engrafted "*para physein*" and not through its own merits. Balthasar does not fear tendentious dialogue so long as power relations are not in the balance; indeed, he thinks that Christians have a lot to learn from the living Jewish community from which Christ himself emerged even if Christians will sometimes need to do *intellectual* battle on behalf of their faith, and even if no full agreement is in sight until the *eschaton*.

Chapter Four

Judaism, the Nations, and Christological Hospitality

This final chapter broadens our discussion to take into account Balthasar's theology of religions outside of biblical religion. At the most general level, this chapter argues that Balthasar offers a capacious, Christocentric theology of religions, one that finds partial truths scattered throughout civilization and calls them into the Christian form to be interpreted, fulfilled, and redeemed. Balthasar wants to argue that to call these truths into Christianity is not to change them into something else, but rather to fulfill their own aspirations in an ever-greater and surprising consummation. Balthasar labels his own method "integration," a term that springs from his view that the Incarnation reveals God's desire to call the goods of creation into relation with his purposes in the world, yet without eliminating or squelching differences.

Within this general argument, a number of more specific claims are being made. First, Balthasar's theology of religions serves as an *a posteriori* Christian apologetic very much akin to the work of the Alexandrian fathers. It is perhaps important to maintain Balthasar's notion of "integration," rather than slip into its obvious cousin, "inclusivism," because Balthasar's approach remains *a posteriori* in a way not required by inclusivist theologies of religion. Balthasar's discussion of metaphysics in *GL4* will feature prominently in this chapter because it is in that volume, which is often ignored, that Balthasar argues for a gentile preparation for the gospel analogous to the preparation in the Old Covenant. It is in this sense especially that his approach approximates that of the Alexandrian Fathers, especially Clement of Alexandria, and gives us a rich understanding of his method. Second, and relatedly, Balthasar's view of the truths found in creation is much more expansive than imagined by some of his critics. He appeals to the traditional tropes of *Logos spermatikos* (seeds of the Logos) and *spolia Aegyptorum* (spoils of Egypt) to indicate what we might call Christological hospitality, and grounds this hospitality to truth, wherever it is found, in God's passionate love for creation on the one hand, and the creature's ec-static wonder at the meaning of all being on the other. For Balthasar this fundamental ec-stasis of the human person comes to formal realization in different types of discourse, namely, mythical-poetic, philosophical, and religious, and these different discourses themselves admit of a great variety of worldviews. Balthasar thinks that looking at Western cultural history through the eyes of the covenant reveals that an extra-biblical pedagogy exists for the gentiles, and that this pedagogy itself shows that the discourses of myth, philosophy, and religion ask for integration that, like the Old Covenant, they cannot find in themselves. It is this call of Being and its pluriform human response that is presented in our first section. It is important to note here, too, that Balthasar's extensive treatment of Greco-Roman discourses of religion, poetry, and philosophy constitutes a rejection of any hard opposition between properly New Testament Christianity and "hellenistic" culture. Balthasar certainly wants to emphasize the theological relatedness between Judaism and Christianity, and, as I have argued, he wants to prioritize this relationship. Nevertheless, this priority does not lead him to denigrate human transcendence found outside of this covenantal relation. In this sense, Balthasar is in line with contemporary biblical scholarship's emphasis on Greco-Roman materials.[431]

Section two shows precisely how Balthasar contrasts Jewish revelation to that of the "nations" and the reasons he gives for placing Jewish revelation on a higher theological plane than gentile metaphysics. Here we will also discuss some of the differences between the approaches taken to Christian theology of religions by Balthasar and by Karl Rahner. Our final section describes how it is that Balthasar sees in the form of Christ the opening for the integration and fulfillment of all religious, mythical, and philosophical truth.

Incarnation as Erotic Integration

LIKE THE ALEXANDRIAN FATHERS BEFORE HIM, Balthasar thinks that God granted humanity not only the Law and the prophets, but also a gentile preparation for the gospel through philosophy and extra-biblical culture.[432] Balthasar's *Glory of the Lord* focuses this second pedagogical prong on an apologetic account of Western mythic, philosophical, and religious discourses both as disclosive genres and in terms of their material analogies to the form of Christ. We will recall that our previous discussion of form focused on two characteristics: (1) the relation between surface and depth (form and splendor, expression and meaning), and (2) the indissolubility of form. We now need to expand this understanding so that its full fruit for a Christian theology of religions can be grasped. As D. C. Schindler and others have pointed out in relation to the first characteristic, for Balthasar, *Gestalt* includes the idea that an indissoluble form also requires what Balthasar calls "antecedent conditions".[433] The second characteristic has to do with the dynamism of form, that is to say, Balthasar thinks form or taking shape occurs through a dramatic process of becoming or form-ation, especially evident in the development of personal and communal identity. This suggests that at the heart of form-as-formation is a notion of the contemplative structuring of eventful encounters with what is different or other in both a horizontal (culture, gender, history, etc.) and vertical sense (God), and thus dialogue. For Balthasar, identity is never simple, but instead includes difference within itself. Both ideas can be clarified by recalling what we have said about the Old Testament and the form of Christ.

For Balthasar, the Old Covenant is a pedagogy or "antecedent condition" necessary to the legibility of New Testament disclosure. The Old Covenant gives to the New Covenant the primary context within which it can be grasped in all its dimensions. In addition, the Old and New Covenants take into themselves different cultural antecedents (indeed, the very notion of a "covenant") and give them new content through their developing relation to Yahweh. The covenantal final form then includes and depicts the dynamic and dramatic relation of freedoms between Israel and others (Egyptians, Canaanites, Babylonians, etc.) and Israel's relation to its God. Israel's form is not something separate from these cultural antecedents, and from these relationships, but it is not reducible to them either. Rather, Israel takes form in its uniqueness by virtue of its encounters and its dialogue with cultural antecedents (horizontal) in theo-dramatic (vertical) interplay. A final point to observe here is that Balthasar's notion of form-as-formation, as *Bildung*, presumes that the content of particular encounters is significant. In other words, in the formation of personality or identity, whether of an individual or community, it is neither the mere fact of encounter, nor solely the way in which an encounter makes one cognizant of her self-transcendence as such, that is central, but rather the actual material of concrete historical encounters that contribute to the shaping of one's identity. The particularity and singularity of identities, that is, of personal and communal form, is predicated on historical eventful encounters and reflective or contemplative appropriation of their significance.

This brief discussion of form pulls together many of the elements that shape Balthasar's theology of religions: encounter, dialogue, and contemplative integration. If Christian identity has its source in the encounter with divine glory as revealed in Christ, nevertheless, this glory penetrates human reality at its deepest point. Like Israel, Christianity ought to view its identity in relation to and dialogue with all things human in a spirit of discerning receptivity. As for writers such as Georges Bernanos and François Mauriac, so for Balthasar there can be nothing human that is alien to the Christian. Moreover, at the theological level proper, for Balthasar the possibility of truth outside the Church has everything to do with the unity of God and God's plan as Creator, Redeemer, and Sanctifier of the world.

Balthasar speaks to this unity in terms of *eros*, evidently agreeing with Denys the Areopagite that no other term, not even *agape*, gets at the passion with which God seeks out his Bride in "creation, revelation, and Incarnation."[434] God's antecedent work as Creator inspires human *eros* or seeking, questing self-transcendence towards Being that defines the *homo religiousus* as such. We should not "denigrate the act of human self-transcending," Balthasar writes in one of his essays.[435] He maintains the same view in his trilogy: the human spirit lies "open to understand the being of all that is. It contemplates the being of all that is, searching out its transcendental, fundamental determination...."[436] To perceive form, that is, to perceive that in each disclosure in the world lies an "exterior which appears and an interior depth," is a fundamental characteristic of being human.[437] Human spirit, then, encounters the world in all its variety and communicates the meaning of these eventful encounters in various kinds of form such as artistic, literary, musical, mythic, philosophical, and religious works. More importantly, Balthasar argues that these expressions are in principle valid because Being itself is a gift of God that expresses divine love and fidelity. Form and structure are not betrayals of the flash-like events of revelation, but rather gifts that allow for human communication and contemplation of God's beneficence as Creator.[438]

Based upon this divine manifestation in the very Being of the world, and humanity's responsive attention to this disclosure, Balthasar contends that Christian theology has an interior relationship to humanity's various attempts to represent the meaning of existence. While Balthasar rejects any linear ascent from worldly forms to biblical revelation, he will go so far as to say:

> *Biblical revelation occurs in the same formal anthropological locus where the mythopoeic imagination designed its images of the eternal. And, to be sure, the living God of Abraham, Isaac, and Jacob will likewise exhaust all philosophical theories about God, world, and man even to the reversal of their meaning and content; but this too occurs precisely at the point where man once looked out over the last horizon of Being, the point where he struggled with the meaning of that ultimate reality which gives meaning to all existence.*[439]

In this passage, taken from *GL*1, Balthasar describes the intrinsic anthropological link between metaphysics or the "truth of the world" and the truth of God that comes through revelation. The mutual *ecstases* of God's love manifest in creation, and in the human spirit's quest to grasp its own meaning and the meaning of all that is, allow for the possibility of genuine perceptions of God's *doxa* throughout culture as preparations for the gospel. More to the point, revelation will come to the human person as a genuine answer to the questionability of his or her own existence. The "I" that is the human subject naturally seeks a word from a Thou.[440] Thus biblical revelation comes not as an adventitious piece of information, but rather as the most intimate form of answer possible.[441] Of course the caveat should not go unnoticed: "even to the reversal of their meaning and content." Balthasar's vision of Western culture is no Pollyannaish or romanticized philhellenism. It will frequently be the case that only through judgment, that is, through a confrontation with the Cross, can a cultural form find its place within the opening into eternity that is the eschatological form of Christ. *GL*4, however, holds off explicit theological critique and instead culls the Graeco-Roman field for empirical evidence of analogies to Christian revelation, and for criteria internal to different types of metaphysical discourse that, in the end, cannot be reconciled from their own resources.[442]

Thus, Balthasar can begin to advance what is a massively integrationist theology of religions grounded in both the capacity of Creation to receive and reflect divine glory and the Redeemer's capacity to bridge the gap, by way of Cross and Resurrection, between Creation and Creator. For Balthasar, the ubiquity of grace provides no warrant for ecclesial anxiety:

> *The positive character of revelation and the Church is not destroyed by the fact that God is at work beyond the boundaries of the positive historical revelation and of the Church which bears witness to this revelation, nor by the fact that he calls to his kingdom and bestows his grace on whomever he will, in his sovereignty: rather, the positive character of revelation and the Church is thereby attested and proclaimed, for the clearly-defined historical form of God's self-revelation has essentially the function of a sign of salvation set in the midst of the cosmos.*[443]

The Church is not the exclusive locus of divine action in the world, but because it receives a definitive divine revelation, it does have the capacity and responsibility to proclaim where God is active outside the Church, to be a sign that has its measure outside itself in the revelation of Christ.

Balthasar's erotically aspirated covenant theology provides him with a theological grounding for two tropes common to the Alexandrian fathers in their own deliberations on the relation of Christian to extra-biblical truth: the *Logos spermatikos* and the *spolia Aegyptorum*.[444] He can now view the self-revelation of God's Word as the recollection and recapitulation of the shards of truth lying scattered about in the cultural forms extant in the world:

> *The logoi spermatikoi of ultimate forms of human and worldly fate which lie scattered in the myth, could be gathered together into the definitive form of revelation in Jesus Christ. Thus genuine art (rooted in the myth) would enjoy a relaxed relationship to what is Christian, for there is no reason why an illuminating and directing light may not fall from the form of revelation upon the significant forms of art which refer to the whole.*[445]

The Logos gathers and shapes or gives full intelligibility to the *logoi* found throughout cultural expressions. Balthasar thinks that by attending carefully to different cultural expressions of ontological significance, theology can get a more accurate assessment of what reason can truly accomplish apart from biblical revelation *and* assess the distance between metaphysical disclosures and revelation.[446] His method of integration is designed to accomplish this dual task. What I want to do briefly here is explore the meaning of "integration" and its theological presuppositions.

Balthasar rarely speaks self-consciously about his theological method, presumably fearing all that "method" implies in contemporary discourse: controlling, dominating, *a priori* thought. Yet when he does name his method, he consistently employs the term "integration" and contrasts this method to an evolutionary dialectics:

> *Perhaps this quick panoramic view is sufficient to explain why we wish to characterize our method as one of integration and not of evolution. Today "evolution" is in favor: it is by denying the old that one breaks through to the new and, in order to justify this turning aside, discredits the tradition (by means of psychology when necessary) and so persuades the contemporary world that it is quite pointless to make the tradition one's own or even to come to know the tradition at all.*[447]

Balthasar is not speaking merely of Christian tradition here, as he makes clear soon after:

> *... the Christian ought to have a sensibility for human tradition which must be integrated precisely if the way into the future is to be found: as the way from a totality that is still implicit (with its equilibrium) to a totality that is made explicit (where the equilibrium is laid open, but not abandoned).*[448]

For Balthasar, "integration" is not a method in the instrumental sense, but rather more like the opening of a space within which ontologically disclosive discourses can find an eternal justification and validity. Balthasar contends that partiality, which he associates with heresy, is always inferior to an integrative vision: "The more truth a partial perspective can integrate into itself, the greater is its claim to be true."[449] In the same context, that of a kind of pre-theological phenomenology, Balthasar is eloquent on the relation between integration and love:

> *Love is the opposite of sectarian insistence on being right. Love's inclination is to acknowledge the validity of another's truth sooner than its own. It has the freedom to affirm all truth, even truth that it does not immediately survey and is not in a position to judge—provided it has its origin in love. But love is also clear-sighted enough to see the full distance separating each respective partial truth from the totality and can thus order truths hierarchically. Love knows which truths*

> *include the others and which are included by them. Therefore, it can appropriate what is in each instance the broader and higher standpoint, and this capacity will be its strongest weapon in the dialogue among world views. Love vanquishes its opponent less through acuteness than through fullness. Love shows him that what he has to say is already included in its standpoint, is perhaps already better accounted for in it. It does not pass judgment; it merely shows and leaves the judgment to the evidence of its radiant revelation.*[450]

In no way is such a method *a priori* or controlling, but rather it exercises a kind of humility before the truth of the other. Theologically speaking, integration becomes another name for salvation through judgment. *Crux probat omnia* (the Cross tests all things), however, does not suggest for Balthasar that all things will be negatively judged by the Cross; rather, they will be measured and integrated within Christian revelation, while providing Christians with a deeper and richer engagement with their own revelation than they could have had apart from this encounter. Indeed, in contrast, for instance, to Jürgen Moltmann,[451] Balthasar thinks that Greek and Roman cultural works provide analogies not only to God rationally conceived, but also to God as revealed through Covenant and Cross. This discovery requires an expansion of theological intercourse to include cultural works beyond and outside the philosophical. Just as personal identity can be enriched by dialogue and encounter, and cannot be itself apart from these encounters, Christian identity gains illumination and breadth through its relations with others.[452]

This significance of dialogue for Balthasar will become more evident as we progress through a discussion of the different genres that Balthasar sees as metaphysical expressions of the human encounter with innerworldly beauty, goodness, and truth, and the ways in which these expressions gesture to a genuine encounter with divine *doxa*. We will take these genres in the order that Balthasar chooses, beginning with myth, and following with philosophy, and then religion. The aim here is not to repeat Balthasar's treatment, but rather to see the hospitality of Balthasar's Christocentrism, better grasp the nature of his apologetic, and simultaneously see how various elements of his discussion continue his battle against Marcionism and Prometheanism. Indeed, the very fact that created reality can image Christian revelation points to a positive relation between the Creator and the Redeemer that Marcionism would proscribe.

The Rehabilitation of Myth: The Homeric Canon

BALTHASAR'S REHABILITATION of mythical forms of discourse connects with many of our earlier themes. This rehabilitation at once brings myth into proximity with Old Covenant revelation and into conflict with modernity's philosophical clamoring for demythologization. In Balthasar's view, modern philosophy, in its empiricist, Cartesian, Enlightenment, and Hegelian manifestations, has been overzealous in its attempts to exclude mythical discourse, thus excising any valid conceptualization of divine transcendence or of the dialogical relation between the divine and human.[453] Modern philosophical reason presents little in the way of a dialogical relation to the depths of being. Instead, revelation often becomes reduced through logic to a speculative doctrine of God—one that, in many cases, turns philosophical *eros* into either an elevation of the self to divinity or an ascent into the One. Either way, the conditions necessary for genuine Christian prayer and praise appear to vanish.[454] We have seen this previously in our discussions of modern Marcionism and Prometheanism. Here we look at how for Balthasar Homer presents a resistance to modern Prometheanism analogous to that of the Old Covenant, and thus the beginnings of an alternative gentile pedagogy that one can no doubt also discover in non-Western mythic thought.

Balthasar contends that Homer develops the basic criteria for mythic-poetic discourse over which struggle will occur in the poetic, philosophical, and religious traditions that follow him. The central Homeric insight mirrors both that of the Delphic Oracle and one of the primary axioms of Old Covenant pedagogy: "Know thyself" and know that you are not God.[455] It is this basic difference-in-relation, that is, divine transcendence in free relation with the mortal world found in Homer, that makes possible grace, prayer, dialogue, divine freedom, and the singular, unrepeatable events that reveal the gods and their attributes. Insofar as other mythical, poetic, and philosophical discourses lose or weaken this basic insight, Balthasar claims, they lose the context or the conditions for all that flows from it in Homer's poetry.

The virtues of Homer's form, however, do not end with this fundamental accord with the Old Covenant vision. Like the Old Covenant again, Homer joins divine transcendence to an unsparing vision of human sweat, toil, misery, and death. This existential realism, on Balthasar's reading, gives the West a second metaphysical criterion: interpretations of being must be faithful to the concrete suffering of human beings and to the fundamental image of human beings as facing death. Euripides is Balthasar's exemplar here, as he provides an almost seamless connection to Golgotha: the "great, valid cipher of the Christ event."[456] Unlike Stoic theodicy, Euripides and Homer never gloss over human suffering for a superficial vision of wholeness or unity. Moreover, Homer can even grant to suffering its own form of *gravitas* which, in turn, gives suffering a dignity that it does not find in many other poets. Odysseus, the suffering righteous one, is also Athena's chosen one who becomes exalted and able to pass judgment on others, but only in the wake of his suffering. Balthasar thinks that Euripides and Sophocles develop this insight further, and he can even go so far as to find a substitutionary-sacrificial role for suffering that is grounded in love.[457] Clearly, then, Balthasar rejects the claim that reason is incapable of forming, from its concrete engagement with human existence, an analogy to divine embodiment or to Christ crucified, and he rejects this claim because he discovers that human reason, in its poetic manifestation, has in fact done so.[458] Of course, for Balthasar it remains to say that the form of Christ will be "ever greater" in its dissimilarity to the content of Homer's *Odyssey*.

Balthasar argues that the Homeric form is able to join its vision of divine transcendence and anthropological realism to a profound sense of divine presence and even indwelling in the world through a particular hero. Beauty in Homer comes from the radiance of being indwelt by the god who cares for her mortal charge and elevates him to happiness and human flourishing through grace or favor. Beauty is an eventful, theophanic gift, as are all things: "Everything—even the evil but above all what is noble, what raises man to his greatness and truth—comes from above, is gift."[459]

The condition for this indwelling and the proper human response is strongly reminiscent of the human side of Old Covenant righteousness: the "humbled holding-firm in obedience to the invisible will of the gods."[460] The hero is the one who lives a life devoted to the god. These elements form for Balthasar the basic Homeric "double doctrine":

> ... *a primal opposition, an unbridgeable distance between gods and man—and man's complete devotion to the gods. The first principle contradicts the philosophical tendency towards an enclosing of being in itself as identity, and the second resists any containment of man within himself.*[461]

Put otherwise, we might say that Homer's viewpoint is one of divine-human dialogue and human transcendence through grace, gratitude, humility, and service. Here we have the paradox that service and gratitude provide the conditions for transcendence. Balthasar suggests that for Homer, human transcendence, at least formally speaking, finds its ground in divine transcendence, and apart from this theandric context, humanity closes in on itself in a suffocating immanence. In Homer, Balthasar thinks he has found another ally in the battle against Prometheanism.

Balthasar presses the analogies to covenant-being further and draws what can only be an analogy to the Old Testament prophet. Like the prophet, the poet too must be obedient to the voice that comes from above and within. It is Homer's task, through contemplation (*theoria*) and creativity (*poesis*), to offer praise, to see the gifts of the gods and bring them to light. If the hero bears some resemblance to the exalted suffering servant, then the poet is akin to both prophet and psalmist. He holds up a mirror to civilization while bestowing praise on the gods. Balthasar's final statement on Homer is remarkably positive:

> *Can the balance between god and man, grace and nature, suffering and consolation be maintained in the light of the glory shown and accomplished here? Yet even when this must fall apart, what a promise lay in such a beginning for the next millennia.*[462]

For scholars schooled in Bultmannian demythologization, Balthasar's assessment of myth will be disorienting. Significantly, however, it raises the possibility that mythical discourse can be ontologically disclosive and perhaps reveals aspects of the divine-world relationship that philosophy is often unable to represent. For a theology of religions, this discursive shift means that far more cultural material becomes religiously significant than if "myth" and poetry were excluded for only the more theoretical or philosophical-style works. More specifically, for Balthasar myth has a unique ability to represent the singularity of events, the variety and multiplicity of worldly being, dynamic, personal divine transcendence, and the possibility for human transcendence given the right spiritual disposition. Mythical discourse sets up a dualistic, theandric reality in which a struggle of freedoms plays itself out. It becomes clear that, for Balthasar, Homer's world is a world thoroughly recognizable to one educated in Old Covenant pedagogy and therefore is capable of providing its own kind of preparation for the gospel.[463]

Platonic Integration

BALTHASAR SUGGESTS THAT THE MOVEMENT from myth to philosophy comes from a basic question posed to the Homeric world: Is the relation between the god and hero universally valid?[464] Several questions follow from this. Is the epiphanic moment or even "indwelling" also an ongoing characteristic of being or creation? Is the glory that marks the relation between the gods and heroes accessible to all human beings? Is a personal portrayal of the divine appropriate? In other words, Balthasar finds that the direction of philosophical questioning moves from particularity to universality; inquiry begins to ask about whether myth depicts "the entire situation of human kind."[465] In doing so, myth moves towards the philosophical expression of "universality" and "necessity,"[466] and this movement inevitably ushers in criticism of the myths themselves as parochial and imagistic. Balthasar characterizes this discursive trend, substantially if not always chronologically, as a move from image to concept, and thus a movement of abstraction.[467] Hellenistic philosophy now "evacuates it [myth] of its original content and subdues it to its own categories."[468] Balthasar undoubtedly considers the conceptual and universalistic orientation of philosophy part and parcel of human thinking, and it will pass this universal orientation on to Christian theology. A Christian apologetic must therefore address itself to philosophical reason as much as to mythical or imagistic forms of thought. As he writes near the beginning of *GL4*:

> *If Christian proclamation and theology ... is in all seriousness to make a claim of absoluteness on everything that is, then Christian proclamation must have its roots both in the historical sphere (only things which exist are real) and also in the metaphysical sphere (only as being is that which exists universal).*[469]

Christianity needs philosophy to protect it from becoming a mere "positivistic science of the historical facts of revelation," [470] or worse, an external and authoritarian imposition on human freedom.

We must admit, however, that Balthasar is suspicious of philosophical discourse, at least as it is historically realized. This does not mean that he wants to eschew reason for some brand of fideism.[471] But as philosophy emerges as a historically discernible discourse, Balthasar thinks it arises as a violent form of thought: "Where philosophy first comes to our notice, with Parmenides and Heraclitus, it is tuned to a pitch of overbearing ferocity."⁴⁷² The suspicion, even at this early stage of its arrival, is of titanism, and therefore it bears a connection not with mythical discourse as such, but with some of its content:

> *Reason, which wants to assure itself of the viability of its own transcendence into being, into the immutable, divine world, must at least "bracket off," methodically suspend, the act of glorifying God; its undertaking will therefore necessarily assume at least the appearance of titanism, of the storming of Olympus by its own power: "the spectacle of the Titanic nature of which our old legends speak is re-enacted* (ten palaian Tisaniken physin).⁴⁷³

The contrast between myth and philosophy is that between divine-world opposition (or the Homeric "double doctrine") and what we might recall as the pedagogy of the Old Covenant, on the one hand, and a movement of philosophical discourse towards identity on the other:

> *Here one suddenly senses the distance between the world of myth—where God and man are in basic opposition—and the world of philosophy, where in principle the kinship (συγγένεια) of both with each other must be pressed to the point of identity.*⁴⁷⁴

If the divine transcendence inherent to mythical discourse is lost, then it will turn out that the dialogue and prayer inherent to mythical disclosure are also "cut off at a stroke."⁴⁷⁵ Philosophy, for Balthasar, frequently runs towards total vision through monological reason and ends in identity. Unlike faith, which receives its criteria from "above" itself, and therefore requires transcendence, relation, and dialogue, reason knows by its own criteria: "Knowledge is that for which man possesses the criteria for verification in himself, in his reason"⁴⁷⁶; "In place of the daring of the heart there is knowledge which keeps itself to itself."⁴⁷⁷

Balthasar's judgments on philosophical discourse, however, are hardly all negative and, in contrast to Martin Heidegger, do not posit a fall from a pre-Socratic garden into the unfortunate ontological amnesia of Socrates and beyond.⁴⁷⁸ Philosophy has too much to offer Christianity, and Christians must reap its harvest if a true integration is to occur. Balthasar attempts to return to Plato some historical dignity; Plato, he contends, moderates, refines, and balances both the tone and the content of this origin. Ferocity turns to irony, and being and becoming are now expressed in their unity.[479] On Balthasar's reading, Plato conceives of all things as made of both becoming and a reflection of something beyond change, something immutable, and therefore something divine. Plato's world bears the epiphanic marks of myth, but no longer in episodic fashion; instead, the world's universal intelligible structures manifest the divine. Plato will be able to argue that all Being is beautiful in its particular manner, and, through the particular forms that it takes, Being opens itself to participation by way of knowledge.[480] The goal of this participation, Balthasar observes, is not a mere vision of the beautiful or the good, but a "begetting" or fruitfulness in the good. One ascends from the cave only to return to it to free others; one ascends in erotic love to the Good, and returns to realize this good in the practical context of the *polis*. As in John's Gospel, so in Plato's philosophy, fruitfulness for the community is the *telos* of contemplation.[481]

What is legitimate here, Balthasar argues, is the desire to know Being in its universal properties and the self-forgetfulness and transcendence that, for Plato, are prerequisites for true knowledge. If the hero is exalted through his obedience to the god, and the poet serves the *polis* by singing the praises of divine glory, then the philosopher achieves glory when she obeys the truth of things, serves them, and rightly orders them.[482] Through this right ordering of the soul and state on true or objective values, the philosopher serves her fellow citizens, even if they do not see it–even if they execute him. Philosophical knowledge, in Balthasar's reading of Plato, is a knowledge born of service, self-sacrifice, and openness to the things that are, rather than Promethean power and self-seeking. The beautiful soul is the soul ordered not by its own appetites or desires, but by reason, excellence, and truth; the beautiful soul has recollected or returned to its true, natural self and is now harmonious. Moreover, if Being is knowable by this soul, it is because Being discloses itself as objectively beautiful, true, and good. This, Balthasar contends, is the legitimate *eros* of philosophy: to "strive for the unconditionally Ultimate, True, Good, and Beautiful."[483] In answer to the question it poses to myth, philosophy can say that all Being, in different gradations, is both epiphanic and intelligible.

Whereas Balthasar does argue that modern philosophical movements too often banish mythical revelation or divine-world difference, he does not think that Plato or pre-Christian philosophy ever takes it as far as post-Christian philosophy will; in other words, pre-Christian philosophy never asserts a full identity between the world or humanity and the divine essence. At this point in our discussion this should not surprise us. We recall that on Balthasar's reading, it is only in the wake of Old Covenant divine transcendence and messianic eschatology, joined to a deformation of traditional views of Christ's *kenosis*, that modern Promethean and Dionysian movements arise. Plato may approach the line, but never quite breaches it, never succumbs to the total identification of the world or the human with the divine.[484] Balthasar observes that some differentiation, however insufficient, is always present. Moreover, Platonic philosophy does not always try to overcome the in-breaking of revelation from above by placing it in its own categories. At its boundaries, philosophy frequently turns to myth for the answers its own discourse cannot give.[485] This suggests for Balthasar that pre-Christian metaphysics is more likely to see the human person as inherently questionable, as inherently in need of a transcendent word or a word from the Transcendent than will modern post-Christian metaphysics.

The difference between pre-Christian and post-Christian philosophy, however, should also alert us that Balthasar does not want an anti-philosophical theology. Such a theology could never be a genuine integration of human discourse or an authentic penetration into God's work in creation. Balthasar makes this clear in the first volume of *Theo-Logic*:

> *By its very nature, theological insight into God's glory, goodness, and truth presupposes an ontological, and not merely formal or gnoseological, infrastructure of worldly being. Without philosophy, there can be no theology.*[486]

In his *Theology of Karl Barth*, Balthasar suggests that because grace effects a change in the human person both "ontically" and "noetically," philosophical reflection always takes place within the "theological a priori" of the call to grace. This point has two corollaries. First, no clear separation can be delineated between pure natural thinking and thinking moved by grace. In other words, the theologian can adduce no *a priori* upper limit assigned to the possibilities for the truth of such reflections.[487] He can even say that philosophers will often be "crypto-theologians."[488] Second, the Catholic theologian will welcome the appearance of truth wherever it might be found. At this point, Balthasar is at his most Christologically hospitable: "... space has been opened up inside the all-comprehensive Yes to revelation for everything in creaturely thought that can be and has been redeemed."[489] Indeed:

> *The content of revelation, as the highest ratio—the personal, divine Logos itself—needs all the forms of the worldly logoi of truth in order to present its inexhaustible fullness: the abstract and general as well as the concrete and individual. Theology must work from below, where, as Newman loved to show, all the truths of cultures and peoples are gathered up by the Church and made serviceable to theology. But theology also works from above, where the divine Logos wants to enrich all logoi in his mission to the world and lead them back to the Father in himself.*[490]

Excursus on *The Truth of the World*: A Covenantal Ontology

OUR DISCUSSION OF BALTHASAR'S gentile pedagogy or gentile preparation for the gospel has focused thus far on cultural manifestations of analogies to covenant revelation. Thus, we have observed the accessibility of an authentic relation with divine glory through the eventfulness, prayer, dialogue, suffering, piety, realism, and obedience found in mythic poetry on the one hand, and the self-forgetfulness, service, love of truth, desire to be fruitful for one's community, and discovery of the epiphanic nature of universal Being found in philosophy. Balthasar undergirds this generous reading of the classical tradition—and in principle, at least, other cultural traditions—with his investigation in *TL*1 of the ontological and anthropological substratum that makes possible the authentic doxological encounter-response we find in a variety of mythic-poetic and philosophical discourses. It will become clear that his philosophic-metaphysical considerations in this, his most purely philosophical text, remain informed by his covenant theology, without suggesting that this phenomenology is either inaccessible to or without persuasive power for non-Christians and non-Jews on the one hand, or merely deduced from the form of revelation on the other. In addition, our discussion of *Theo-Logic* supports our anti-Marcionite / anti-Promethean reading of Balthasar prosecuted throughout. Of course these three elements are inter-related. To the extent that Balthasar's covenant theology and his assessment of extra-biblical revelation are related to his philosophical metaphysics, it stands to reason that his ontological considerations would be anti-Marcionite. In part, this anti-Marcionism comes from the very fact that he positively relates Old Covenant themes to his discourse on truth. Specificity will come from the covenantal disposition of the subject toward being, the epiphanic and positively mysterious character of being, the very notion of truth as *emeth*, the refusal to eliminate justice as he turns to discuss love, and Balthasar's sense that service and praise lie at the heart of what is real. The upshot of all this is that Balthasar's text on truth supports the contention that his theology is hospitable to the possibility of truth, goodness, and beauty discovered outside of ecclesial precincts and inhospitable to Marcionite Prometheanism.

The ontological truth of the world, in Balthasar's view, has two fundamental qualities: *aletheia* (unconcealedness) and *emeth* (trustworthiness). Reality shows itself, according to Balthasar, which never means that knowledge can exhaust it. Indeed, reality always exceeds our grasp[491] as a particular form of existence points to a plenitudinal, always greater essence that gives itself appearance or sense-apprehensible form for us.[492] The world that offers itself to "vision" is not mere image or appearance, but also essence, ground, interior light, and depth.[493] Reality shows itself (*aletheia*) and thus can be known in its depths, even with a kind of certainty or deep trust (*emeth*).[494]

Balthasar's inclusion of the Hebrew *emeth* is a non-incidental riposte to Heidegger's restriction of authentic philosophy to a Greek-German linguistic axis on the one hand, and also a rejection of the idea of philosophy as quest without answers or as opposed to truth as correspondence.[495] *Emeth* comes from the "trustworthiness" of God lying at the foundation of Israel's covenant and for Balthasar is reflected in the foundation of the truth of Being as well. The excessive nature or prodigality of Being[496] equally reflects what Balthasar describes as the extravagant self-giving of God in the covenant and the paschal mystery. The truth of Being, he observes, can never be exhausted. Instead, knowledge opens greater contexts and intellectual vistas and reveals what remains unknown. Thus, knowledge always beholds the ontological promise of ever-greater revelation of truth and consequently reveals mystery at the very heart of knowing.[497] Truth, for Balthasar, is like a "seed"[498] that promises growth and fruitfulness. *Emeth*, then, serves to stave off the sheer "opacity"[499] of Being that we find in, for instance, Kafka's *The Castle*, but also does not represent a closing off. Rather, knowledge supports desire for greater knowledge, which desire is an implicit awareness of mystery as ontological excess; as in Israel's covenant, and also for Balthasar in the final form of the biblical canon itself, so in our experience of Being, *emeth* is a beginning and gateway.[500]

From the vantage point of the subject, this beginning originates in desire (*eros*) and in the senses. The subject is both already in the world, and desires to know and act upon the world of which she is a part. While Balthasar certainly allows for intentionality in acts of knowing and willing, it would be accurate to say that receptivity is logically prior in his phenomenological account. Due to its sensate way of receiving the world, he thinks, the subject experiences the "unchosen necessity of being broken open to receive, through the subspiritual gateway of the senses, the life and truth of the other that comes uninvited, pouring into the domain of its intellect."[501] For Balthasar, as for Heidegger, the subject is never closed in upon itself, but is "always already engaged with the world."[502] The subject's response to the manifest gifts of Being is one of receptivity, attentiveness, readiness, discernment, action, and creativity.[503] Reminiscent of his ontic discussion of Plato and some of the poets, Balthasar suggests that the subject as knower becomes a self-forgetful "space" wherein entities can attain their epiphanic *telos* for the benefit of both the object that gains a "word" or a "voice," and for the conscious spirit that desires to know and act.[504] In Balthasar's covenantal ontology, the truth of being is found even in the death of appearances, that is, in singular revelations of an essence that in their very disappearance paradoxically reveal their perduring underlying ground whose potential is never exhausted by a single instance. Likewise, the subject must renounce the rewarding engagement with a multitude of singulars to allow for conceptual knowledge. The act of knowing appears here as a kind of paschal or Eucharistic hospitality and service to an epiphanic and self-giving and self-surrendering world, all of which reflects the Creator.[505]

However, this hospitality would seem to have an enemy for Balthasar, and by now we should not be surprised that the enemy is Promethean idealism. Balthasar contends that idealism would posit the world and its objects as extensions of the subject's mind, and thus one's interlocutors (as conscious subjects or entities in the world which bear an analogy to them) are never free to be anything but what our mind allows in this profoundly non-dialogical *modus operandi*. By contrast, Balthasar suggests that the subject's expropriation in the act of knowing convinces the subject that the world and its objects are exterior to it.[506] In the unity of being and thinking,[507] the subject experiences not only the capacity to "measure" these objects, that is, to make intellectually true judgments about them, but also the knowledge that the subject herself falls within the truth of the world, and thus can be "measured" as well.[508] She is being-*in*-the-world, and not separate from or creator of it. Thus, the subject finds herself granted a share in an intellectual light she did not create.

It is in this description of being and knowing that we find Balthasar opposing Promethean Idealism to a "Marian" and covenantal phenomenology. The Promethean idealist experiences the unity of being and consciousness and decides that the latter created the former and that objects known are, in some sense, an extension of the knower. Balthasar contrasts this non-dialogical view to what, based upon our previous discussion, we can call his covenantal and Marian view of knowing:

> *For the more the subject grows by its knowledge in the certainty of the truth, the greater the distance between its own measured measure and God's measuring measure must appear to it. The truth proper to the creature is not so much the possession of the absolute truth as the readiness to receive it again and again. Again and again, it receives its self-consciousness by proceeding from its indifferent attentiveness to possible truth to the active service of the truth of the world. It becomes aware of its closeness to God's truth only in its distance from that truth.*[509]

If Promethean idealism represents, for Balthasar, the death of dialogue, it is the recognition of an original distance between God and creature that allows a subject to recognize other, free-standing subjects over-against oneself precisely because one does not see oneself as the genesis of all others. Indeed, for Balthasar, self-consciousness itself is "received" through the manifold encounters with the world and with other conscious subjects. Only with this recognition, he thinks, can we account for inter-subjectivity or dialogue:

> *Truth now appears in the world as distributed among countless subjects, which in their original posture of readiness are open to one another and which await from one another the communication of the part of the truth that God has granted them as a share in his own infinite truth.*[510]

Thus, it is the perceived otherness of God that is the condition for openness to others *qua* other, without whom we end up alethically impoverished. Hospitality here is rooted in divine transcendence, recognition of our creaturely status, and a covenantal purging of Promethean idealist vision.

For Balthasar, dialogue is an ontologically grounded event that brings us to ourselves. It stands to reason that the other should be received not merely as other, but also as truth-bearing gift.

Balthasar brings this epiphanic view of Being and the knowing subject into clear relation with his notion of form. There is, he thinks, a kind of analogy to interpersonal, conscious, free self-giving within the world of inanimate and animate, but non-human objects. All that appears, Balthasar argues, appears as an image that both discloses and veils an inner depth or ground. The appearance hits and breaks open the senses so that the mind can know a depth lying beneath; thus the image or appearance can be—and for Balthasar is—described as surrendering so that its interiority can be disclosed.[511] The knower can judge an interior present because she knows her own form as an interior with a surface image. So, for Balthasar, the image or surface reveals a depth to be known only through its appearance; moreover, the depth shows itself as an essence that holds within an abundance of possibilities for realization, each one unique.[512] Epiphany, then, leads the knowing subject into a depth both revealed and concealed in the image, and into a realm of abundant possibility / promise never exhausted in any particular realization. For Balthasar, mystery is not based upon cognitive shortfall or on a kind of resistance to truth as correspondence and intentional knowing. Instead, mystery is rooted in the very abundance and excess[513] that lie at the heart of being and that become more apparent the more the subject comes to know. Balthasar shows us how the world itself is dialogical[514] and epiphanic, neither episodically nor statically, but in Being's giving itself over and letting itself be known, and the knower performing an analogous kind of self-forgetting service to this order to bring disclosure to fruition in knowledge and action.

Balthasar's stress on depth and surface in mutual, dynamic,[515] and ineluctable unity, that is, on the unity of form, shows its relevance to philosophical critique in his review of the rationalist or mystical idealist position on the one hand, and the skeptical position on the other. The rationalist account suggests that images point to an essence not intrinsically related to the appearance. We can think of this as an allegorical view of being. One may penetrate to the essence and leave the image or appearance behind. Alternatively, one can be skeptical that there is any depth at all underlying appearances or signs. On this view, reason must confine itself to the tracing of signs which inherently present no rationality or underlying laws of operation. The skeptic sees only the images and not their essence or depth;

the rationalist or idealist mystic opts to close his senses and seeks only what lies beneath: "And so in the end it becomes incomprehensible why there is any appearance at all."[516] Both options end in some kind of formlessness, or "empty mystery,"[517] whether a superficial or aestheticizing series of images without depth or an ineffable depth that takes no meaningful shape in the world. Balthasar's entire ontology seeks to navigate beyond a totalizing and formless apophaticism, which, theologically speaking, would proscribe divine speech and thus issue in its own kind of Prometheanism,[518] and a kind of *kataphatic* ontology or rationalism that would destroy the mystery of plenitude and the wonder built into it. For him, neither total ineffability nor total transparency do justice to human experience or to the God of Creation and Covenant.

If, at the beginning of *TL*1, Balthasar speaks of truth as *aletheia* and *emeth*, and if Being breaks open the senses and thus expropriates humanity as knowing subjects, we might label this kind of epiphany as Being's *kabod*, that is, Being's ability to catch and hold our attention, thus carrying human persons beyond themselves in ec-static existence. Truth, he says, comes upon us and calls for decision.[519] Now, Balthasar's Old Covenant pedagogy moves from theophany into the depth of relationship over time rooted in *emeth*, and this truthful God makes possible the expropriation of covenant-being leading to the ever-greater revelation of God's self-giving and abundant love. Cyril O'Regan has pointed out that Balthasar's *TL*1 exhibits a similar movement, that is, from *emeth / kabod* to the specification of both as love. Love, for Balthasar, is the measureless measure of all things.[520] For Balthasar, justice sees things as they are, whereas love sees things both as they are and as they could be in the eyes of God; love gives more than is required: "the law of love is to be in the movement of giving itself away."[521] Human beings, he thinks, are to be the administrators of this love that goes beyond, but never forsakes, the responsibilities of justice. Indeed, "true love always fulfills justice."[522]

The analogies we find to the form of revelation, then, are not for Balthasar accidental. Rather, they emerge out of the human response to and participation in the Gift of Being, and find space within the Son's all-inclusive Yes to the Father, in the mutual glorification of Savior and Creator. Given this metaphysics of Gift and participation—what we are calling his covenantal ontology—Balthasar refuses a kind of extreme apophaticism or "formless" theology of religions that would employ the utter transcendence of God to empty out theological language of its specificity. For Balthasar, God always remains true (*emeth*) to his self-revelation, and as revealed, God is known as always ever-greater. Mystery is not the emptying of form and content, but instead connotes a fullness of form that bears only analogous relation to worldly forms. In other words, Balthasar's rejection of Promethean idealist metaphysics is also a rejection of theology of religions discourse that would view revelation as more nearly allegorical than sacramental, with God's revelation in history only "pointing" to an Ineffable variously named by the many religions. What Balthasar's metaphysics shows, both in *GL4* and in *TL1*, is that his emphasis on the particularity and singularity of Christian revelation makes this same revelation no less universally compelling.

Religion

RELIGION IS BALTHASAR'S THIRD DISCURSIVE TYPE. He conceives religion as an inherently syncretistic operation that attempts to reconcile the metaphysical insights fundamental to the genres of myth and philosophy. Some attempt at this unity becomes especially necessary once myth encounters philosophy. Following Hegel, Balthasar observes that in the face of de-personalizing philosophical criticism, the myths soon become pale, sickly versions of themselves, unable to spark the first naïve conviction they once inspired.[523] Moreover, in this defeat much of what saved philosophy from becoming a completely insular discourse departs. Balthasar again adopts Hegel's analysis by giving this cultural development a political edge: Roman philosophical religion, as it appears in Varro, for instance, is designed to reduce the gods to the Roman Imperium, and to substitute for divine freedom and transcendence omnipotent Fate, "in which the philosophical hegemony of men or the political hegemony of Rome manifests itself—and ultimately deifies and absolutises itself in the climax and summit, the representation of the imperial office."[524] The message is clear: If myth can become a dangerous and closed tribal ideology, then philosophy can be every bit as insular and ideological; conversely, if philosophy can indicate a rational adherence to truth, myth and poetry can likewise point to a profound personal fidelity to reality as it shows itself, "diamond hard."[525] With its universalist orientation, then, philosophy begins to undermine mythical content, concreteness, and vitality. Myth will respond by trying to compete through a rationalization of its own stories, where it then forfeits the contributions essential to its form and encloses divine glory within the cosmos, or it will insist on esoteric and fantastic epiphanies known only to a few, but not communicable outside the sect. Religion, he concludes, is unable to maintain the insights of the two kinds of discourse through a genuine reconciliation. In this analysis, we are left with meaningful fragments, but fragments nonetheless.

It is important to notice, however, that Balthasar partly includes Christianity in the discourse of religion. In one of the most telling comments in all his discussions of religion, Balthasar takes a firm stand on the significance of the Incarnation and God's real solidarity with humanity, and thus with human modes of discourse. This passage is worth quoting in full:

> *We may indeed do so [proclaim the gospel] announcing with Karl Barth in tones of loud conviction that Christianity is not a religion, or, with Kierkegaard, that it is not a philosophy, or, with Bultmann, that it is not a mythology. But God would not have become human if he had not come into positive inner contact with these three forms of thought and experience. The evidence for this contact and this contamination is provided by the Bible itself, which attains its final and (for the Christian) binding form precisely in the great age of religion and syncretism. Those who want to "purify" the Bible of religion, philosophy and myth want to be more biblical than the Bible, more Christian than Christ. What is invariably left after these supposed exorcisms is a pitifully abstract affair, that seeks to hide its wretchedness by exalting the slogan of "holy poverty", the "absolute seriousness" of its own impoverishment, as the* unum necessarium, *latching on to "the Word" in one way or another, as if this Word, ascending to the Father, had not sent forth the Holy Spirit upon Church and world.*[526]

Balthasar does not hesitate to notice the Bible's own "syncretistic" borrowings from cultural materials.[527] He concludes:

> *This all points clearly to the fact that human thinking does not happen without concepts (philosophy) and images (myth), and the relation between "religion" and revelation is thus bound to be an intimate interior penetration of just this intense kind.*[528]

The more obvious point here is that insofar as divine revelation really occurs *for human beings*, then this revelation will take place in humanly accessible patterns of thought, yet precisely through these patterns will reveal its object as transcendent, as ever-greater. Balthasar thinks that each and every form found in the Old Covenant can also be found outside that Covenant; how these forms are embraced and placed in relation to Yahweh, and in relation to God's Incarnation, is what transforms or orders them. The Incarnation shows that there can be no adventitious relation between nature and grace, but rather grace is mediated through the realm of nature and history. Christianity cannot avoid this mediation, and, more importantly, should not want to.

Of course this also means that nature cannot assert any absolute autonomy from grace. What has proven impossible, he thinks, is for philosophy and myth to integrate themselves from below. The bridge, as he puts it, is never built.[529] Philosophy strives to both rid itself of myth and to maintain the warmth and beauty of a religious worldview. In Balthasar's view, however, philosophy's de-mythologization process is largely delusional (both then and now). On the one hand, de-mythologization involves the de-personalization of the gods and the enclosure of reality within the divine cosmos. The divine now becomes synonymous with order, and the gods are reduced to elements of the cosmos. Yet this order still comes "from above," and on Balthasar's reading philosophy never does rid itself of its mythological baggage. Its vision of order, harmony, and the divine still derive precisely from the images and metaphors that it found there. Even more importantly, from a Christian perspective, is what is lost in this process: the experience of glory as a personal Thou who eventually reveals himself as that which makes reality beautiful, good, and true, yet transcends each of those transcendentals in his own *doxa* as personal, sovereign, self-abandoning love. Instead, philosophy devolves into a dialectic between "god-fearing pantheism" and "god-less atheism"—really flip-sides of the same coin for Balthasar.[530]

Similar problems occur, Balthasar thinks, when religion must try to incorporate philosophy. Once philosophy as critical thought emerges, religion cannot avoid its challenge. Here we find prayer, grace, sacrifice, all the elements of religion—but now, on Balthasar's reading, enclosed within "a more comprehensive frame of reference based on pantheistic identity."[531] Dialogue, the I-Thou relation, and sacrament all "rest upon a monistic foundation," even if the ecstatic experiences are said to come from without or from grace and are never reduced to mere psychological experience. Porphyry seems an exception, however, in that he does allow for a "'true showing' (αὐτοψία) of the divine in its 'glory,'" where "its appropriate form of manifestation is possible: the higher the rank of a divinity, the clearer and more beautiful and free from illusion is its appearance."[532] What remains impossible in this realm of thought, however, is that the divine should "humble itself to serve human beings."[533] Perhaps more importantly, Balthasar notes the trenchant critique of Porphyry by Iamblichus which leads, in a Hegelian direction, to the integration of all forms of "dialogic faith into the monological knowledge of reason."[534]

Yet Balthasar makes room for two figures who each transcend the general trend and who give to Christianity a religious preparation for the gospel and elements of expression that flow into the heart of the tradition. Plotinus[535] and Vergil each offer a distinctive *kairos*, and a moment of thought in the "mode of Advent expectation."[536] Vergil presents a historical drama in which Homeric Greece serves as the Old Covenant to the Roman New. This historical action takes place in relation to a divine realm that shines through and calls for a response from the poet that is an unconditional affirmation, a Yes, to all being, even in the face of real human corruption and suffering. Plotinus fashions a form of thought in which the world manifests, at every level, the divine brilliance that radiates through the totality of being but evades capture within this world or the totality of being (at least on one reading). The *exitus-reditus* structure of Plotinus' thought becomes crucial for Christian self-expression in the centuries to come and bears retrieving precisely because it gives a schema for both the *eros* of the creature for the divine and for the divine's desire to express itself in each and every being.[537] Nevertheless, Balthasar does not think that these systems can maintain themselves in the glory they perceive. Like Augustine, they try to ascend, but fall back. More specifically, Vergil's poetry moves towards an inner-worldly Roman utopia that threatens to once again make the gods subservient to the state and reduce divinity to immanence. The analogy to Balthasar's discussion of the Old Covenant and Judaism is clear: just as a Judaism shorn of its covenant norm can threaten to become a strategy for innerworldly kingdom creation, so Vergil's Rome threatens the same. More importantly, the analogy is to modern Promethean states that locate glory in the nation.

Plotinus' religious philosophy, though certainly a work of profound contemplation, stands in an ambiguous twilight that can be interpreted either in Christian theological terms or in terms of a pantheistic idealism. Whatever the interpretation, however, Christian self-interpretation takes into itself the categories and content of these systems, and then opens them up to serve the expression of God's Logos.

Aside from the important material analogies between ancient religion and Christianity, two crucial points emerge from Balthasar's discussion. The first is the inability of Graeco-Roman religion to integrate philosophical and mythical elements. Balthasar thinks that this inability itself is a designation of our *humanum*; it speaks at once of the transcendent communion or communion with the Transcendent that humanity desires (*eros*), and the inability of the world to satisfy this longing in itself or from its own constructions. Human beings, in Balthasar's view, are seekers. The second is the need for Christianity to enter into the structures of human reasoning and worldly disclosure. Balthasar believes that the Incarnation demands such a non-coercive *suasio* by virtue of its own formal disclosure of God's desire to enter into the deepest structures of worldly existence, not excluding birth and death. Revelation without reason, and reason without revelation, are doomed to the failures of authoritarianism and totalitarianism.

Judaism and the Nations

"INTEGRATION," ON THE SCALE THAT BALTHASAR PROPOSES, is a daring and perilous enterprise. In the currently designated post-modern situation[538] of theology, "integration" sounds the threat of the univocal, the same, the imperialistic, and even the Hegelian. Now a passage we quoted earlier—"Catholicism embraces everything, leaving nothing out"[539]—may be heard in more nearly threatening than welcoming tones: a religious *pax romana* that "integrates" through forced submission. Balthasar is aware of these concerns and addresses them at the very beginning of his New Covenant discussion in *GL7*:

> *Nevertheless, God does not destroy the work which he has begun, like a Shiva who destroys the world in his dance: rather, he perfects in the identity of the "person" of the One the "distinction without mingling of natures." It is far more difficult to hold on to this in thought, than to maintain a final commingling of everything or even only a Hegelian progressive "resolution" of the differences into the synthesis ... and thus what is not identical coincides, and is yet thereby preserved in its particularity.*[540]

Here, we can see that the Incarnation proves the hermeneutical key to Balthasar's theology of religions in its opposition to Hegelian systematizing. Interpretation by way of the Incarnation signals a commitment to the particularity or difference-in-unity of metaphysical disclosures.[541] The glory of the Incarnation is, for Balthasar, what can interpret and validate the disclosures of glory found throughout world culture without either conflating an extra-biblical religion and Christianity or seeing extra-biblical religion as a logical way station to the Incarnation. For Balthasar, the Creator's work finds its validation through the redemption of temporal ontological disclosure within the broad opening up of God's interior life that is Christ's eschatological mission.

It is equally true that Balthasar's incarnational theology of religions leads to a rather direct rejection of the Barthian and Kierkegaardian hostility to analogy and seeks to replace this hostility with a kind of discerning hospitality.[542] We have previously discovered this rejection in Balthasar's discussion of religion. Now, we can join this discussion of ancient religious discourse to his more formally stated position. Balthasar contends that there will be "traces" of God's Logos found "everywhere," since through Christ's life, death, and resurrection nature is freed to "pursue its ultimate goal."[543] So long as we do not equate "traces" with the religions as such, we can even recognize a "(hidden) history of the *ecclesia ab Abel*," that is, elements of the Christ-form, extant throughout culture.[544] We know that for Balthasar these traces emerge from the contemplative appropriations of the human encounter with Being drawn forth by the erotic drive toward transcendence, on the one hand, and God's erotic self-giving in creation on the other. Among these traces of God's Logos, Balthasar includes Lao Tzu, Socrates, Buddha, and the guru, each of which can be viewed as genuine intimations of Christ insofar as they exhibit self-renunciation in order to become vessels for the infinite.[545] The intense self-effacement of Zen Buddhism and the genuine transcendence of the human person discovered by Hinduism,[546] Balthasar suggests, are high points of extra-Christian disclosure. It is also evident through the foregoing analysis of *GL*4, and through Balthasar's work in *TD*1, that the universality of the Christian *Gestalt* emerges from actual contact with human culture in its expressions of joy, suffering, questioning, aspiration, and its multiple attempts to address the mystery of death. For Balthasar, Christ's Incarnation penetrates these fundamental structures of human existence, and thus bears a distinct solidarity with humanity. Thus, the form and content of Christian revelation gives itself to the human being in the same anthropological "place" that all other discourses do, and the concrete universality of Christian claims emerges from the depth of God's penetration into historical existence.

This solidarity has its ground in the human response to God's call in Being itself, and this "erotic" call-response grounds for Balthasar the Second Vatican Council's view of the human person as religious seeker. He observes throughout culture a human desire to return to a lost unity in full communion with the source of all being. Appealing to Augustine's unquiet or restless heart (*cor inquietam*), Balthasar observes that for gentile religion, this restlessness positively propels *homo religiosus* towards communion with what is absolute and simultaneously gracious:

> *Touching on their view of the Absolute, what we can expect on the average is that two images overlap: the thought of a dependence, and thus of a certain (free) graciousness, and the thought of the inadequacy to, and the ever-greater dissimilarity with, the ultimate ground.*[547]

The religious desire, he thinks, will be to find and remain in vertical communion with the absolute, which may be conceived as local, anthropomorphic deities (e.g., Roman or Greek), or as universal principles that would grant grace and / or stability in an ever changing world (e.g., Being, the One, Logos, fate, *dîke*). The attempt to establish this communion can take the form of mysticism, philosophy, ritual, psycho-somatic technique, etc. In any case, it is clear that Balthasar finds this legitimate desire for communion and this expression of the *analogia entis* throughout the religious forms. He thinks that religion reveals humanity's nature as seeker (Acts 17), the human origin and goal in God that begets this seeking, and the distinct awareness of not being God. This, of course, is all positive from a Christian standpoint and presents for Balthasar strong evidence of God's providential preparation for the gospel throughout culture and history.[548] The insights taken from the broader, supernatural providence of God in Creation permeate the covenant borders and enter into the form of Christ itself. Creation and Covenant, world and Church, then, are not for Balthasar mutually exclusive divisions, but mutually penetrating spheres that nevertheless retain their difference.

Balthasar addresses this most clearly in *TL3*, where he considers issues of Church-world relation in view of the Spirit given to both Church and world. We quoted earlier a passage from *GL4* where Balthasar, criticizing a certain Protestant form of theology that would see revelation as opposed to the world, writes, "as if this Word, ascending to the Father, had not sent forth the Holy Spirit upon Church and world."[549] Balthasar makes several observations here that are important. First, he observes that Christ becomes human for the redemption of the world,[550] not merely for the Church, and that the obverse view is heresy.[551] Balthasar observes that the apocalypses must be seen together with the synoptic gospels so that a Spirit Christology involves both the cosmic and missionary (anthropological) dimensions of Christ's redemptive work. Second, he notes that in a number of instances, Scripture proclaims people faithful prior to baptism based upon the work of the Spirit.[552] In short, Balthasar sees the mission of the Son and Spirit as cosmically and humanly inclusive. Indeed, he concludes that Christ and the Spirit in principle transcend any division between Church and world.[553] This leads him to a number of interesting theological inferences.

In *TL3*, the principled soteriological breaching of the Church / world division (not to say distinction) justifies a kind of "to and fro" movement from Church to world in missionary activity that seeks genuine inculturation, and from the world back into the Church's own precincts and depths so that the unity of truth does not end up as incoherent fragments. The purpose of this second movement would be to grasp how partial truths formerly separated from their home in the Christian *Gestalt* can be re-integrated into that form and seen in their true splendor. So the Christian movement outward to others finds its complement in a movement of retrieval where such cultural elements, such as universal rights,[554] can be re-inscribed within Christian discourse without a tragic loss of transcendence. This discovery of genuine Christian elements outside ecclesiastical boundaries, once again, should not surprise if Balthasar's insistence on John 3:8, "the Spirit blows where it will," is taken to heart. And here he extends the Alexandrian *Logos spermatikos* trope to include the *pneumata spermatika*.[555] Thus Christians should not be surprised to find elements of Christian truth, or even the Gospel itself, everywhere. Now, having opened up the important issue of inculturation, enabled by the breaching of the Church-world difference by Christ and the Spirit, we still need to mark Balthasar's approach off from some others that remain significant and popular.

It is perhaps not surprising that Balthasar continues to refuse a trend in modern theology toward the relativization of Israel's covenant vis-à-vis Greek and other extra-biblical sources. In contrast to Schleiermacher,[556] Kant,[557] and, more recently, John Hick,[558] Balthasar reaffirms the traditional priority of Israel's revelation and what he considers an ineluctable difference inscribed into the biblical *Gestalt*:

> *Here the distinction between "Jews" and "gentiles" becomes striking: Israel is and always has been the people of God, predestined to find its fulfillment in the Church. As for the "nations," on the other hand, while they are watched over by a general (supernatural) providence, they are not given a distinct theological mission and personality prior to Christ's call; and even after being called by him, they cannot receive such a mission and personality except within the unity of the Church. No national messianism has any theological significance.*[559]

Balthasar clearly thinks that on a Christian view, Judaism receives a personal call that characterizes its covenant and gives it a unique mission in history. He joins this reading of Israel to his reading of Acts of the Apostles, chapter 17. If gentile religion shows humanity's desire to commune with that which is absolute above the vicissitudes of this world, then Judaism works in the "reverse direction."[560] Following Heschel's statement, Balthasar observes that for Judaism, "God has gone in search of man."[561] For Israel, reflection on religious experience and "spiritual practice" will take a backseat to active readiness for the command / mission that issues from God. This makes sense if in fact they are not attempting to find communion with God, but to maintain right relations with God and community that God has already established.[562] His work suggests that this fundamental orientational difference leads to other differences between Judaism and the nations. For instance, while he observes formal similarities between Christianity and extra-biblical religion throughout his work, he also thinks that the content will often sharply diverge. So Athena takes on human form to grace or favor Odysseus; yet Odysseus' violent acts of slaughter hardly mirror the culmination or recommendation of the Gospel. By contrast, the Old Covenant shares the same content as the Gospel, namely, salvation through judgment, and will gain its most true and coherent form in Christ. Of course the content of certain Euripidean dramas may venture closer to the form of Christ, but nothing in Greek thought would seem to penetrate toward the Gospel with the level of intensity of the prophetic staircase or the suffering servant, and no cultural form bears the clarity of revelation lifted out of the mass of the cultural and historical process to gain a definitive form.

If Balthasar finds the human desire for vertical communion with Absolute Being to be the essence of religion as a discursive genre, one fully consonant with Christian form, he also thinks that for extra-biblical religion the blessing will also be the curse. In particular, he thinks that such "vertically" oriented religious systems lack the ability to positively ground and thus fully affirm the world of experience, time, multiplicity, and difference. Instead, the world, necessarily emanating or accidentally falling from a divine unity, even if it has some good qualities expressive of divinity, will not be viewed as an ontologically and epiphanically rich reflection of its Creator's freedom, wisdom, and love. Using the terms we established in our excursus, we can say that for Balthasar, extra-biblical religion will generally view the world as more nearly allegorical than sacramental.

Balthasar believes that Judaism, spurred on by its covenant relation to the God of Creation and Covenant, will be more concerned for the world and for history as the loci of God's action. It is clear from our former discussion that Balthasar finds the *analogia entis*, understood by him as similarity in ever-greater dissimilarity, in the Old Covenant, and absolutely clear that in Judaism we have the preeminent preparation for the gospel. Judaism provides the very covenantal categories in which God's self-interpretation "for us" takes place. In Balthasar's view, Judaism originates with God's opening up of his own life to Israel and initiating the communion yearned for in religion more broadly. Of course this view of the relation between Jewish and gentile pedagogies removes Alexandrian historical claims that Plato learned from the Law of Moses, and replaces that view with a Christian phenomenology. Gentile religion does not directly learn from Israel but is rather taken up into Israel's movement toward the New Covenant. Israel represents the fulfillment of the religious desire by way of God's trustworthy action at the root of Creation and Covenant, and, he suggests, passes that religious desire for ongoing communion into the form of Christ.

Balthasar also finds much to praise in modern Jewish intellectual culture, especially in its consistent rejection of and intervention against theoretical systems that suffocate the prophetic cry of suffering humanity and proscribe God's in-breaking call of the singular human being, and, especially in the case of Franz Rosenzweig, its stress on dialogue.[563] Moreover, in lieu of an extra-biblical "vertical" religious striving, Balthasar thinks that Judaism's primary concern lies along the horizontal-historical axis with special focus devoted to the transformation of the future. One important thread ties these vertical (gentile religion) and horizontal (Judaism) axes together: as they depart from their mythical origins towards philosophical sophistication, he believes, both will often leave behind a personal god for impersonal categories or laws, whether the laws of economics, fate, *dîke*, or an absolute grasped as "ineffable," or for a transcendent formlessness in stark juxtaposition to a world composed of finite forms.[564]

We will investigate in our next section how Balthasar thinks Christianity propounds a unique universality that joins the vertical communion of gentile religion with the ongoing historical mission that marks Jewish eschatology. But we have come to a point where a brief discussion of the differences between Balthasar and Karl Rahner is now appropriate, and we can begin with the last sentence of our passage quoted above: "No national messianism has any theological significance." Here, Balthasar exhibits a cultural anxiety that goes beyond inter-religious dialogue. Certainly his emphasis on Jewish singularity and soteriological uniqueness has biblical roots; but it is also reasonable to think that Balthasar has in mind the kind of conflations that occurred in Nazi Germany between Christ and Hitler, where Hitler was envisioned as the German messiah and Germany stood in for Israel as the bearer of a world mission.[565] Balthasar makes this concern explicit in *Theo-Logic* 3, where the difficulties of missionary inculturation become evident:

> *One difficulty of missionary work is the fact that the truth of the Christian revelation cannot be embraced in its fullness apart from its prehistory, that is, the experience of Israel. Every "inculturation" that attempts to replace Christianity's prehistory with the history of a particular culture will necessarily fail to attain the catholicity of Christian culture and introduce some kind of nationalization of Christianity. Hitler's "German Christians" should be a constant warning for us here.*[566]

Once this confusion between biblical revelation and particular cultural formations occurs, Christianity forfeits any prophetic culture critique, whether culture takes the form of economic exploitation, secularist utopianism, or religious fanaticism.[567] Quite obviously, Balthasar thinks theological pluralism is not an ecclesially or biblically faithful option. On his view, there is only one plan of salvation, and Judaism is the bearer of it for the nations.

This biblical view is directly related to Balthasar's problems with Rahner's own theology of religions and to what he considers the leveling effect of Rahner's "supernatural existential." In other words, he argues that Rahner's formulation of the issue of grace in terms of the supernatural existential makes God's self-revelation to Israel and in Christ instances of a more general divine revelation that occurs in and through human transcendental subjectivity.⁵⁶⁸ In Rahner's view, the encounter with and ability to know categorical objects serves to inform the knowing and willing subject of her own transcendental movement towards an infinite, non-objective, unthematic horizon. Notice that this pre-apprehension (*Vorgriff*) does not so much inform the subject about the categorical object itself, or how in that singular object one can find an epiphany or trace of the divine life, but rather makes possible the subject's own self-transcendence towards an infinite horizon or towards the absolute itself.⁵⁶⁹ This self-possession, if read in a Christian direction, can reveal to the subject that she is a forgiven and loved creature, that is, the subject of genuine salvation, divine intimacy, and care.

Here, of course, we encounter Rahner's creative development of the theological phrase "supernatural existential." For Rahner, this pairing of terms helps illuminate how Christians can affirm that saving grace can be from Christ and in the Church, yet at the same time available universally as saving grace. Rahner does not equate the Church with what is occurring in other religions.⁵⁷⁰ Rather, he thinks that other religions can provide the concrete and social occasion for someone coming to live a genuinely Christian form of life, and by implication to utter a real Yes to grace, which is always already present as an offer in supernaturally elevated subjectivity.⁵⁷¹ The concept of the supernatural existential is Rahner's way of articulating the universal experience of grace as both constitutive of human existence (existential), and as freely given and independent of human nature (supernatural).⁵⁷²

Balthasar critiques Rahner's thought on a number of levels, but we need not take the time to review the issues between these two titans of Catholic thought. We can restrict our concerns to Rahner's supernatural existential and ideas related to it. At the root of Balthasar's critique is Rahner's systematic use of Kantian categories of the transcendental and categorical, in connection with the supernatural existential. Balthasar believes this combination threatens to make the self-understanding of a particular religion marginal, and either to measure concrete religious traditions by a transcendental subjectivity that sits above all religious forms, or subsume other religious forms into a kind of "anonymous Christianity."⁵⁷³ The first difficulty, then, is that the transcendental-categorical pair, regardless of the importance of the categorical element, is unable to "justify the incomparable nature of *this* definite categorical that is foundational for Christian catholicity."⁵⁷⁴ The singularity and singular significance of God's action in history, rooted in the biblical *Gestalt*, will suffer relativization through its transmutation into a Kantian structure behind which, perhaps, lurks a formless infinite.[575]

In terms of our earlier discussion, we can say that Balthasar thinks Rahner allows philosophical discourse to control revelatory content and form, and thereby begins to narrow or foreshorten the Christian form while leveling out the difference between Judaism and extra-biblical religion. The supernatural existential is part of the problem: Balthasar argues that the biblical *Gestalt* does not support a view that all religions are receivers of a personal word of God and a theological mission; Israel receives this mission to and for the nations, and this mission occurs within and through the events of history. Indeed, Balthasar also thinks that the content implied by the supernatural existential, and by Rahner's marginalization of the Atonement,[576] evacuates key elements of the biblical form:

> *For nature, defined as creatureliness, "ensures" that grace is "only" grace and does not turn into nature, meaning a natural participation in God's nature. It also "ensures" that the gospel of grace appear not only as love (which is what it is in God) but also as law and command, as reverence, religio, distance and fear of the Lord. Fear is not abolished, nor is distance eliminated, when grace is given to nature but shows up now in its authentic form in Gethsemane and on the Cross and is transfigured as a "holy fear of the Lord" lasting into eternity.*[577]

From Balthasar's point of view, then, Rahner's discourse shares in the tendency of modern thought to relativize Israel's revelation and thus marginalize the God of the Old Covenant (who is also the God of the New). Moreover, Balthasar does not think that the content of other religions supports this framing of the issue. He observes that many religions have at an early stage a personal view of God but forfeit this understanding under the pressure of philosophical critique. The doctrine of the supernatural existential, however, must hold that the religions do receive a personal word of God if it holds that the religions *qua* religions provide for the gift of saving grace. This does not mean that Balthasar rejects Rahner's contention that grace is socially mediated and universal, only that religions as such should be considered the carriers of divine revelation and saving grace based upon a confluence of Christian doctrines.

For Balthasar, no appeal to the transcendentality of the subject can get around or rise above the actual, public form and content of a particular religion. The degree to which a religious path and goal have something in common with Christianity is open to *a posteriori* interpretation, which would then require the sort of comparative approach that Balthasar takes in *GL*4, *TD*1, and *TL*3. Balthasar's incarnational or Chalcedonian hermeneutic would recommend, instead, an acceptance of tension between Christianity and other religious forms until the *eschaton* when these tensions will be overcome. In this way, differences can be honestly and openly discussed, while commonly perceived truth and holiness can be appreciated by the religious interlocutors in question. From the side of Christian theology, Balthasar has shown that this "appreciation" has a thick theological and philosophical rationale. Moreover, as we have seen, Balthasar would not dispute, and in fact positively argues, that elements of particular cultural forms, whether specifically religious or not, can point in the direction of Christian revelation and salvation.

What Balthasar would dispute is the idea that religions as total forms can be anonymous forms of Christianity apart from a call to conversion, "crucifixion," or judgment. In other words, Balthasar thinks that different religious systems possess truth and goodness, but in terms of truth, most religions will also view themselves as total systems. This means that a particular truth or ethical claim will find its place, meaning, and relative significance within that "system." The Cross, here, points to the need for all systems to move to salvation through judgment, and, in a free appropriation of this judgment, conversion. The Cross is the hiatus that breaks with inner-worldly form to re-form it in view of God's own image.

Balthasar's view of aesthetic form plays an important role here. For Balthasar, religions—and not just religions, but philosophical, political, economic, and social systems as well—will often see themselves as total and universally valid presentations of truth, beauty, and goodness, and thus will frequently resist Christian claims, or any critique, for that matter. Insofar as truth claims matter, and matter in the form that religions conceive them among their more literate spokespersons,[578] then universal and contradictory claims cannot be reconciled at the same level of discourse. Insofar as Einstein's relativity theory is a universal theory of space, it cannot be reconciled with Newton's equally universal claims. Newton's mechanistic physics might still help grasp some elements of physical reality, but as a general theory it can no longer claim universality. In religion, a view of ultimate reality as fate (whether philosophically or mythically articulated) or an absolute principle is not the same as a personal, loving God. At the level of the divine, these two claims would contradict, but if one is subordinated to the other, they can be reconciled. The gods might be subordinated to cosmic fate in what Balthasar labels a cosmocentric view, or God might write into nature some kind of law subject to his freedom, as Balthasar seems to think occurs in Deuteronomy. In addition, Buddhist "emptiness" might be integrated within the Christian's utter availability for a mission of service or witness (e.g., Paul's mission), or a Buddhist sense of "letting-be" can be integrated at the anthropological level, as the disciple allows God's will to overtake her own, or at the theological level where the Father lets be the world in its difference and even sinfulness within God, or again as the Son opens space for the Spirit to be for the world. These are all integrations within the personal and inter-personal revelation of God's love for the world.

A Cruciform Theology of Religions

BALTHASAR IS A CHRISTOCENTRIC THEOLOGIAN, but he thinks that christocentrism need not be narrow or exclude truth, goodness, and beauty discerned apart from biblical revelation. Indeed, it is part of God's providence to prepare for the gospel in nature, history, and through interpersonal relation. The crux of the issue, for him, is whether and in what way Christianity makes a claim to universality from a particular revelation. For Christians, universality must show itself from the particular center that is God's self-exposition (*autos exēgesato*) (Jn. 1:18) in Christ and demonstrate its solidarity with human joys, suffering, and aspirations, as *Gaudium et Spes* has set out in its famous opening salvo. In other words, universality must be concrete not only in the sense that Jesus realizes God's universal saving will in his person, but also in that he does this because he, and the Christian church, makes genuine contact with human culture in its myriad manifestations. In a general sense, he argues that religion manifests a fundamental human desire to return to a lost unity in full communion with the source of Being, to live good and fruitful lives for one's community, and even to transform the world in hopes of putting suffering to an end.

As we have seen, on Balthasar's view we have a vertical axis (gentile religion) and a horizontal axis (Judaism), both of which contain crucial elements that cannot be foregone in any synthesis. Communion with the divine and transformation of a decidedly unjust world are not options that should be juxtaposed, as they are, for instance, in Marxism. However, Balthasar believes that these two axes cannot reconcile themselves from within either gentile or Jewish religion, at least not as an abiding form.[579] Neither, then, can achieve the true universality they nevertheless assert. Only Christianity, he contends, can reconcile the horizontal and the vertical axes in itself.

The crucial point, once again, is the Incarnation. Balthasar points out that while the Incarnation certainly represents a judgment (*krisis*) of the world's sin, this judgment is nevertheless wrapped or enfolded into a primary and encompassing divine Yes to the world. It is from this central affirmation that Balthasar concludes the world is loved by God even in the present and in its sinful state. This is, of course, only to repeat the Johannine view that God sent his Son because he loved the world, even in its darkness. More importantly, Balthasar thinks that Christianity alone truly affirms the goodness of the world in its present tense, that is, in any present, and maintains the full dignity of the individual, while not foregoing the past or the genuine human desire for vertical communion and future transformation. Traveling down the vertical axis, Christ is God who seeks and makes possible through his self-abandonment a reconciled communion with the Father; but he also makes possible, in his continued "liquifaction"[580] or self-gift through Eucharist and in the Spirit, true communion with one another across national boundaries. This vertical opening on communion is simultaneously the presence of the Alpha and the Omega, the horizontal beginning in solidarity with all human traditions, and the eschatological future that promises to fulfill all genuinely human aspirations. Here is where Balthasar's notion of Jesus' "dual time" is important. On the one hand, Jesus' time is the eternal present that constitutes the "already" of the Kingdom and the erasure of the salvation history / world history contrast, at least in principle; on the other hand, Jesus continues with the Church's pilgrimage, the Kingdom's "not yet," through historical time in the love and service of one another, and in efforts to transform discordant communities and lives into reconciled communities attuned to God's consummatory will. If the present cannot be sacrificed for the future, or the horizontal for the vertical, it is also true for Balthasar that the Incarnation, which always includes for him the "full journey of the Word" through the Resurrection, proscribes any relativization of individual lives for the sake of the collective. Christ's Incarnation and bodily resurrection display God's enduring care for the individual human being and the individual's perduring identity in God. This does not suggest, of course, that sacrifice for others can be ruled out; what it does indicate is that sacrificial love must be freely given, and never coerced in view of utopian designs.

The Trinity is crucial to Balthasar's view that Christianity provides a uniquely positive ground for the world of multiplicity and becoming, but Trinitarian doctrine, he thinks, must be grounded in Christ's incarnate mission. Apart from this mission, the Trinity becomes an abstraction of unity in difference, three in one, a tripartite logic or "bloodless myth," to invoke Aidan Nichols' phrase.[581] While certainly unity-in-difference and three-in-one have their truth, these Christian claims find their warrant to the extent that they form the background assumptions or conditions for the possibility of the biblical accounts of creation, revelation-covenant, and Christ's *kenosis* and mission. The Trinity becomes important in our present context because it speaks to the ultimate positive ground for the world, its temporal constitution, and its eventfulness.[582] Indeed, Balthasar reads Christ's descent from the Father as a fundamental confirmation of Genesis' claim that God's world is good and, even after sin, worth redeeming. Jesus' Father is no Zeus, who looks down upon the barbarism of his subjects, declares them incorrigible, and seeks their destruction.[583] Instead, the God of Israel's covenant condescends to open up a "sphere" of relation that lets difference and freedom, even to the extent of the unfreedom that is sin, be within the divine life itself. Difference, then, means the positive difference of a world that is not God and all the intra-worldly ways of not being God that nevertheless, in some fashion, reflect divine Being. Difference itself, for Balthasar, finds its ground in the Otherness of Father, Son, and Spirit within God, in the letting-be that is simultaneously spontaneous self-giving as the Father gives himself completely for the Son, and the Son returns the gift in the Spirit. This means that the world is not without Logos, without reason for being, but is rather grounded in the spontaneous letting-be of difference that is inner-Trinitarian love. Like the essential difference the world bears to its Creator, becoming, event, and even surprise—each of which are part and parcel of history, temporal being, and especially covenant being-identity—find their ontological possibility in the ever-greater spontaneous self-giving of intra-Trinitarian communion. For Balthasar, temporality finds its ground in the "interval" of Father-Son communication, space in the "diastasis" of the persons, and surprise in the super responsive love of the persons for one another.

For Balthasar, then, the Christian view of the world is rooted in the events and form of covenantal being in the world. Temporality, event, surprise, and newness are not incidental to the covenant but characterize Israel's very relation to God over time, and nowhere is this more the case than in Christ's life, death, and resurrection.

The resurrection is of particular significance here, for Balthasar reads the resurrection not only as a pledge for eternal life, but also as the Creator's validation of Jesus' life, teaching, and suffering love. The brokenness of death is bound to throw into question all missions, all purpose, all human striving, all meaning or form. The resurrection, then, is the surprising re-formation of a form given and broken for others, and thus a validation of such a life by the Creator. Apart from the resurrection, there is no form, only shattered pieces of truth that cannot legitimate themselves before the mystery of death. For Balthasar, God remains faithful to his Creation in Redemption, and thus remains a God of form beyond formlessness. As Mongrain points out, precisely because we are permitted to share in the paschal mystery, a life of suffering and service for others can become a life of joy. We can also put this in terms of our discussion of covenant. The community's existence as expropriated for God is an existence devoted to the incarnation of righteousness, mercy, and loving-kindness, that is, the community's participation in the deification of creation in all its truth, goodness, and beauty. So Balthasar's emphasis on the resurrection serves as a remarkably anti-Marcionite validation of the Creator and Covenant God's love for the world. This continues in the Spirit. We have seen that for Balthasar, the Spirit breaches the line between Church and world. The Spirit forms the Body of Christ and gives to that community, and individuals in it, the gifts necessary to continue the redemptive mission of the Son in ecclesial missions for the world. In other words, the Spirit continues to give shape to eccentric lives, that is, to lives centered not on themselves, but on those to whom they are given over in love.

We might also observe the anthropological correlate of the dynamic inner divine life that Balthasar presents. For Balthasar, the present or "presence" does not indicate self-satisfied knowing, as it does in contemporary critiques of logocentrism, or manipulative, instrumental reason, but rather stresses a spiritual posture of availability, attentiveness, and readiness to receive a mission that participates in Christ's own mission for the world, that is, a mission to help better tune the world to God's own Trinitarian harmony. Just as Christ's "presencing" in the Incarnation and in the Spirit stretches back and forward, so the disciple's mission stretches back for its reference in the Incarnation and forward, in the Spirit, to God's consummating Kingdom.

What we have labeled Balthasar's Christocentric hospitality is a way to emphasize that, for Balthasar, the Christian form invites into itself the truth and holiness discovered beyond ecclesial borders. Moreover, engagement with extra-Christian disclosure is not, for Balthasar, extrinsic to Christian self-understanding, but rather intrinsic to the form of Christ itself, and thus ought to be intrinsic to Christian identity. Failure to engage the world is failure to follow the path of the incarnate One. We have also discussed Balthasar's cruciform apologetic, his view that Christianity uniquely joins vertical and horizontal religious axes for a concrete universality that enters into, redeems, and fulfills the deepest aspirations of all the religious and extra-religious cultural forms of the world.

Conclusion

IN THIS FINAL CHAPTER, I SOUGHT TO EMPHASIZE the ways in which Balthasar maintains the priority of Judaism for Christian belief, and thus to discuss his theology of religions within the context of concerns for Christian-Jewish relation that animates the rest of this text. Judaism, for Balthasar, is called out from the more general religious quest of the nations for a special mission in history. This mission determines its very being. It is important to observe the complexity of Balthasar's move here. Normally, the claim that there is a generalizable reality called religion, in which Judaism and Christianity share, would appear to make these religious traditions an instance of a general human propensity to be judged by how well each tradition fulfills that propensity. Thus, an idea of religion would come to judge actual historical religions. Due to his reading of the Incarnation, however, Balthasar is able to hold together Christianity's deep penetration of religious forms, and thus its share in religion, with the singularity and transcendent fullness of the Christian form that finds room in itself to house religious truths. He does not offer a Hegelian evolutionary model, but rather an incarnational integration that provides reasons for Christians to continue dialogue with past and present religious expressions. It is important to notice that Balthasar's method of integration is deeply rooted in his view of the Incarnation, and is not a stand-alone form of argument for him. Integration is grounded in the intimacy and interpenetration of nature and grace given in Christ's own life. This interpenetration returns us to our passage from Bernanos in the introduction:

> *"The Truth" for us is everything Christ was from his childhood to his death, and the eternal and infinite dimension of this truth was revealed in the Resurrection. Even the most humble of truths was redeemed by Christ, ... just like anyone at random from among us Christians. The humblest truth, I say, has a share in the divinity of him who deigned to put on our nature—thus making us* consortes ejus divinitatis *[partakers of the divine nature]*.[584]

For Balthasar, the mission of the Logos gathers and orders all the truths and goods given by the Creator and disclosed through a variety of discursive genres and individual works. Here lie the preparations for the gospel strewn about throughout time and culture. Insofar as philosophical, mythical, and religious forms speak to the Creator-creature difference, the human longing for communion with God and neighbor, a desire for a more just and kind world, and the personal and gracious being of God, and do not shy away from human suffering and misery, they prepare for the Gospel; even in their most "humble" of truths, they find a home in Christ.

Throughout the first and second sections, I also argued that Balthasar's discussion runs contrary to the Prometheanism he sees in modernity. Both Homer, and to a lesser extent, Plato, offer a negative or apophatic pedagogy of significance: Homer with his dual canon of ineluctable immortal-mortal difference and his refusal to prettify human existence, Plato with his negation of mythical insularity and the narrow circumscription of beauty or glory by the heroic model. Positively, Homer and his followers provide a genuinely theandric context that supports prayer, eventful beauty, grace, and acts of divine freedom on behalf of humanity. Plato too provides positive education in his striving for truth, his self-forgetfulness, and his universal determination of the transcendentals as properties of Being. I also argue here that Balthasar rejects the Barthian and Kierkegaardian antipathy to analogy. The age of religious syncretism, for him, marks not an unfortunate hindrance to Christianity, but rather a *kairos* that provides Christian revelation with plural connections so that its essential universality can make actual contact with the cultures of the world.

In section three, I argued that Balthasar's openness to truth and goodness beyond biblical religion does not lead him to relativize Israel's priority. Balthasar makes clear that, from his view of the Christian form, Judaism maintains a unique place and role. Its special election and mission in history is an ineluctable element of the biblical form, and thus of the form of Christ. Indeed, Israel takes into itself many of the religious forms of surrounding cultures and makes them available for fulfillment by bringing them into proximity to the New Covenant. This section is also the locus of a discussion of Rahner and Balthasar. If Balthasar veers away from Barth's "narrow" Christocentrism, he also thinks that Rahner tends to relativize Jewish revelation vis-à-vis other religions especially through his discussion of the supernatural existential and "anonymous Christianity." Of course Balthasar agrees with Rahner that God calls all human beings to salvation, but thinks that Rahner's particular use of philosophical categories overwhelms the biblical form. In other words, he does not think that Rahner's use of Kantian terms can effectively represent the singular events of God's freedom on behalf of Israel and the world. Equally important to notice is that Balthasar does not promote a logical reduction of all things to Christ. He rejects the Hegelian "evolutionary" view in favor of an integration that awaits its final form only in the *eschaton*. In the meantime, Jew and gentile retain their differences, even if in Christ we can gain a glimpse as to how those differences might ultimately be resolved.

In the last section, I presented the apologetic side of Balthasar's integrationist theology, where he argues that the religious yearnings of non-biblical religion, and the world-transforming drive of covenant and kingdom, get transcended and folded into Christ's vertical descent into the horizontal plane of historical existence. From above and from below, Christ penetrates the deepest aspirations and experiences of humankind, and elevates this humanity to participation in his own life for the world. This discussion then rose up into the Trinity to discuss what Balthasar thinks sets Christianity apart from other religious traditions: its sacramental embrace of the world even in its present suffering and sin. Of course, this embrace is a sacramental one, and that means that included in such an embrace is the transformative service that seeks to reconcile the world to Gods' will for a world of mutual forgiveness, care, justice, and mercy. As we have seen, Balthasar thinks that Christian Trinitarian doctrine provides a unique ground for difference, multiplicity, variety, and surprise.

Conclusion

The Introduction promised a three-fold argument: (1) Balthasar offers an anti-Marcionite theology designed to counter a major Marcionite revival in modern thought and culture; (2) Balthasar's theology offers a positive Christian appraisal of Judaism; (3) Balthasar's ecclesial and Christocentric theology is deeply hospitable to truth, goodness and beauty discovered beyond ecclesial borders. We can call these to mind in order.

(1) The first promise stands fulfilled through several venues. Balthasar's theological aesthetics of form proposes an interpretative structure that rules out canonical excisions or final supersession popular to ancient and modern forms of Marcionism. For Balthasar's ecclesial theology, the biblical canon stands as an integral whole with its magnetic center and measure in Christ as the Father's self-exegesis or expression. The canon is a form that not only points to something that transcends it, but bears God's self-interpretation for us. This formal unity is, for Balthasar, also a dynamic unity as the good things of creation get taken into God's covenant with Israel, and God's covenant itself develops new forms of encounter and relationship. If Christians often speak as if the covenant is an undifferentiated thing, Balthasar's work on the Old Covenant offers a welcome complexification designed to exhibit a covenantal unity amidst many different forms of relation. Thus, creation and covenant pour into God's deepening eschatological self-expression which is unreadable apart from all that went before, including theophanic, covenantal, apocalyptic, sapiential, messianic, and, of course, prophetic encounter-disclosure.

The unity of this revelation is no mere historical connection for Balthasar; rather, it is both a union from within Israel and from a theological continuity between the God of Jesus and the God of the Jews. It is the eschatological nature of God's self-revelation in Christ that validates all the forms of revelation found in the Old Covenant. Even when new or somewhat different meaning must be applied to Old Covenant motifs, Balthasar can note that this is itself a practice of Israel as it time and again reinterprets its key symbols as events of revelation disclose new aspects of their relation to God.

For Balthasar, Christ is the concrete realization of the two sides of the Covenant. He reveals the meaning of Israel as expropriated people called to be righteous, just, merciful, truthful / true, and humble as they strive to manifest God's true image in history as a blessing upon the nations. He reveals God as paradoxically sovereign and extravagantly self-giving, a God of the covenant who opens himself to the suffering of the world and can thus redeem it. So, Christ brings unity to the covenant from below and from above, thereby giving Israel's mission validity in eternity. In Christ, Israel becomes a blessing upon the nations. But apart from Christ, it seems, Balthasar believes that the faithful of Israel's covenant with God remain a blessing for the nations as they reflect God's covenant will for their people in their worship, their praise, and their instantiation of God's righteousness and mercy in the world. Thus, post-biblical Israel, for Balthasar, speaks to the living covenant between God and God's people and also serves to remind Christians of their concrete historical responsibilities. A Christianity separated from living conversation with Jews is a Christianity prone to becoming a Gnostic or Marcionite self-parody.

(2) Balthasar's antipathy to Marcionite deformation opens up a deep and positive engagement with Judaism. Judaism, for Balthasar, stands in a unique and uniquely positive relation to Christianity. Central to Balthasar's treatment of Jewish-Christian relation is his emphasis on Paul's Letter to the Romans. It is here, he contends, that Christians ought to focus, and where they will find the continuing validity of God's promises to and covenant with Israel. Indeed, he argues that the fundamental content of Israel's covenant and that of Christianity is the same: salvation through judgment. In addition, Balthasar observes that Israel's rejection of Jesus as Messiah should not be reason to think that Israel will be lost, for not only does Romans 11:26 tell against such a conclusion, but neither Romans nor the New Testament witness would appear to override God's gracious election and mercy by virtue of human failure. Balthasar helpfully reminds us that both judgment and mercy are responses to guilt, and neither is a simple function of human cause and divine effect. For Balthasar, God's threats outweigh neither God's fidelity to his promises nor his mercy. Instead, the temporary rejection of Israel stands subordinate to their election. Israel's "rejection" stands as part of God's plan to allow gentiles into a new relationship with the God of Israel. Balthasar presses the point when he obliterates Jewish guilt for the Crucifixion by way of Peter's discourse on the grace and necessity of Christ's death and the people's ignorance of what they were doing (Acts 3:17-19). The Crucifixion, for Balthasar, is fundamentally about divine judgment on human sin and God's exorbitant

mercy, and not about Jewish guilt. Indeed, he reminds us that neither Israel nor the Church holds a monopoly on infidelity or on fidelity to God's covenant.

Balthasar, of course, goes much further. He sees in Israel's temporary rejection a kind of redemptive suffering for the nations as they share in the sufferings of the innocent Messiah, and he writes that the "Messianic and salvific suffering is present in a hidden way in the judgment and suffering of Israel."[585] Balthasar believes that his reading of Romans should end Christian mission to the Jews. Romans 9:4 shows that Israel remains God's chosen people. His vision, here, is of a "convergence of the two separated halves of the people of God."[586] Israel, for Balthasar, looks forward, with Christians, to a final consummation where God's peace becomes fully manifest and redemption in Christ will be shared (Romans 11:25-29). Finally, we noted that Judaism, insofar as it continues its mission as a model of the redeemed life, that is, as it continues to critique idolatrous religion, adheres to and worships the One God, and makes real in the world God's righteousness and mercy, participating in God's work of reconciliation. Of course we have entered some caveats to this overall positive Christian appraisal of Judaism on Balthasar's part. Nevertheless, Balthasar's sometimes unfortunate phrasing and questionable use of Joachim aside, the overall impression of his thought is that of a deep and thoughtful appraisal of Jewish-Christian relation where neither interlocutor comes away theologically unscathed, but both are better for the relation.

(3) Balthasar's hospitality to truth, goodness, and beauty discovered outside ecclesial boundaries is grounded in essentially three elements of his thought: (1) the analogy of being; (2) the *Logos spermatikos* doctrine of the Alexandrians; (3) the extension of this Alexandrian teaching to include the Holy Spirit. On Balthasar's view, the Creator discloses divine Being through the mediation of created reality as that which both reveals and conceals divine glory. Through the quest of the human spirit for what is most worthy of praise and gratitude, and the many attempts to give insight form and articulation, poets, artists, philosophers, and others approach at a variety of distances the revealed mystery of Christ. The epiphanic or ontophanic richness of creation joined to ec-static human transcendence yields a vast array of cultural analogies to the form of Christ. Christians are not the first to think that contemplation ought to bring forth fruit for the community in service. Nor are they the only ones to imagine that

humble obedience to truth might yield suffering, but that it may be worth the cost. Through our reading of *GL4*, we saw that Balthasar views the Incarnation as God's Word penetrating all manner of cultural expression. Of course it is true to say that, as he himself observed, he was never able to do the same relative to religions of the East save for a few positive and negative notes here and there. But to observe what Balthasar neglects is not the same as to say his integrative vision is unworthy of pursuit. Indeed, it may suggest the opposite conclusion. For Balthasar, if it is true that Christ intersects all truly human attempts for transcendence, then Christians ought to follow Christ into the varieties of religious and cultural expressions and ought to be open to truth everywhere, but of course not with an undiscerning eye. Integration involves knowing the form of Christ and discerning just where, in this form, an alien expression can come to shed its light and broaden one's perspective.

The Alexandrian *Logos spermatikos* doctrine forms another avenue of Balthasar's hospitality. Balthasar takes up Justin's view that seeds of the Logos can be found throughout the cultural landscape as preparation for the Gospel. Balthasar appears to go even further when he extends the *Logos spermatikos* motif to the Spirit, who for him can bring the Gospel to those beyond formal ecclesial boundaries. Here, the Spirit's close tie to the Son's mission expands rather than contracts Christian hospitality.

It is important to observe that Balthasar's theological hospitality is not without criteria. In other words, the truths of creation and the seeds of the Logos require integration within the Trinitarian vision of Christian revelation. To the extent, for instance, that a religious teaching has as its context a purely inner-worldly eschatology, cannot give a quasi-sacramental account of creation, is unable or unwilling to relate to God primarily as sovereign, self-giving love, flees from the value of creation's multiplicity as a glorification of God, views history as a site of divine-human free interaction, etc., such a teaching, from a Christian theological perspective, requires conversion. This hardly negates the illumination provided by others, grasped as we noted earlier as "truth-bearing gift." It only points to the basic Christian premise that all worldly truth must be ordered by the truth revealed in Christ. However, we should also observe that apart from all truth gathered from all those who bear truth, Christ cannot be grasped as all-in-all. Thus, it is incumbent on the Christian who truly seeks to praise God in all things to receive all that is true.

A Word on Ineffability and Dialogue

BALTHASAR'S ENTIRE THEOLOGY IS ROOTED in the pluriform encounter with divine glory and the grounding of these pluriform encounters in the God who is, in some mysterious way, both One and Communion, or perhaps One in Communion. So on the theological plane, Balthasar's theology is profoundly dialogical. Trinitarian economy reveals a dialogical or communion version of God's interior relationality that is the condition for the possibility of God's work in history. As we have seen, Balthasar also has a deeply dialogical ontology, as Being communicates itself for us, and we seek to give voice or a coherent word to this wondrously variegated expression. This dialogical ontology, what we have labeled covenant-being-in-the-world, is at the root of his hospitality to the other, grasped as truth-bearing gift.

It is important to understand, then, that Balthasar's dialogical prescription is rooted in Christian theological and theologically accented philosophical discourse and not in a discourse external to the community. We might extrapolate, then, and suggest that different religions will find resources within their beliefs and practices, that is, within what they hold beautiful, good, and true, that warrant dialogue. Certainly Jewish authors have been at the forefront of dialogical thought rooted in the call of God to God's people. In addition, non-theistic traditions may well discover reasons for dialogue from within their own communal resources. It is, then, what has form and what is in fact "effable" in these traditions that will frequently serve to warrant dialogue with members of other communities.

This view flies in the face of philosophical positions, such as that of John Hick, that would suggest that only "ineffability" supports inter-religious dialogue. Hick's view, discussed briefly in the introduction, would argue that the unknowability of the divine, save for a generalizable notion of Transcendence, alone supports peaceful relations and dialogue among religions. My suggestion here is that, in fact, such a prioritization of ineffability is foreign to the different religions, and thus substitutes a philosophy of religion for the actual religious complexes which do have their formal or determinate boundaries, concerns, beliefs, and practices. Balthasar's theology shows an understanding of these formal points that necessitates concrete, a posteriori engagement with the religious traditions of particular and determinate communities. No philosophical position can get around this if it is to be a genuine dialogue.

These are formal points that might be complemented by a consideration of whether it matters that one has a personal or impersonal view of the divine. For Hick, of course, the importance of such a decision is minimal given that the transcendence of the divine is such that no human figurations of it will be mutually exclusive in the infinite divine life itself. By contrast, for Jewish and Christian theology, for most Islamic theology, and even for theistic traditions of the East, the answer here would be in the affirmative. Balthasar's theology supports dialogue precisely because of its faith in the Trinity as a personal and relational ground of all that is, in God as the One who seeks relation with Israel and all humanity, and in the relational or covenantal ontology rooted in this covenantal form. Relation presumes persons, as does Christian spirituality. It stands to reason that for Christians all of these interpersonal reasons for dialogue would vanish if the personal divine were to be swept away.

From another angle, we can observe that Balthasar's opposition to Prometheanism and Marcionism is also an opposition to a kind of philosophical apophaticism or negative theology that would seek to marginalize concrete Jewish and Christian revelation, or, for that matter, the content of other religions, in favor of a doctrine of divine ineffability. Such a doctrine, he thinks, can find little support in Scripture and would appear to contradict God's truthfulness in self-disclosure. Balthasar's entire corpus militates against any rendition, whether Kantian, Heideggerian, or Barthian, that threatens to undermine form, either metaphysically or theologically, in view of a formless absolute or metaphysics of formlessness. Indeed, such radical formlessness would call into question Jewish and Christian gratitude for pluriform created reality and their joint vocation as "Shepherds of Being." Instead, Balthasar articulates an ontology and theology of excess, wherein no form ever exhausts disclosure's possibility and all forms testify to the "more" at the heart of Being. This ontological "more," for Balthasar, reflects the "ever-greater" dynamism of triune communion that never contradicts itself lest it fail to be Logos.

Such an emphasis on form, in Balthasar's work, is complemented by his theology of the Cross. The cruciform character of his thought means that his emphasis on form will not become a superficial aesthetic. Rather, for Balthasar, the brokenness or shattering of all form through this world of suffering and injustice can be overcome only through the self-abandonment, the love, that enters into the suffering of others and thereby redeems form from formlessness. In other words, for Balthasar, such redemption cannot be had apart from a trust and hope rooted in Christ's crucifixion and resurrection. Apart from the resurrection, a life lived for others ends only in death and shattered portions of truth; with the resurrection, a life for others gains eternal validity and all those pieces of truth come to glorify God and find a place in the ever-greater hospitality that is the divine life.

Acknowledgements

A first book must present the most difficult challenge for an acknowledgements, for one's making explicit of debts comes so belatedly that there is seemingly no end to the list. Selection, then, is both invidious and necessary. From Saint John's, in Collegeville, MN, I learned a capacious, intellectual, and deeply prayerful Catholicism to which, someday, I hope to do justice. William T. Cahoy, or Bill as we know him, incarnated this spirit with remarkable energy, humility and hospitality. I hope that in some small measure his intellect and critical eye for the pretentiously obscure has rubbed off just enough here. At Saint John's, I also had the good fortune of meeting Kevin Mongrain in what began a now decades-long friendship and theological conversation that informs every page of the present work, which he graciously read and re-read always lobbying for clarity of thought and expression. I don't know that Elizabeth Johnson would approve of Balthasar's theology or my appreciation for it, but possible theological differences notwithstanding, she taught me that fidelity to the tradition called for creativity and cultural engagement and encouraged her students to find their own theological voice. She also went some lengths to help me find my first academic job and for that I am forever grateful. Out of some combination of fraternal love and Christian charity that eludes me, my brother, Chris, proofread every last iota of this manuscript. I remain in awe of his generosity. Tom Guarino read and commented on the entire manuscript. His comments are invaluable, his friendship an unexpected gift. Cyril O'Regan gave me the confidence to engage Balthasar in the first place and this book would never have happened had he not graciously invited me to his Yale seminars on *Glory of the Lord* and *Theo-Drama* in what seems like a distant age. John Jones at Crossroad is a simply wonderful editor who helped me find my post-dissertation voice and get it onto the page. His patience shames the angels.

Finally, I must thank my wife, Julie, whose fully incarnate love lends joy and energy to all my days.

Notes

Introduction

1. *NA*4.
2. Kevin Mongrain, *The Systematic Thought of Hans Urs von Balthasar: An Irenaean Retrieval* (New York: Herder and Herder, 2002), pp. 133–153.
3. See Raymond Gawronski S.J., *Word and Silence: Hans Urs von Balthasar and the Spiritual Encounter between East and West* (Grand Rapids, MI: Eerdmans Publishing Company, 1995), pp. 24–26.
4. Francis X. Clooney, S.J., *Hindu God, Christian God: How Reason Helps Break Down the Barriers between Religions* (Oxford: Oxford University Press, 2001), p. 16–17. Clooney, however, thinks that Balthasar's type of theological approach is helpful for comparison because in its formal lines of thought it can be found in Hinduism as well (p. 17). It is perhaps worth mentioning that Balthasar admits his inability to represent the religious traditions of Asia and that his discussion is "all too Mediterranean" (*GL*1, p. 11). What he will do is differentiate Christian theological positions from Asian religious traditions ("discern the spirits") insofar as he can, or at least show where the serious issues would lie for anyone who sees no significant difference. He will also draw out important similarities, for instance, between Zen Buddhism and Christianity.
5. Joseph DiNoia, *The Diversity of Religions: A Christian Perspective* (Washington, D.C.: Catholic University Press, 1992).
6. See Kevin Mongrain, *The Systematic Thought of Hans Urs von Balthasar: An Irenaean Retrieval* (New York: Herder and Herder, 2002). It will be clear from both the Introduction and from the first chapter that I share Mongrain's view that Balthasar's theology is directed against modern returns of Marcionism and Gnosticism. For a more rigorous treatment of Gnosticism's return in modernity than is offered by Balthasar himself, see Cyril O'Regan's two works, *Gnostic Return in Modernity* (New York: State University of New York Press, 2001) and *The Heterodox Hegel* (New York: State University Press of New York, 1994). In *Gnostic Return*, O'Regan nicely differentiates Gnosticism from Marcionism, a differentiation which Balthasar often fails to make. See especially, pp. 61–63. I will not be adverting to the issue of distinction within this text as Balthasar's genealogy *qua* genealogy is not my main issue.
7. The most obvious example of this is his *The Moment of Christian Witness* (San Francisco, CA: Ignatius Press, 1994).
8. See Francis Clooney, *Hindu God, Christian God: How Reason Helps Break Down the Barriers between Religions* (Oxford: Oxford University Press, 2001). Clooney writes on Balthasar in chapter three.

9. See *Dare We Hope "That All Men Be Saved"? with a Short Discourse on Hell*, trans. Dr. David Kipp and Rev. Lothar Krauth (San Francisco: Ignatius Press, 1988). It is important to point out, however, that Balthasar opposes any view that would theoretically necessitate universal salvation, since such a view would restrict divine freedom within the confines of a philosophical system and reduce the significance of human freedom.

10. See chapter seven of Henri de Lubac, *Catholicism: Christ and the Common Destiny of Man*, trans. Lancelot C. Sheppard and Sister Elizabeth Englund, OCD (San Francisco: Ignatius Press, 1988; first published as *Catholicisme: Les aspects du dogme* in 1947 by Les Editions du Cerf, Paris). De Lubac's reflections here are rooted in his fundamental conviction of the solidarity of all humanity in origin and destiny, a view that is at the heart of the claims of *Nostra Aetate*, *Gaudium et Spes*, and also, I would argue, *Lumen Gentium*.

11. See *Church: The Human Story of God* (New York: Crossroad Publishing Company, 1990), p. xvii, where Schillebeeck juxtaposes a statement from the Council of Florence-Ferrara (1442) to the Second Vatican Council's *Lumen Gentium* (*LG*) 16. Of course much tension on this point emanates from the tension within *Lumen Gentium* itself if we compare *LG* 14 with *LG* 16.

12. For an example of this kind of reading of these developments, see John Hick, "The Non-Absoluteness of Christianity," in *The Myth of Christian Uniqueness: Toward a Pluralistic Theology of Religions*, ed. John Hick and Paul F. Knitter (New York: Orbis Books, 1987), pp. 16–36. Hick claims that both Protestant and Catholic Christianity have moved away from an exclusivist past toward an inclusivist present, but that this inclusivism is not as positive as it may sound for it still holds that salvation occurs through Christ, and that even if salvation occurs outside the visible Church, the assumption is still that only Christians really know how it occurs. Hick then contends that any claims to Christian superiority in the opportunities that Christianity offers for salvation must be defended empirically and not assumed based on Christian premises. For Hick, salvation means a movement from being self-centered to being Reality-centered. He then says that "It [Christian superiority] can no longer be established simply by defining salvation as inclusion within the scope of the divine pardon bought by Christ's atoning death. From that definition it does follow that Christianity, as Christ's continuing agency on earth, is superior to all other religions. But this kind of arbitrary superiority-by-definition no longer seems defensible, even to many Christians" (p. 23). This sentence seems to assert that Christians conceive the Crucifixion as a way to assert their superiority rather than the event of grace that they trust as the salvation offered by the one God to and for a world alienated from God. Is Hick's claim that Christians need to surrender their most precious beliefs and experiences for the pluralist position to work?

13. John Hick, *An Interpretation of Religion: Human Responses to the Transcendent* (United Kingdom: MacMillan Press, 1989).

14. A variety of critiques of the pluralist position now exist. See, for example, William A. Christian, Sr.'s *Doctrines of Religious Communities: A Philosophical*

Study (New Haven: Yale University Press, 1987), Paul Griffiths' *Apology for Apologetics* (Eugene, OR: Wipf and Stock, 2007), James L. Fredericks, *Faith among Faiths: Christian Theology and Non-Christian Religions* (Mahwah, NJ: Paulist Press, 1999), Tomoko Masuzawa's *The Invention of World Religions: Or, How European Universalism Was Preserved in the Language of Pluralism* (Chicago: The University of Chicago Press, 2005), and Joseph DiNoia's, *The Diversity of Religions*, cited above. A recent debate between Terrence Tilley and Gavin D'Costa in *Modern Theology*, spurred by Tilley's defense of Jacques Dupuis' theological pluralism in light of "Dominus Iesus," may also be of interest. See also D'Costa's edited response volume to Hick and Knitter, *Christian Uniqueness Reconsidered: The Myth of a Pluralistic Theology of Religion* (New York: Orbis, 1990).

15. It perhaps bears mention that Kant himself was no pluralist. For him, Christianity alone is pure, moral religion; this Christianity, however, is a Christianity divorced from its Jewish roots and interpreted according to Kant's own moral philosophy. Hick is aware of this and notes that he is drawing from Kant's epistemological theory, not from his *Religion within the Limits of Reason Alone*. More recently, Jacques Derrida has explicitly called upon Kant's idea of *Religion within the Limits of Reason Alone* for his own discussion of religion. For Derrida, Kant is right to limit religion to reason alone but wrong to think that this rational religion is to be found within Christianity or in terms of Kant's view of reason. See Jacques Derrida, "Faith and Knowledge," trans. Samuel Weber, in *Acts of Religion* (New York and London: Routledge Press, 2002), pp. 40–101. For his call for a Kantian retrieval, see especially pp. 47ff. and 50–51.

16. Hick no doubt recognizes what he has done, but thinks that if Christians assert revelation, grace, and faith as their entrance into divine reality, then their positions are closed off to reason. Two things can be said here: first, if the pluralist position cannot do justice to actual religious claims and experience, then it is no longer genuinely pluralist; second, for Catholic theology, revelation, grace, and faith do transcend reason by bringing it to its fullest realization, not by negating or destroying it. The basic truth, here, is that the one God transcends human reason but also descends so that faith's intellectual assent can be given to revelation.

17. Alternatively, the paschal mystery might be extruded altogether from the pluralist reading of Jesus. Then, Jesus can be considered a guru, rabbi, or spiritual teacher of some sort who reveals but does not atone. Here, knowledge, rather than God's action for us in Jesus Christ, brings salvation. Again, singular actions in history would need to be downplayed. Once these moves are made, of course, others must follow. Views of sin, God as Creator, doctrines of creation, etc. would need complete revision. It is only fair to note that Paul Knitter, in his latest book, *Without Buddha, I Could Not Be a Christian*, seems to have gone decisively beyond his pluralist position to something like a comparativist stance. See the review by James L. Fredericks in the April 2010 edition of *Commonweal Magazine*.

18. This is one of the main points of Clooney's *Hindu God, Christian God* and lies at the foundation of his comparative method. It is helpful to remember that

Balthasar makes no claim to being an expert in Eastern religions. Indeed, his comments on them, positive and negative, should be read as issues to consider when thinking through Christianity's relation to other religions rather than definitive statements. He makes this clear in the last paragraph of his foreword to GL1. In other words, these statements are attempts to "discern the spirits" but are clearly open to revision with new data.

19. Jacques Dupuis, S.J., *Toward a Christian Theology of Religious Pluralism* (Maryknoll, New York: Orbis Books, 1997 and 2001), pp. 10–11.

20. Rosemary Radford Ruether, *To Change the World: Christology and Cultural Criticism* (New York: Crossroad, 1981), p. 31.

21. For Hick, see *The Myth of Christian Uniqueness*, p. 31.

22. See Ruether, *To Change the World*, pp. 42–43. Jesus' Cross and Resurrection "found *our* people, ... mediate hope in the midst of history *for us*" (p. 43). By this "for us" Ruether does not mean all of humanity, but only Christians; other equally valid religious events, experiences, and people mediate hope and salvation to others in other cultures. With respect to Judaism, a strong doctrine of the Incarnation may seem to allow for anti-Judaism and perhaps even Nazi anti-Semitism. But there is something else to consider in terms of cultural criticism. When the uniqueness of the Incarnation is relativized, and the Spirit set free from Christ, the Spirit can be said to incarnate itself in particularly charismatic figures. These new 'incarnations' can be diabolical. See Christopher Morse's examples of German Protestant sermons in *Not Every Spirit: A Dogmatics of Christian Disbelief* (Valley Forge, PA: Trinity Press International, 1994), pp. 35–36.

23. At least at the level of high intellectual engagement. The story at the pastoral level would require a more complex discussion—but certainly emphasis on some biblical texts as opposed to others has a serious role to play.

24. *The Scandal of the Incarnation: Irenaeus against the Heresies,* selected and introduced by Hans Urs von Balthasar, trans. John Saward (San Francisco: Ignatius Press, 1990), p. 3.

25. Henri de Lubac, "Letters to my Superiors," in *Theology in History,* trans. Anne Englund Nash (San Francisco: Ignatius Press, 1996), p. 432.

26. Ibid.

27. Henri de Lubac, "A New Religious Front," in *Theology in History,* trans. Anne Englund Nash (San Francisco: Ignatius Press, 1996) pp. 467–468. This text was published in Switzerland in 1942, was therefore most likely known by Balthasar, and, according to André Latreille, also circulated in occupied France. See the text note on page 457.

28. Ibid., p. 466. By "central," I mean Auguste Comte, Hegel, Wagner. De Lubac is strongly critical of Hegel. See pages 459–460.

29. Ibid., p. 486.

30. Hans Urs von Balthasar, *Bernanos: An Ecclesial Existence*, trans. Erasmo Leiva-Merikakis (San Francisco: Ignatius Press, 1996), p. 179.

31. Ibid. Put this way, election has nothing to do with nominalism / voluntarism since it coincides with God's Wisdom.

32. *Explorations in Theology: IV: Spirit and Institution*, p. 103.

Chapter One

33. Hans Urs von Balthasar, *In the Fullness of Faith: On the Centrality of the Distinctively Catholic*, trans. Graham Harrison (San Francisco: Ignatius Press, 1988), p. 27. He is referring here to Jesus and making the argument that Jesus is Catholic in this sense. This indicates the massive form of theological integration that Balthasar intends.

34. Although my concern is mainly with Marcionism, I am not arguing that this is the only way to Prometheanism for Balthasar. In fact, when he differentiates—and he often does not—Gnosticism provides a second route. He will usually see Marcionism as a form of Gnosticism. Cyril O'Regan has provided a helpful narrative way to distinguish Marcionism from Gnosticism. Whereas Marcionism shortens the biblical canon by severing the Old Covenant from the New, Valentinian Gnosticism (and modern versions of it such as Hegel's philosophy of religion) extends the biblical narrative into the heavens. This does not necessarily lead to any better evaluation of Judaism or the Old Covenant or any greater emphasis on divine transcendence, and just as easily becomes Promethean. O'Regan's distinctions, I think, improve upon Balthasar's use of these categories and give them far more rigor, but they do not serve to invalidate Balthasar's insights. See Cyril O'Regan, *Gnostic Return in Modernity* (New York: State University of New York Press, 2002), pp. 61–65.

35. "Testament" here must be taken in its broadest theological sense, that is, in terms of a living relationship between God and God's people. F.F. Bruce notes that "Testament," in terms of Scripture, translates the Latin *testamentum* which translates the Greek *diathēkē*, used to indicate a will, but "used more widely of various kinds of settlement or agreement, not so much of one which is made between equals as of one in which a party superior in power or dignity confers certain privileges on an inferior, while the inferior undertakes certain obligations towards the superior... It is usually rendered by our word 'covenant', and its most distinctive usage relates to an agreement between God and human beings." See F.F. Bruce, *The Canon of Scripture* (Downers Grove, IL: InterVarsity Press, 1988), p. 19.

36. Alois Grillmeier, S.J., *Christ in Christian Tradition: From the Apostolic Age to Chalcedon*, trans. J.S. Bowden (New York: Sheed and Ward, 1965), p. 451. Grillmeier writes, "At the same time, it (Logos-Sarx Christology) was also of supreme religious significance because the whole relationship between God and the world seemed to be expressed in the unity of *Logos* and *sarx* in Christ. The Incarnation was in fact the greatest expression of the relationship of God to his creation. It was the task of fourth-century theology, in its christology, to preserve the transcendence of God while still demonstrating this highest degree of his immanence. This is where the real problem of the Arian and Apollinarian heresies lay. Their mistake was that

they applied philosophical frameworks to the interpretation of Christ without having made the necessary corrections" (p.176; cf. p.126 in direct reference to neo-Platonism). See also Jaroslav Pelikan, *The Christian Tradition, vol. 1: The Emergence of the Catholic Tradition (100–600)* (Chicago and London: University of Chicago Press, 1971). Pelikan, speaking of Marcionism and Gnosticism, writes that "the most important early heresies were not Jewish, but anti-Jewish in their inspiration" (p.71). He also notes that Tertullian's response to Marcion is a Trinitarian response (p. 75).

37. See Robert Louis Wilken, *The Spirit of Early Christian Thought: Seeking the Face of God* (New Haven: Yale University Press, 2003). Wilken writes: "The notion that the development of early Christian thought represented a hellenization of Christianity has outlived its usefulness. The time has come to bid a fond farewell to the ideas of Adolf von Harnack, the nineteenth-century historian of dogma, whose thinking has influenced the interpretation of early Christian thought for more than a century.... a more apt expression would be the Christianization of Hellenism, though that phrase does not capture the originality of Christian thought nor the debt owed to Jewish ways of thinking and to the Jewish Bible" (p. xvi).

38. Hegel read secularism as a result of the Incarnation and the death of God and evaluated this movement in a positive light. See Georg Wilhelm Friedrich Hegel, *Lectures on the Philosophy of Religion: The Lectures of 1827*, ed. Peter C. Hodgson (Berkeley: University of California Press, 1988). This becomes especially clear in Hegel's discussion of reconciliation (pp. 452–470) and in his discussion of "The Realization of the Spiritual Community" (pp. 481–491). Cf. Hegel's *The Phenomenology of Spirit*, trans. A.V. Miller (Oxford: Oxford University Press, 1977), pp. 459–463 (paragraphs 759–764).

39. *GL*1, p. 533.

40. Tertullian, *Adversus Marcionem*, I.1.5, trans. Ernest Evans (London: Clarendon Press, 1972).

41. *GL*1, p. 656.

42. *Martin Buber and Christianity: A Dialogue between Israel and the Church*, trans. Alexander Dru (New York: The MacMillan Company, 1961), p. 109. First published in 1958 as *Einsame Zweisprache*.

43. *The Scandal of the Incarnation*, p. 3.

44. See *Martin Buber and Christianity*, pp. 15–18.

45. Balthasar explains his decision to begin his trilogy with "glory" in these terms in the first volume of *Theo-Logic*: "Our choice to begin with 'glory' is comparable to what was once called apologetics or, if you will, fundamental theology. Our idea was that today's positivistic, atheistic man, who has become blind not only to theology but even to philosophy, needed to be confronted with the phenomenon of Christ and, therein, to learn to 'see' again—which is to say, to experience the unclassifiable, total otherness of Christ as the outshining of God's sublimity and glory. Of course, man's constitution affords him a certain anticipatory understanding of this experience (*The Glory of the Lord*, vols. 4 and 5). However, the true presence of this glory first comes

into view only in the salvation history of the Old and New Testaments (vols. 6 and 7), and it is unfolded explicitly by the great Christian theologians. This option seemed even more needful given its underdeveloped role in contemporary, postconciliar attempts to reform Catholic theology, where it tends to get resubmerged under the rationalism with which many exegetical accounts of the phenomenon of Christ simply replace the older rationalism of the Neoscholastics" (*Theo-Logic: Theological Logical Theory*, vol. 1: *The Truth of the World*, trans. Adrian J. Walker (San Francisco: Ignatius Press, 2000), p. 20; see also p. 28).

46. These texts can all be found in *The Nag Hammadi Library*, ed. James M. Robinson (San Francisco: Harper & Row, 1988).

47. *The Scandal of the Incarnation: Irenaeus against the Heresies*, p. 3. Valentinian Gnosticism revels in fantastic and complex myth, stresses private and comprehensive knowledge of the divine as the way to salvation, and thoroughly allegorizes and expands Scriptural discourse. Von Balthasar gives the basic lines of Gnostic thought on pages 1–11. He addresses Marcionism in particular on pages 3 and 5 and Gnosticism's genealogical flow in modernity on pages 4–5. He also uses the parasite-host analogy for Gnosticism's relation to Christianity here.

48. *TD4*, p. 460.

49. Much of Tertullian's first book of *Against Marcion* is taken up with the oneness of the Supremely Great God and the errors of Marcion's dualism, but includes what will become the major theme in Book II, namely, that the "separation of Law and Gospel is the primary and principle exploit of Marcion" (I.19.19).

50. Tertullian, *Adversus Marcionem*, trans. Ernest Evans (Oxford: Clarendon Press, 1972), 1.1, p. 5.

51. *TL3*, p. 263.

52. *TL3*, p. 264.

53. Insofar as we can link Prometheanism with "protest" atheism, we can see that Tertullian's observation of Marcion still applies. A kind of obsession with the experience and issue of evil can easily lead to some variety of theological dualism.

54. Ludwig Feuerbach, *The Essence of Christianity*, trans. George Eliot (New York: Harper, 1957), p. 35. The italics are mine. Also, on God as Trinity: "Man's consciousness of himself in his totality is the consciousness of the Trinity.... That which theology designates as the image, the similitude of the Trinity, we must take as the thing itself" (p. 65). In other words, Feuerbach turns Augustine on his head: where Augustine takes the *imago trinitatis* to be an imperfect analogy in us to God, Feuerbach takes the doctrine of the divine Trinity to be an imperfect expression of human self-consciousness.

55. Feuerbach writes: "The Israelite trusted himself to do nothing except what was commanded by God; he was without will even in external things; the authority of religion extended itself even to his food. The Christian religion, on the other hand, in all these external things made man dependent on himself, i.e., placed in man what the Israelite placed out of himself in God. Israel is the most complete presentation of Positivism in religion. In relation to the Israelite, the Christian is an *esprit fort*, a

free thinker. Thus do things change. What yesterday was still religion is no longer such today; and what today is atheism, tomorrow will be religion"(p. 32). Balthasar nearly always discusses Feuerbach in relation to Hegel and Marx, each of whom are more prominent figures for him. He views Feuerbach as another link in the chain that identifies the divine with the human and its projects in history. For examples, see *TD3*, p. 420 and *TD4*, p. 144. Of course Feuerbach is also a key figure for Henri de Lubac in his *The Drama of Atheist Humanism*, trans. Anne Englund Nash (San Francisco: Ignatius Press, 1995), pp. 19–73, for which Balthasar wrote the foreword. Elsewhere, however, Balthasar gives plaudits to Feuerbach for his discovery of the dialogical principle.

56. Balthasar's comment that whereas Karl Rahner chose Kant and he chose Goethe, while it can illuminate an important move against anthropocentrism and for a contemplative form of poetry, can also be misleading to the extent that Balthasar would be seen as uncritical of Goethe. Near the end of his treatment of Goethe, in *GL5*, we find that "The great conclusions to Faust are successive final hieroglyphs. Glory passes from God to the cosmos, to what Heidegger will call Being" (p. 408). This is the cosmocentric form of titanism that emerges in modernity.

57. Ibid.

58. See Peter Henrici, S.J., "Hans Urs von Balthasar: His Cultural and Theological Education" in *The Beauty of Christ: An Introduction to the Theology of Hans Urs von Balthasar*, ed. Bede McGregor and Thomas Norris (Edinburgh: T&T Clark, 1994), p. 18.

59. For a helpful discussion of this important trope and its understanding in Christian tradition, see Thomas Guarino, "'Spoils from Egypt': Yesterday and Today" in *Pro Ecclesia* 15, no. 4 (Fall 2006), pp. 403–417. This trope is very important to Balthasar, as we will see later in our discussion.

60. *GL5*, p. 409.

61. See *GL5*, pp. 410–412. Balthasar writes that "many classical myths retain symbolic expressivity, indeed take on a greater expressivity where the fate of modern mankind takes on a more tragic form—the myths of Prometheus and Dionysius, for instance—but the titanic or divine figures themselves are not thereby reanimated" (*GL5*, p. 412). Balthasar does not believe that these gods, as genuine gods, can be resurrected in modernity since they always live in the critical question: are they real or are they merely names by which "we designate our universal fte" (ibid.)? Cf. 412n.4, where Balthasar references his own work on this topic, *Apokalypse der deutschen Seele* (1937–1939).

62. This term, of course, comes from Max Weber, but is also recently picked up and used to describe a religio-political meta-narrative of Western culture by Marcel Gauchet in his *The Disenchantment of the World: A Political History of Religion*, trans. Oscar Burge (Princeton: Princeton University Press, 1997). Charles Taylor writes the foreword.

63. The term "history of effects" is that of Hans-Georg Gadamer and comes from his *Truth and Method*. It indicates a critique of objectivist hermeneutics that

fail to take into account the way in which a work comes into consciousness through a series of historical connections and naively believes that one can simply interact with a text in a hermeneutical vacuum apart from a tradition of interpretation. For Gadamer, this tradition of interpretation should be examined as a history of a work's effects that condition its reception and interpretation. See *Truth and Method*, trans. Joel Weinsheimer and Donald G. Marshall (London: Continuum, 2004), pp. 298–305.

64. See *TD2*, pp. 175–180, *GL6*, pp. 100–103, *TD2*, pp. 398–405 on the issue of the heightening tensions of human beings in the wake of the free self-revelation of God and the demythologization enacted by Israel's revelation.

65. God's glory is above heaven and earth, yet he is omnipresent in both (*TD2*, p. 175). Man will try to conquer or storm heaven (ibid., p. 176).

66. *TD2*, pp. 177 and 395.

67. *TD2*, pp. 177–178; cf. ibid, pp. 348–349. Tertullian, Irenaeus and others will recognize this utter transcendence of God as an argument for monotheism, even if Balthasar believes that too many of the "Platonizing" fathers failed to fully grasp God's transcending of the cosmos. For Tertullian, if the title "God" means Supreme Greatness, then by definition there can only be one. See *Adversus Marcionem*, 1.3.3.

68. So, for instance, on Hölderlin: "The darker his path and the firmer the grip of night, the more resolutely does Hölderlin maintain his attitude of prayer and total affirmation" (*GL5*, p. 336). The difficulty for Hölderlin, however, is the loss of analogy and the replacement of analogy by cosmic identity (*GL5*, p. 331).

69. We will discuss this at length in the following chapter.

70. This is especially clear throughout *Theo-Logic* 3, but see pp. 251–275 specifically.

71. A number of scholars have pointed to the importance of Henri de Lubac for Balthasar's formation. Kevin Mongrain argues, persuasively I think, that although Karl Barth was an important figure for Balthasar, it is de Lubac who gives him his primary theological framework and impetus. Earlier, Peter Henrici had noted the importance of de Lubac as well. See Mongrain, *The Systematic Thought of Hans Urs von Balthasar*, p. 10.

72. This is Balthasar's point in his discussion of Leibniz in *Love Alone Is Credible*, trans. D.C. Schindler (San Francisco: Ignatius Press, 2004), p. 28. As opposed to the early Fathers, in Leibniz, "the cosmological horizon no longer serves to provide evidence for Christianity, but has instead absorbed Christianity into itself and left no trace."

73. On Hegel's negative view of human nature and creation, see Cyril O'Regan, *The Heterodox Hegel* (New York: SUNY Press, 1994), pp. 141–187, especially, 151–169 and 170–171.

74. Peter Henrici, .S.J., "Hans Urs von Balthasar: His Cultural and Theological Education" in *The Beauty of Christ: An Introduction to the Theology of Hans Urs von Balthasar*, ed. Bede McGregor and Thomas Norris (Edinburgh: T&T Clark, 1994), p. 17.

75. "*Doxa* [glory] stands against *doxa*, beauty from below against beauty from above: beauty as entanglement and as a decadent, seduced sliding into the power of lust and the lust for power stands against the beauty of the adoration and service (Mt 4.10) of the one God of glory, whereby the servant not only experiences glory but is himself wrapt about with glory: 'Then the devil left him, and behold, angels came and ministered to him' (Mt 4.11)" (*GL1*, p. 664).

76. Balthasar clearly believes that the Church is not immune to the temptation to substitute "love of power" for the "power of love." In *TL3*, he writes, "Let us put it more simply [than Wilhelm Dantine]: the final criterion by which a 'discernment of spirits' is vindicated is this: whether secular power devotes itself to the pure service of Christian, powerless love or whether Christian love uses secular power in order (allegedly) to attain its purposes and goals. This has been a problem ever since the 'Constantinian shift', and we see it in the Crusades, in the Inquisition, in the liquidation of the Jesuit missions (Paraguay and Peking), and in the various instances of political 'restoration'; it is a problem today where mission is confused with propaganda in many 'movements' that loudly advertise their Church credentials. Discernment of spirits must be active above all wherever 'Satan disguises himself as an angel of light' (2 Cor. 11:14), wherever a well-meaning Peter needs to be reprimanded and unmasked as a 'Satan', that is, a tempter, because he is "not on the side of God, but of men (Mt 16:22–23). Church institutions as such are no more satanic than any secular power administered with a sense of Christian responsibility, but the tendency toward power, the tendency in all personal and social areas, to slip out of the umbrella of greater love and seek autonomy, calls for constant vigilance in the pneumatic discernment of spirits. And by 'love', here, we do not mean a virtue to be wielded by human beings; rather, we mean that grace which needs constantly to be asked anew of the *Pater pauperum*, a grace that can only be received by those who are 'poor in spirit' and can only be poured into hearts by God himself, as his own love in the Holy Spirit (Rom. 5:5)" (*TL3*, pp. 265–266).

77. Kevin Mongrain has demonstrated the importance of Irenaeus' work to Balthasar's "architectonic" and he is borne out in *TL3* where Balthasar has an entire section entitled "The Father's Two Hands" (pp. 165–219).

78. Von Balthasar is aware that antiquity affords some special figures access to the divine; his point is that in Christianity divinization or partaking of the divine nature or being born of God is open to all (See *TD2*, p. 401 and n.5).

79. Henri de Lubac, *The Drama of Atheist Humanism* (San Francisco: Ignatius Press, 1995), p. 45. De Lubac is referring specifically to Nietzsche here.

80. Balthasar writes: "as for the distance between himself and God, which pre-Christian man took for granted, he can jump over it and settle down in God's realm as if it were his own" (*TD2*, p. 407).

81. *GL5*, p. 285.

82. Ibid.

83. *GL5*, p. 291; The "Enlightenment and Idealism stripped Christianity of dogma to such an extent that nothing more can prevent its total absorption into a transcendental philosophy" (ibid., p. 15).

84. *GL5*, pp. 291–292 n. 14 and pp. 294–295.

85. Ibid.

86. Ibid. See Balthasar's comments on Shaftesbury opening up this possibility. Balthasar also notes that Shaftesbury's criticism of the Jews for engaging in speculation on the afterlife is misplaced. In fact, he says, the Old Testament shows remarkable reserve with respect to such issues. See also *GL1*, pp. 651–653 on this issue. There, Balthasar sees this reserve as part of Israel's courage and as part of its task in preparing for Christ's resurrection.

87. *GL1*, p. 104.

88. *TD4*, p. 458.

89. *TD4*, pp. 457–459.

90. *TD4*, p. 447.

91. Gianni Vattimo, *After Christianity*, trans. Luca D'Isanto (New York: Columbia University Press, 2002). See especially, pp. 25–41. See also my "Contesting the World and the Divine: Balthasar's Trinitarian 'Response' to Gianni Vattimo's Secular Christianity," *Modern Theology* 23, no. 4 (October 2007), pp. 525–559. I discuss Lessing and Thomas Altizer in relation to Vattimo's use of Joachim there.

92. In addition, Marx holds that history is, by definition, a scene of struggle and class war. This is, for him, the nature of history until it reaches its *telos*. This again would not be a Jewish view of history. Balthasar is sometimes clear and sometimes not that he intends as his target "secularized" Judaism. "The effective challenge comes from a secularized Israel that, frustrated in its Messianic hope, tries to promote salvation in and through the technological age. It is explicitly atheistic and anti-theistic vis-à-vis the ancient God, Yahweh, who has failed; and it is explicitly anti-Christian, insofar as Jesus' claim to fulfill this salvation in himself is proved to be a pitiful failure, doomed in its very concept" (*TD4*, p. 440).

93. *TD4*, p. 457–459.

94. See Cyril O'Regan's discussion of Joachim and Hegel in *The Heterodox Hegel* (New York: SUNY Press, 1994), pp. 263–279.

95. Ibid., p. 274.

96. Ibid.

97. Ibid., p. 264.

98. *Mysterium Paschale*, pp. 62–63.

99. *GL5*, p. 548.

100. *GL5*, p. 580. Balthasar does not hesitate to use the term "anti-semitism" to describe elements of Hegel's work. For Hegel, Israel, including post-biblical Jews, are consigned to utter rejection by God (ibid.).

101. *TD4*, p. 440. The political-cultural edge of this movement should not be missed: "Marxist anti-theism organizes and channels all the pagan, diffuse anti-Christian atheism and gives it a shape, a plan, a striking force" (ibid.).

102. Balthasar explains the terms "pre-Christian" and "post-Christian" in *TD2*, pp. 344–345. He also links "pre-Christian" to "pre-biblical" (ibid., p. 344 n.17), biblical thought breaking open the mythological, cosmocentric universe. The distinction between pre- and post-Christian occurs again in the context of Balthasar's discussion of Martin Heidegger in *GL5*. Although Heidegger receives many plaudits throughout Balthasar's work, his ultimate judgment on Heidegger and a whole swath of modern thought that attempts to retrieve Greek thought is that they do so in an attempt either to consume Christianity within some other system or to oppose Christianity outright. In a telling statement, he writes: "The return to classical antiquity, in order to find a way out of the confusion of the late Middle Ages, would have been successful in the long run only if antiquity had been understood as an Advent-like openness looking to Christianity, not as a comprehensive ('cosmic-religious') form in which Christianity was embedded as a potentiality (perhaps the greatest one of all), nor indeed as a base for an anti-Christian reaction" (*GL5*, p. 451). Balthasar chooses Clement of Alexandria over Heidegger in seeing Greek thought as preliminary to Christianity and not as a thought form that can consume Christianity. Cf. the discussion of Heidegger, ibid., pp. 429–450, esp. pp. 447–450. The term "pre-biblical" indicates that Balthasar will link the Old Covenant intimately to the New, whereas extra-biblical thought will be considered generally in a tertiary position. The issue of Old Covenant revelation in relation to extra-biblical thought will become important as we proceed.

103. Tertullian thinks that Marcion had an "unhealthy interest in the problem of evil—the origin of it—and his perceptions were numbed by the very excess of his curiosity" (*Adversus Marcionem*, 1.2, p. 7). Of course the polemical character of Tertullian's attacks need not return.

104. Balthasar also sees an asymmetry between pre- and post-Christian thought vis-à-vis Christian revelation. Whereas "pre-Christian" thought exhibits "elements (*logoi spermatikoi*) of the reality that is only fully manifested in Christianity," (*TD2*, p. 344) and does not lose sight of the *analogia entis*, post-Christian Prometheanism takes up Christian elements and deforms them by omitting the *analogia entis* and confusing or conflating the divine and the human or redemption and creation. While "No Greek would have dreamed of confusing himself with a god" (*TD2*, p. 346), according to Balthasar, this confusion runs rampant in post-Christian modernity. Pre-Christian thought is redeemable by Christianity because it respects the difference between gods and mortals. By contrast, post-Christian thought exists in an agonistic relation to Christianity that Christian theology itself must be aware of if it is to address these thought forms appropriately, which at times will mean outright rejection (*TD2*, pp. 348–349).

105. This strand of development involves Nominalism, runs through empiricism, and even includes *a priori* philosophies that do not attend to the world outside the self and mind for manifestation of divine glory.

106. In his own language, Michael Buckley makes this argument forcefully in his *At the Origins of Modern Atheism* (New Haven: Yale University Press, 1987).

107. *GL7*, pp. 510–511 n. 1. Cf. *TD5*, p. 170: "Bloch's attempt, which is closer to the Exodus atmosphere of the Bible than Marx (and better acquainted with Hegelian logic), is a radically secularized Messianism." Walter Kasper similarly distrusts secular utopianisms and, with Karl Löwith and Sergei Bulgakov, sees these as failed attempts to secularize Christian hope. See Kasper, *The God of Jesus Christ* (New York: Crossroad Press, 2000), pp. 36, 199, 329n.114. Like Balthasar, Kasper argues that the loss of Trinitarian theology leads to atheism. Michael Buckley makes a similar claim at the beginning of his major work, *At the Origins of Modern Atheism*. Buckley contends that during the Enlightenment, for various reasons both historical and philosophical, philosophy moved from its role as preamble to faith to the center of Christian thought where it competed with non-Christian philosophy. Atheism is fundamentally a rejection of a non-Christian view of God, that is, a vacuous theism. See Buckley, pp. 33, 38, 39, 47. Speaking of the apologetic offered by Marin Mersenne in the 17th century, Buckley asks, "But what happened to the theologian?" (p. 64). Again: "Neither Christology nor a Pneumatology of religious experience figure in his apologetic" (ibid.). The final section of Kasper's text is called "The Trinitarian Confession as the Answer to Modern Atheism" (ibid., p. 315). Kasper is careful, however, not to argue that philosophers are undeserving of philosophical answers to their questions. What he wants to guard against is an abstract and empty theism somehow becoming a substitute for concrete Christian monotheism rooted in the God of the Scriptures and tradition.

108. Balthasar does view the Old Covenant as somewhat "heteronomous," but only as compared with the New. "Accordingly, it is hard to avoid seeing an element of heteronomy in the old Law. Only in the preaching of Jesus and the post-Easter meditation upon it in the light of the Holy Spirit does the womb of the Father's divine freedom open so wide and so deep that we begin to suspect what the "fulfillment of finite freedom in infinite freedom" might mean" (*TD2*, p. 229). Kant now becomes a catalyst for Fichte's identification of the self with absoluteness; in other words, Kant in *TD2* is being read as a figure who inadvertently enables Prometheanism. The Kant texts cited are later texts, namely, his *Anthropology (1798)* and *Metaphysics of Morals (1797)*. Kant's rational moral subject must seize the absolute moral law and identify himself with it (*TD2*, p. 421).

109. *GL7*, p. 509.

110. *GL7*, p. 510. Balthasar takes us from Otto's Wholly Other to Cusa's non-aliud to a Trinitarian depiction of God's closeness to us as in-the-non-other (*TD2*, p. 194). While Balthasar thinks it appropriate and biblical for the creature to see itself as an other to God, or to see God as a Thou, the creature should not think that this is how it looks from God's perspective. Given God's unity, there can really be no other "outside of" God; rather, the creature only exists as a gift within God, within that which is the "Other in the non-Other." Balthasar is making the radical sameness in difference of the Trinity the ground for the existence of the finite creature *within* the divine infinite being (*TD2*, pp. 193–194). Balthasar does think that there is progress between the Old Covenant sense of glory and the New Covenant sense of glory. He

writes that "We must admit that the Old Testament form of relationship between Yahweh and the people (or mankind as a whole) somehow implies the idea of an opposition between the Divine 'being' (in heaven) and a multiplicity of human 'being' (on earth)" (*TD2*, pp. 229). We should also take note of the word "postulate" used here by Balthasar, recalling Kant's notion of a postulated God necessary to make moral sense out of the world. The same term is used several pages earlier: Speaking of the creature's invitation into the sphere of the divine life, Balthasar writes that "This is something the creature would never have dreamed of; he would never have postulated it for himself, either subjectively or objectively" (*TD2*, p. 400).

111. *GL7*, p. 511.

112. Balthasar makes this especially clear in *TD4* during his reading of the Book of Revelation. He compares the angel who throws burning coals on Jerusalem (Ezek. 10:2) with Revelation 8:5, where an angel similarly throws fire to the earth, and comments: " ... it is clear that the actuality of the first event is wholly preserved in the second. And this in spite of the fact—again—that the work of Christ has been accomplished, in the midst of time, valid for all past and for all future time" (p. 18). Christ remains judge for von Balthasar, even more so after he has accomplished his mission in time. Following the example of de Lubac, he is committed here to paradox: "We must hold fast to the paradox that goes right through this book: Christ's completed work gives him power to break the seal of world history and unveil it; yet this very opening of the seal brings about a growing sense of fear and foreboding as the end of time approaches. It is not even clear whether the salvific effects of Christ's death become somehow latent in order to allow the aspect of pure judgment to move into center-stage, or whether this salvific efficacy itself summons the opposing powers to the battlefield for a final decisive conflict" (ibid.; cf. p. 21: "In this way we can grasp something of the paradox of the Book of Revelation: the Lamb can appear as the ultimate Victor and as the Lord of all history, while at the same time he is depicted riding out to do battle and to slaughter" (19:11ff.)). The paradoxes of the Book of Revelation defy systematization and open a "window into the ever-greater world of God" (ibid.). Also, the Book of Revelation opens "perspectives that, once opened, can never be shut" (ibid., 19). Von Balthasar is reading Revelation's apocalyptic against an apocalyptic that would possess full knowledge of history in its coming events.

113. Against Promethean evolutionism, von Balthasar pits a more nearly Augustinian view of history: " .... world history is not a demonstration of progressive integration—Augustine was right—but is characterized by an increasing polarization" (*TD4*, p. 21). His mention of Camus's *Les Justes* three different times in a short space is relevant here. Camus seems haunted by the notion that without a God we must judge ourselves. His characters take to themselves the evil of the world in a heroic act, but one of them suspects the pridefulness of this act. Von Balthasar contrasts this with Jesus' act of obedience to the Father. Jesus does not heroically take on the suffering of the world, but accepts it as part of his obedience to the Father's will.

114. Joseph Komonchak, "Returning from Exile: Catholic Theology in the 1930s," in *The Twentieth Century: A Theological Overview*, ed. Gregory Baum (Maryknoll, New York: Orbis Books, 1999), p. 43.

115. On positivity and representation see especially *Lectures on the Philosophy of Religion*, pp. 145–151.

116. *GL*1, p. 131.

117. *GL*1, pp. 135–139. See also *GL*1, pp. 53–56 where Balthasar is speaking about Karl Barth.

118. *GL*1, p. 239.

119. Ibid.

120. *GL*1, pp. 138–139. The Bultmann point is made on p. 56 where Balthasar is juxtaposing Barth to Bultmann.

121. For a helpful discussion of this early period of canonical struggles, see Joseph T. Lienhard, S.J., *The Bible, the Church, and Authority: The Canon of the Christian Bible in History and Theology* (Collegeville, MN: The Liturgical Press, 1995).

122. *GL*1, pp. 18–19.

123. Joseph Komanchak captures the essence of this way of doing theology in his discussion of Henri de Lubac: "Theology should not be conceived as simply 'the science of revealed truths,' simply an understanding *of* the faith; what is needed is an understanding of all reality *by means of faith*, an integrated fundamental theology in which the invitation to faith is mediated, not by extrinsic demonstration, but by an exposition of how revelation and grace illuminate and empower the human mystery." Joseph Komonchak, "Returning from Exile: Catholic Theology in the 1930s," in *The Twentieth Century: A Theological Overview*, ed. Gregory Baum (Maryknoll, New York: Orbis Books, 1999), p. 43. Italics are in the original.

124. *GL*1, p. 150.

125. *GL*1, p. 118.

126. *GL*1, p. 151. See also pp. 18 and 118: "The appearance of the form, as revelation of the depths, is an indissoluble union of two things. It is the real presence of the depths, of the whole of reality, and it is a real pointing beyond itself to these depths." Cf. *TD*2, pp. 21–36. See also Cyril O'Regan's discussion of form in "Newman and von Balthasar: The Christological Contexting of the Numinous," in *Église et Théologie*, 26 (1995), pp. 165–202.

127. Balthasar would want to note that the experience of beautiful form and the experience of divine revelation are analogous, not univocal experiences. In the experience of innerworldly beauty, an identity of being obtains between the work and the receiver of the work; this is not the case between God's being and ours, so that the encounter with God in Christ requires that grace elevates us, in faith, to be able to receive such revelation as divine revelation.

128. See *GL*1, pp. 30–31, and especially p. 529.

129. *GL*1, p. 618. See also the example of Mozart, p. 539. Balthasar expressly addresses this view against Gnosticism and for a Johannine contemplative view.

Love will be the "warrant of objective knowledge in the realm of trinitarian revelation" (ibid.). Cf. ibid., p. 467: "The first prerequisite for understanding is to accept what is given just as it offers itself."

130. See *GL*1, pp. 20 and 31 on trying to get "behind" the form of revelation, whether Platonically in a way that severs body and soul or as in modern historical criticism of Scripture: " ... and for this reason we can 'go behind' this form only at the risk of losing both image and Spirit conjointly. Only the final result of the historical developments which lie behind a text—a history never to be adequately reconstructed—may be said to be inspired, not the bits and scraps which philological analysis thinks it can tear loose from the finished totality in order, as it were, to steal up to the form from behind in the hope of enticing it to betray its mystery by exposing its development. Does it not make one suspicious when Biblical philology's first move in its search for an 'understanding' of its texts is to dissect their form into sources, psychological motivations, and the sociological effects of milieu, even before the form has been contemplated and read for its meaning as *form*?" (*GL*1, p. 31). Balthasar considers the perception of form "a universal phenomenon" (ibid., p. 151) and refuses to oppose Greek to Jewish form, at least on a general level (ibid., pp. 151–152).

131. *GL*1, pp. 535–536.
132. *GL*1, p. 533.
133. *GL*1, p. 625.
134. *GL*1, p. 619.
135. *GL*1, p. 658. Balthasar also comments, provocatively, that "In the figure of the two Testaments, which are really but one Testament, time attains theological form: time becomes the clay from which God creates a measure of revelation for eternal life...." (ibid.).
136. *GL*1, p. 625.
137. "The testimony of the Old Testament is the testimony time bears to eternity, which with Christ enters into time. This is a testimony that constitutes one intelligible form with what it attests, and without this total form the testimony itself would remain impenetrable. For the eyes of faith, the 'riddle of Israel' does not exist, not even the riddle of Israel's continued existence until the Last Judgment" (*GL*1, p. 658).
138. *GL*1, p. 657.
139. *TD*3, p. 367.
140. Ibid.
141. *GL*1, p. 656.
142. *GL*1, p. 657.
143. *GL*1, p. 543.
144. *GL*1, p. 466.
145. *GL*1, p. 534.
146. *GL*1, p. 536.
147. Ibid.

148. *GL1*, p. 542.
149. *GL1*, p. 467.
150. *TD3*, p. 72.
151. *TD3*, pp. 64–65.
152. *TD3*, p. 73.
153. *TD3*, pp. 73–74.
154. *TD3*, p. 68.
155. *TD3*, p. 62.
156. *GL1*, p. 534.
157. *TD3*, pp. 88–89.
158. *TD3*, pp. 112–113.
159. Ibid.
160. *TD3*, pp. 118–120.
161. *TD3*, pp. 65–66 n. 18.
162. *GL1*, p. 649.
163. *GL1*, p. 635.
164. *GL1*, p. 648.
165. *GL1*, p. 635.
166. *GL1*, p. 649.
167. *GL1*, p. 648.
168. *GL1*, p. 649.
169. *GL1*, p. 646. Balthasar writes, "The decisive thing here is that the temporal relationship of the Old to the New Testament not only represents the relationship of time to eternity, but bears it within itself in the manner of a sacrament that contains and communicates what it symbolizes in the likeness of what is seen. This sacramental possibility is possessed by the Old Testament in virtue of the grace of the New: because the Word to which Israel should listen is the one that will come in the flesh."
170. *GL1*, p. 651.
171. Not included here, for instance, is Balthasar's treatment of the history of Being (*Seinsgeschichte*) from Scotus through Nominalism, Machiavelli, early Utopianisms, Hobbes, and Francis Bacon. The Old Testament de-divinization of the cosmos is relevant here, but the sacramental nature of the cosmos is lost. Thus slowly but surely, human, autonomous power comes to be a dominating facet of understanding. On Scotus, Nominalism, and Suarez, see *GL5*, pp. 16–29; on early Utopians, see pp. 286–287, and pp. 287–289 for Hobbes, Bacon, and Machiavelli. A key theme running throughout Balthasar's work, evident in our discussion with respect to exegesis, is the loss of mediating discourses between a theology of the Word and faith. Philosophy, poetry, myth, art, exegesis all stand to relate revelation to human understanding and endeavor.
172. *GL5*, p. 298.
173. *GL1*, pp. 652–653.
174. *GL1*, p. 656.
175. Ibid.

176. *GL1*, p. 657.

177. *TL3*, p. 269. God's invitation effects a real change in the sinner, for Balthasar, and the Church is then to proclaim this offer of freedom borne by the Holy Spirit.

178. *GL1.*, p. 647.

179. Ibid.

Chapter Two

180. What Balthasar typically calls Prometheanism can also be named "nihilism" in the proper sense that Heidegger intends the term in his reading of Nietzsche. Nihilism, in this sense, indicates that the "place" that was the center of meaning, value, truth has been "dis-placed" and now must come to reside in the human as opposed to the divine understood as a transcendent reality. See Heidegger, *Nietzsche*, vol. IV: *Nihilism*, trans. Joan Stambaugh, David Farrell Krell, Frank A. Capuzzi (San Francisco: Harper, 1982), pp. 4–5. This displacement, on Heidegger's reading of Nietzsche, occurs to all such transcendent realities including Platonic forms, Aristotelian substance, and Kantian postulates. In short, humans must become divine, as Nietzsche puts it in his parable of the madman (*The Gay Science*, #125).

181. Max Weber, *The Protestant Ethic and the Spirit of Capitalism* (Oxford: Oxford University Press, 2001).

182. Marcel Gauchet, *The Disenchantment of the World: A Political History of Religion*, trans. Oscar Burge (Princeton: Princeton University Press, 1997).

183. See *TL3*, pp. 263 and 270.

184. Balthasar and de Lubac each inveigh against neo-Scholasticism that abstracted "pure nature" from nature as the concrete site of God's gracious activity. See especially Henri de Lubac, *Augustinianism and Modern Theology*, trans. Lancelot Sheppard (New York: Crossroad Publishing, 2000) and Balthasar, *TD3*, pp. 414–418.

185. W.T. Dickens, *Hans Urs von Balthasar's Theological Aesthetics: A Model for Post-Critical Biblical Interpretation* (Notre Dame, IN: University of Notre Dame Press, 2003). I am persuaded that I took this phrase from Dickens, but cannot find it at present. Anyone who has read his book, especially chapter three, will notice much convergence in our views. Although much of this chapter was written prior to my reading of Dickens's text, it was also improved by having read it.

186. *GL6*, p. 402.

187. Ibid.

188. Friedrich Schleiermacher, *The Christian Faith*, trans. Rev. Professor D.M. Baillie (Philadelphia: Fortress Press, 1976), pp. 60–62, §12. This is a translation of the second edition of Schleiermacher's work. Schleiermacher observes the historical connections between Christianity and Judaism and clearly thinks monotheism is a religious view superior to those of fetishism and polytheism found in Greek and Roman culture (pp. 34–39, §8), but he also believes that while Christianity introduced

monotheism to non-Jewish cultures, Judaism had many obstacles to belief in Christ, for instance the loss of a genuinely messianic hope or its confusion and a demand to give up the Law, that Greek and Roman cultures did not have. He is trying to make the point that a movement from either Judaism or "heathenism" to Christianity involves a leap into a new religion. For Schleiermacher, "we must assume that Christian piety, in its original form, cannot be explained by means of the Jewish piety of that or of an earlier time, and so Christianity cannot in any wise be regarded as a remodeling or a renewal and continuation of Judaism" (p. 61).

189. See Samuel Balentine's discussion of this drift away from Israelite public ritual in Protestant biblical scholarship. Samuel Balentine, *The Torah's Vision of Worship* (Minneapolis: Fortress Press, 1998), pp. 8–11. Like W.F. Albright and H.J. Kraus, among others, Balentine notes the importance of moving away from a Hegelian reading of Old Covenant history as an evolutionary development away from public worship or cult and towards prophecy and spirit.

190. See Lessing's "Education of the Human Race," in *Lessing's Theological Writings*, trans. Henry Chadwick (Stanford, CA: Stanford University Press, 1972), pp. 82–98, and Kant's *Religion within the Limits of Reason Alone*, trans. Theodore M. Greene and Hoyt H. Hudson (New York: Harper and Row, 1960), pp. 116–117.

191. *GL7*, p. 33.

192. Gerhard von Rad, *Genesis: A Commentary* (Philadelphia: The Westminster Press, 1972), p. 28; cf. von Rad's claim that for Christians reading the Bible there is a continuity in terms of type between the God of the Old Covenant who reveals and conceals himself and the revelation, at times in hiddenness, of Christ in the New Testament (ibid., p. 42).

193. As Ernest Nicholson puts it, "Writing in the 1930s, Gerhard von Rad sounded a protest against the disintegrating and fragmenting effect of Pentateuchal research hitherto, notwithstanding the valuable insights it had yielded into the sources and the information gained concerning the history of Israel, its religion and institutions. He castigated scholars as being guilty of an approach which viewed the Hexateuch as 'a starting-point barely worthy of discussion, from which the debate should move away as rapidly as possible in order to reach the real problems underlying it.'" Ernest Nicholson, *The Pentateuch in the Twentieth Century: The Legacy of Julius Wellhausen* (Oxford: Clarendon Press, 1998), p. 250. For the von Rad quote, see Gerhard von Rad, "The Form-Critical Problem of the Hexateuch." *The Problem of the Hexateuch and Other Essays*, trans. E. W. Trueman Dicken (Edinburgh: Oliver & Boyd, 1966), p. 1.

194. On von Rad as a confessional biblical scholar and member of the Confessing Church in Germany in the 1930s, see Walter Brueggemann and Hans Walter Wolff, *The Vitality of Old Testament Traditions* (Atlanta: John Knox, 1975), pp. 30–32.

195. Ibid., p. 28.

196. *GL1*, p. 641.

197. *GL1*, p. 647.

198. Jon Levenson points out that it is the forsaking of this transcendent reference point that leads to a fundamental difference between historical critics and traditional readers of the biblical text. Thus, historical criticism becomes uninteresting to traditional readers of the Jewish scriptures. See Levenson, *The Hebrew Bible, the Old Testament, and Historical Criticism: Jews and Christians in Biblical Studies* (Louisville, KY: Westminster John Knox Press, 1993). Levenson makes this point most directly and forcefully in his preface.

199. See *GL6*, pp. 402–416.

200. See esp. *GL6*, p. 406.

201. See especially the entirety of section 3 of *GL1* entitled "The Objective Evidence." Much of Balthasar's narrative of aesthetic loss in the modern period has to do with the gradual occlusion of the transcendental of beauty as a genuine and objective transcendental of Being. See *GL1*, pp. 17–79.

202. *GL6*, p. 12.

203. *GL6*, p. 12. The passage that Balthasar quotes is from Scheeben, *Dogmatik*, vol. I (1873), p. 25. On Scheeben, who Balthasar names "the greatest German theologian to-date since the time of Romanticism," see also *GL1*, pp. 104–110. Balthasar is critical of some of Scheeben's work, in particular his "from above" approach, and his sealing off of nature from supernature too strictly due to his polemic against Romanticist conflation of creation and revelation. Nevertheless, he thinks Scheeben makes up for these deficits in later works (ibid., pp. 108–109).

204. *GL6*, pp. 9–10. We should note that Balthasar's emphasis on encounter also differs from von Rad's stress on a particular confession of faith as the center of Israelite tradition formation. Balthasar would also reject any reading of the Old Testament that would have a Law-Gospel dynamic at its center, as Levenson argues is the case with von Rad. See Levenson, *The Hebrew Bible*, pp. 21–25. Levenson cites Brevard Childs' critique of von Rad approvingly.

205. *GL5*, pp. 548 and 580.

206. *GL5*, p. 309 and 548.

207. *GL6*, p. 10.

208. *GL5*, p. 580. Of course Balthasar is not alone in this view. Near the beginning of a Hegelian renaissance in the United States, Lawrence Stepelevich, later to be editor of the journal of Hegel studies, *The Owl of Minerva*, issued a challenge: "Now, a simple litmus test to determine the social desirability of Hegelianism would be the examination of its attitude in regard to Judaism, for there is nothing more refractory to philosophic sublimation than anti-Semitism. If Hegel's philosophic system is either incapable of rising above the cultural psychosis of anti-Semitism, or, worse yet, incorporates it within the system, then the revival of Hegelianism must be, for men of good will, a most unhappy event" (Lawrence Stepelevich, "Hegel and Judaism", in *Judaism*, 24, no. 2 (Spring 1975), p. 215). Stepelevich argues that Hegel was a fundamentally anti-Jewish philosopher, even if he did support emancipation at the socio-political level (pp. 215–224). For a contrary view, see Yirmiyahu Yovel's,

Dark Riddle: Hegel, Nietzsche, and the Jews (University Park, PA: The Pennsylvania State University Press, 1998).

209. *GL5*, p. 581.

210. For instance, see Hegel, *Encyclopedia of the Philosophical Sciences*, paragraph 564 in *G.W.F. Hegel: Theologian of the Spirit*, ed. Peter C. Hodgson (Minneapolis: Fortress Press, 1997). Yet the story is complicated by the fact that Hegel's rejection of epistemic limitations on knowledge of God would find agreement in Balthasar, as Hegel is arguing that given the definition of Christianity as "revealed" religion, any philosophy claiming to interpret this religion, but also claiming that God remains unknown, simply has no right to claim itself as such an interpretation. Balthasar, however, will want to distinguish between different kinds of knowing, that is, between reason and faith, in a way quite different from Hegel. For an intensive discussion of Hegel's rejection of apophaticism, see Cyril O'Regan, *The Heterodox Hegel* (New York: SUNY Press, 1994), pp. 31–44.

211. In *LPR*, Judaism stands in an ambiguous position. On the one hand, in Judaism one moves beyond a religion of natural, non-subjective beauty to a religion of sublime subjectivity, that is, to a religion that has a God who is universal and personal, and who is not reducible to aspects of nature, but can reveal himself through events in nature as what is sublime. As for Balthasar, so for Hegel it is Judaism that separates world from God or disenchants the world (see *LPR*, pp. 357–364). For Hegel, Roman religion takes up the subjectivity of Jewish religion but gives this subjectivity a universal purpose or mission; unfortunately, this universal mission remains a finite mission of domination and cannot comprehend the infinite (*LPR*, pp. 409–410). Of course, for Hegel Judaism is then headed toward a kind of logical supercession that will take place as the divine becomes concrete in the Incarnation and in human self-consciousness. Jesus will be the finite one who comprehends the infinite.

212. *LPR*, p. 435.

213. For actual rupture as necessary for the seriousness of the concept of God as reconciled otherness, see *LPR*, pp. 433–434. For the world as negation, see p. 435.

214. *LPR*, p. 463.

215. Cyril O'Regan, "Balthasar and Eckhart: Theological Principles and Catholicity," *The Thomist*, 60, no. 2 (April, 1996), pp. 203–239.

216. This is a thesis that Balthasar deployed as early as his book on Martin Buber. Buber had argued, in *Two Types of Faith*, that Jesus and Paul represented two incommensurable religious views, Jesus being a good, if perhaps too idealistic, rabbi, whereas Paul was a Greek-style metaphysician who had left his Judaism behind and essentially created a different type of faith altogether, one based in doctrines and metaphysical ideas rather than in personal trust. See Martin Buber, *Two Types of Faith*, trans. Norman P. Goldhawk (London: Routledge and Kegan Paul, 1951). Balthasar argues in his book on Buber and in *GL6* that the images and direction of the Old Covenant find their fulfillment in Christ, without which they give rise to a Gnostic or Kabbalistic mysticism on the one hand, or an unrealized eschatology

turned Prometheanism on the other. We will discuss Balthasar's treatment of post-biblical Judaism in chapter three.

217. See *GL6*, p. 15; *TD1*, p. 125; and *TL3*, pp. 185–190 where Balthasar contests facile contrasts between East and West on divinization. On Balthasar's reading, "incorporation into Christ" and "divinization" are nearly isomorphic.

218. *GL6*, p. 19.

219. The term "ontotheology" is often used as a term of opprobrium but can also be appropriated for positive usage. Negatively, it indicates a failure to differentiate sufficiently between God and worldly being. For its positive appropriation, see Peter C. Hodgson's introduction in *G.W.F. Hegel: Theologian of the Spirit*, ed. Peter C. Hodgson (Minneapolis: Fortress Press, 1997), pp. 6–7. Very important on Hegel's philosophy of religion is Hodgson's text, *Hegel and Christian Theology: A Reading of the Lectures on the Philosophy of Religion* (Oxford: Oxford University Press, 2005).

220. *GL6*, 198.

221. Ibid.

222. *GL6*, 199.

223. Ibid.; Is. 60; Acts 2.

224. *GL6*, p. 34.

225. *GL6*, p. 53.

226. Book one of Irenaeus' *Against the Heresies* expresses a similar concern with respect to Gnosticism: "Thus it is that, wresting from the truth every one of the expressions which have been cited, and taking a bad advantage of the names, they have transferred them to their own system; so that, according to them, in all these terms John makes no mention of the Lord Jesus Christ. For if he has named the Father, and Charis, and Monogenes, and Aletheia, and Logos, and Zoe, and Anthropos, and Ecclesia, according to their [the heretics'] hypothesis, he has, but thus speaking referred to the primary Ogdoad, in which there was as yet no Jesus, and no Christ, the teacher of John" (*Against the Heresies*, Bk.1. IX.2.). Irenaeus, *Against the Heresies*, trans. Alexander Roberts, in *The Ante-Nicene Fathers*, vol. 1 (Michigan: Eerdmann's, 1953), p. 329.

227. *GL6*, pp. 54–55.

228. Rudolf Otto, *The Idea of the Holy*, trans. John W. Harvey (Oxford: Oxford University Press, 1958).

229. Cyril O'Regan has made this point in his "Newman and von Balthasar: The Christological Contexting of the Numinous," in *Église et Théologie*, 26 (1995), pp. 165–202.

230. What Balthasar accomplishes here is the biblical contextualization of Christian discourse on the divine attributes and thus also on analogous religious speech. Such a contextualization, we can observe, is promising both on ecumenical and on philosophical grounds. For ecumenism, Balthasar's biblical focus allows him to present a discussion of divine attributes that would, at least in principle, be feasible within a *sola scriptura* framework, while nevertheless advancing a theol-

ogy of glory that in other forms would be inimical to a Lutheran theological stance. Philosophically, Balthasar is able to meet hermeneutic concerns for the historicity of revelation by presenting divine disclosure through revelatory events that occur within the form of the covenant relation. Events point to the nature and character of God, not as to a "homogeneous block of essence," but to a personal mystery of freedom encountered in the very center of people's lives.

231. *GL6*, p. 415.
232. *GL6*, p. 166.
233. Ibid.
234. *GL6*, p. 169.
235. *GL6*, pp. 167–168.
236. *GL6*, pp. 170–172.
237. *GL6*, p. 172; i.e., Isaiah 51:3, 8.
238. *GL6*, p. 172; Is. 42:1–4; cf. 53:11.
239. See *LPR*, p. 154, where Hegel is contrasting representational discourse to conceptual discourse.
240. Concrete here also carries the connotation of "realistic." From a theological point of view, we are always in relation to God whether or not we want to admit this. Thus, we can even live abstractly, as if this relation were non-existent, or concretely in recognition of this relation.
241. *GL6*, p. 87; cf. 91.
242. *GL6*, pp. 91, 95.
243. *GL6*, pp. 96–97.
244. See Merton's brief but insightful essay on Prometheus in *Raids on the Unspeakable* (New York: New Directions Publishing Corp., 1966), pp. 79–91.
245. See Henri de Lubac, *Theology in History: The Light of Christ, Disputed Questions, and Resistance to Nazism* (San Francisco: Ignatius Press, 1996). Balthasar cites de Lubac's text on tripartite anthropology in *TL3*, p. 262 n. 15.
246. *GL6*, p. 100.
247. *GL6*, p. 101.
248. *GL6*, p. 103.
249. *GL6*, pp. 106, 109, 114, 117.
250. *GL6*, p. 114.
251. *GL6*, p. 107. This treatment has its parallel in the fourth volume of *Theo-Drama* where the focus is on "God's long patience" (*TD4*, pp. 205–231).
252. *GL6*, 115–116.
253. *GL6*, p. 123.
254. *GL6*, p. 124.
255. Hans Urs von Balthasar, *The God Question and Modern Man*, trans. Hilda Graef (New York: Seabury Press, 1967).
256. *GL6*, p. 177.
257. Ibid.
258. *GL6*, p. 180.

259. *GL6*, p. 181.
260. *GL6*, pp. 181–183.
261. *GL6*, p. 188.
262. *GL6*, p. 185.
263. *GL6*, p. 192.
264. See Sermon 29, on Psalm 118:1, in *The Works of Saint Augustine: Essential Sermons*, trans. Edmund Hill (Hyde, NY: New City Press, 2007), pp. 50–53.
265. *GL6*, p. 207.
266. Ibid.
267. *GL6*, p. 208.
268. Ibid.
269. *GL6*, p. 215.
270. *GL6*, pp. 222–223.
271. *GL6*, p. 225.
272. Ibid.
273. *GL6*, p. 205.
274. *GL6*, pp. 269 and 295.Von Balthasar is using these later traditional Christian terms to describe the intense union of the divine Word and both Ezekiel and the Servant.
275. *GL6*, pp. 232–234; cf. 235, 244.
276. *GL6*, pp. 237–238, 252.
277. *GL6*, pp. 259–263.
278. *GL6*, pp. 258–263.
279. *GL6*, p. 249.
280. *GL6*, p. 268.
281. Ibid. It should be mentioned that although Job lies outside the covenant, he is included in the staircase. He provides an important block to simplistic theodicies, a rendering of "terror" in the presence of God, and an analogy to the unity of divine glory and abandonment by God suffered by Jesus on the Cross (*GL6*, p. 290).
282. *GL6*, p. 292.
283. Ibid.
284. Ibid.
285. *GL6*, p. 294.
286. *GL6*, p. 295.
287. See Irenaeus, *Adversus Haeresis*, Book IV, 20, 7.
288. *GL6*, p. 297.
289. See Levenson, *The Hebrew Bible*, pp. 10–15 and 41–42. Levenson rejects the theoretical link between Hegel and Wellhausen, while criticizing Hegel's anti-Judaism. His rejection of the link is based on the following points: Wellhausen's model of evolution was degenerative, that is, from Israel to Judaism (in the Jahwist and Elohistic writings from a universal priesthood, free and easy relation to the natural cycles of the calendar, sacrifice unfettered to a central location through the Deuteronomic period and then in the post-exilic period with the writings of the

Priestly author. D and P come to stress a limited Levitical priesthood, emphasis on tithing, the central place of sacrifice, stress on atonement, loss of the free relation to the natural world), whereas Hegel's was progressive; Wellhausen had four stages of development (including the gospel) whereas Hegel's thesis, antithesis, and synthesis are only three, and the state plays no role in Wellhausen's formulation. I would argue that this analysis, while fine for Wellhausen, does not take into account crucial aspects of the Hegelian system. Hegel's progressive view of revelation includes a massively negative moment that in his *Lectures on the Philosophy of Religion* includes creation, the remainder of the Hebrew bible, up to the resurrection of Christ where Spirit takes over. While one cannot map this discussion directly onto Wellhausen's account, there is more similarity than Levenson recognizes.

290. *GL6*, p. 303.

291. *GL6*, p. 370. Balthasar has theological reasons for this related to the nature of history. The newness of Israel's discovery lies in the unique significance that it gives unrepeatable historical events. He believes that Qoheleth and the Wisdom literature retreat from this crucial understanding when they repeat cyclical versions of time found in various world religions. Daniel falters when he places too much emphasis on the moment of transition from history to eschatology.

292. *GL6*, p. 303.

293. Ibid.

294. *GL6*, p. 321. The messiah is most often linked to kingship, a link that in terms of historical time alone, rather than eschatological time, does not allow for vicarious suffering or the descent of God found in the Son of Man imagery in Daniel 7. Balthasar argues that the eschatological messiah must be both continuous with Israel's history in order to be recognized and radically discontinuous because only God can truly bring the divine righteousness / justice that was necessary to fulfill God's own covenant. Here, we see Balthasar's understanding of the relation between nature and grace fully operative. Nature is called beyond itself, and, therefore, beyond any purely intra-historical realization, for its own fulfillment as a share in the divine life. Likewise, the fulfillment of covenant righteousness cannot occur through a purely historical figure, but only in a figure who is at once historical and transcends the historical. This nature-grace relation, found for Balthasar at the origin of the covenant, is what post-exilic messianism failed to see. Thus, it placed its hope in historical figures and did not gain the vision of Daniel's Apocalyptic Son of Man or the suffering Servant of Deutero-Isaiah.

295. *GL6*, p. 322 and 341. Von Balthasar's wording here reveals something of his notion of "concrete" history: Apocalyptic opens up "a living supratemporal dimension of Heaven which accompanies history on earth" (*GL6*, p. 341). History from Balthasar's point of view is never just the bare facts. Real history is permeated by a dramatic interaction between human and divine freedom.

296. *GL6*, pp. 341–343.

297. *GL6*, pp. 351–353, 361

298. *GL6*, p. 361.

299. *GL6*, p. 346.

300. *GL6*, pp. 346–347.

301. *GL6*, p. 375.

302. Ibid. For the contrast, Wellhausen: "When it is recognized that the canon is what distinguishes Judaism from ancient Israel, it is recognized at the same time that what distinguishes Judaism from ancient Israel is the written Torah. The water which in old times rose from a spring, the Epigoni stored up in cisterns," quoted in Levenson, *The Hebrew Bible*, p. 42. Of course it would be odd for a Catholic to opine that canon and priesthood lead to the death of revelation. While on the one hand this might point to the idea that Balthasar is more concerned with an Old Testament justification for Catholicism than with the good of Judaism, this same argument could easily be turned around to suggest that a Catholic dogmatics is better situated for a dialogue with Judaism than is a Protestant dogmatics. Dickens nicely addresses these issues in chapter three of *Hans Urs von Balthasar's Theological Aesthetics: A Model for Post-Critical Biblical Interpretation* (Notre Dame, IN: University of Notre Dame Press, 1997).

303. It is of interest to point out that Balthasar assessed the post-exilic literature far more positively than did Martin Buber. Buber rejected a progressive revelation in Israel and saw much of its Monarchical period forward as a decline from the period of judges. Of course the point of Buber's negative evaluation of the post-exilic literature is contrary to the point either Balthasar or Wellhausen are trying to make through their different assessments. Buber is trying to read against a progressive revelation towards the New Covenant, and this means for him reading against any and all apocalyptic elements springing from what he considered external, Iranian sources corrupting Israel's faith. This corrupt faith is then taken up by Christianity, which becomes an apocalyptic faith unconcerned with the needs of the present world. See Balthasar's *Martin Buber and Christianity*. We will discuss this in chapter three.

304. *GL6*, p. 380.

305. *GL6*, p. 384.

306. *GL6*, p. 385. Here Balthasar argues against Martin Noth, who views this period as the beginning of an attempt at self-justification and an overturning of the entire covenant history: grace turns into an ethic of achievement (*GL6*, p. 385 n. 10). See also Balthasar's comments in *Mysterium Paschale* on Luther's and Hegel's anti-Judaism stemming, in part, from their tendency to make the Cross into a universal law of history whereby paradox becomes a rule. Thus, each author draws a static contrast between Judaism and the New Covenant and moves in the direction of a revival of Valentinian Gnosticism (now in Hegel). See *Mysterium Paschale*, pp. 61–63.

307. *GL6*, pp. 385–86.

308. *GL6*, p. 388.

309. See Michael Wyschogrod, *The Body of Faith: God in the People Israel* (Lanham, MD: Rowman and Littlefield, 1996), pp. 17–21.

310. *GL6*, p. 395; Ex. 4:22.

311. Moreover, the divine wrath on Egypt and mercy on Israel does not represent, he argues, a simple two-sided justice akin to what he finds in the Wisdom or even apocalyptic literature. Instead, divine wrath functions here as the other side of divine election and mercy. God destroys Egypt's first-born only as a function of sparing the first born of the oppressed targeted by the Pharaoh (*GL6*, 396; cf. 396 n.12).

312. He also reads ancient sources in light of the covenant, but that would take us afield of our objectives here.

313. *GL6*, pp. 303–304.

314. Although he does argue that salvation history comes to a halt in the post-exilic period. What this means for post-biblical Judaism will be discussed in our next chapter.

315. Hans Urs von Balthasar, *The God Question and Modern Man*, trans. Hilda Graef (New York: Seabury Press, 1967).

316. *GL5*, p. 11.

317. See George Lindbeck, "Messiahship and Incarnation: Particularity and Universality Are Reconciled," in *Who Do You Say That I AM? Confessing the Mystery of Christ*, ed. John C. Cavadini and Laura Holt (Notre Dame, IN: University of Notre Dame Press, 2004), pp. 63–86.

Chapter Three

318. *Martin Buber and Christianity*, p. 95.

319. Hans Urs von Balthasar, *Explorations in Theology, vol. II: Spouse of the Word*, trans. John Saward (San Francisco: Ignatius Press, 1991). The relevant essay is "The Church and Israel," trans. A.V. Littledale, pp. 289–301.

320. See *TD4*, "Israel as the Model," pp. 211–221.

321. *GL1*, p. 647.

322. *GL7*, p. 33.

323. *GL1*, p. 647.

324. Balthasar will be careful to disassociate divine *eros* from its Platonic implications of "lack" or "need" and therefore from a Hegelian sense that God must create for God's own development. See *TD5*, pp. 79 and 83. For the resignification of *eros* through *agape*, see page 548 of my "Contesting the World and the Divine: Balthasar's Trinitarian 'Response' to Gianni Vattimo's Secular Christianity," in *Modern Theology* (October, 2007). See also *GL1*, pp. 122–123 where Balthasar quotes a long passage from Denys the Areopagite and interprets the divine *eros* as the basis for creation and covenant.

325. Balthasar discusses kenotic theologians in a variety of contexts, but for his most focused treatment, see *TD5*, pp. 223–247. He writes of Hegel that "we can still ask whether Christ is to be regarded, on the one hand, as the unique historical event or, on the other, as the necessary, the highest 'representation' of the most general law of being," p. 226. Balthasar believes Jürgen Moltmann to follow his basic line of thinking on the death of God (ibid., p. 226 n. 15). Balthasar reads

Moltmann as entangling God in the world process, and as seeing history as the actualization of the Trinity (*TD4*, p. 321). His own attempt will be to find a way to speak of God's involvement in history that gets beyond the "tragic, mythological God" of Moltmann, but also to a God more involved in human history and pathos than is Rahner's depiction (*TD4*, pp. 322–323).

326. *LPR*, pp. 415–416, and esp. pp. 433–435.

327. See *TD5*, p. 75 where Balthasar uses Heideggerian language for distinctly non-Heideggerian purposes.

328. *TD4*, pp. 211–221.

329. *TD4*, p. 333.

330. *TD4*, pp. 328–332. See also pp. 325–327 where Balthasar contends that all of the world's possibilities must be positively grounded in the reality of God. He expands on this in *TD5*, pp. 61–99 when he draws out the implications of the Scholastic axiom that the "world is from the Trinity." Balthasar's goal in his doctrine of creation is to provide temporality and the realm of creaturely becoming a positive ground in the divine relations of unity-in-difference.

331. *GL7*, p. 56.

332. *GL7*, p. 55.

333. See *Mysterium Paschale*, p. 125, where Balthasar cites Irenaeus, *Adversus Haereses* III. 18, 5–6. Passages found there include the following: "If, however, He was Himself not to suffer, but should fly away from Jesus, why did He exhort His disciples to take up the cross and follow Him ..."; "For if He did not truly suffer ... when we shall actually begin to suffer, He will seem as leading us astray, exhorting us to endure buffeting, and to turn the other cheek, if He did not Himself before us in reality suffer the same; and as He misled them by seeming to them what He was not, so does He also mislead us, by exhorting us to endure what He did not endure Himself. [In that case] we shall be even above the Master, because we suffer and sustain what our Master never bore or endured." More recently, Shusaku Endo has explored a similar reading of Christ's crucifixion in his renowned novel *Silence*.

334. *GL7*, p. 56. In Jesus' baptism, where he descends into the waters and into solidarity with all sinners, and rises up from the waters to receive the descent of the Spirit upon him, Balthasar perceives the Incarnation as "the encounter, to the point of identification, of the Israel who has been made ready and the God of the covenant who descends to Israel." Wright's text, *The Climax of the Covenant: Christ and the Law in Pauline Theology* (Minneapolis, MN: Augsburg Fortress, 1994) is, however, directly concerned with issues in Pauline interpretation, not with the Gospels themselves.

335. See *GL6*, 412–413, where the formal meaning of the resurrection is the integration of genuine time into eternity. See also David L. Schindler's "Time in Eternity, Eternity in Time: On the Contemplative-Active Life," in *Communio* 18 (Spring 1991), pp. 53–68. See also *GL1*, p. 647, where Balthasar expresses the extraordinary continuity between the covenants: " ... the Old Testament possesses the same 'rightness' or truth as the New: here there is identity, not analogy...."

336. *GL7*, p. 42.
337. *GL7*, p. 58.
338. *GL7*, p. 56.
339. *GL7*, pp. 62–63.
340. *GL7*, p. 63.
341. *GL7*, p. 64. Here Balthasar also introduces the classical notion of the "prior redemption of Mary," a must for him because Mary's faith response is perfectly adequate for the Incarnation of the Word of God (*GL7*, p. 63). Mary will also come to represent "woman" in *TD3*, thus connecting Balthasar with Irenaeus once again.
342. *GL7*, p. 74.
343. *GL7*, p. 124.
344. *GL7*, p. 126. Balthasar cites Jesus' formal authority as the presupposition for the early church's move from the Jesus of history to the Christ proclaimed (*GL7*, pp. 125–126).
345. *GL7*, p. 126.
346. *GL7*, p. 128.
347. Ibid. The authority that Jesus exhibits in judgment and salvation flows out and covers all of the created order as well. Against Marcion, Balthasar stresses the unity between creator and Redeemer throughout his work. The fulfillment of God's deepest intentions with respect to creation gives Jesus the authority to demand the establishment of a just order and a constant struggle against injustice and inhumanity: "active human love—individual and social, personal and acting through structures—cannot be postponed" (*GL7*, p. 129). We can recall that God's *emeth* revealed in the Old Covenant forms the basis of Israel's positive view of creation rooted in the divine promise. The new covenant, based on the divine *kenosis*, goes further in that the Son shows to the Father the goodness of creation, the Redeemer thereby justifying the creator. (See *GL7*, pp. 519 and 522–523.)
348. *GL7*, pp. 207 and 210.
349. *GL7*, p. 140.
350. It goes without saying that this is a tremendously abbreviated reading of Balthasar's biblical discussion. W.T. Dickens is an excellent source for a more detailed analysis. Balthasar is certainly interesting on the issue of poverty in scripture. The "poor" in the New Testament, he observes, can signify a variety of types, including the materially destitute and the socially belittled. On Balthasar's reading, divine grace sides with the poor and against the rich. Yet his emphasis here is on a kind of "spiritual poverty" that recognizes one's total dependence on God. In turn, spiritual poverty fosters a deep availability to God and a readiness to receive a divine commission. Perfect poverty leads to perfect obedience. Jesus demonstrates this relationship between poverty and obedience when he renounces earthly goods and power prior to engaging his own mission. Then, within this mission, poverty exhibits its various dimensions: prayer's confession of utter dependence on God, faith's full confidence and trust, and the Spirit's presence to and for the poor one who acknowledges his or

her need. In linking this poverty to obedience, however, "spiritual poverty" cannot mean a mere change of attitude. Rather, it is a recognition of one's real, ontological dependence, a requirement to become poor, and a mandate to actively and bodily take up one's own mission to the world. (See *GL7*, pp. 132–133.)

351. *GL7*, p. 164.
352. *GL7*, p. 202.
353. I have discussed this in "Contesting the World and the Divine." On Vattimo, see esp. pp. 525–539; on Altizer, see esp. pp. 535–537.
354. This treatment follows closely Cyril O'Regan's discussion in "Newman and von Balthasar: The Christological Contexting of the Numinous," in *Église et Théologie*, 26 (1995), pp. 165–202. See especially pp. 190–194.
355. *GL7*, pp. 243, 364–365, 509–510.
356. *GL7*, p. 509.
357. *GL7*, pp. 39, 218 and *GL6*, p. 302; Balthasar discusses the theme of divine hiddenness at length in *GL7*, pp. 318–389.
358. *GL7*, p. 214.
359. Nevertheless, divine *kenosis* is also ascribed to the Old Covenant: the "mystery of God's redemptive *kenosis* ... consists in the identification of the divine Logos with the man Jesus, an event that is itself in continuity with the antecedent *kenosis* of the Word of God in his covenant with Israel. (The latter continues the covenant with mankind as a whole, which is itself based on the prior creation of creatures endowed with freedom)" (*TD4*, p. 333).
360. O'Regan, "Newman and von Balthasar," p. 191.
361. See *GL1*, pp. 122–123.
362. *GL7*, pp. 229, 243, 316.
363. *GL1*, pp. 509–525, esp. 521; *GL7*, pp. 15–16, 379–380. See also the section on negative theology in *TL2*, pp. 87–123.
364. *GL7*, pp. 248–249. O'Regan once again eloquently captures Balthasar's conception: if for Balthasar, the "lyrical valorizes the moment," then "to become christoform is to surrender to the humility of prose" (O'Regan, "Newman and von Balthasar," p. 194).
365. "In this, kenosis—as the surrender of the 'form of God'—becomes the decisive act of the love of the Son, who translates his being begotten by the Father (and in this, his dependence on him) into the expressive form of creaturely obedience; but the whole Trinity remains involved in this act, the Father by sending out the Son and abandoning him on the Cross, and the Spirit by uniting them now only in the expressive form of the separation" (*GL7*, p. 214). Balthasar makes these claims with some trepidation regarding a Gnosticism whereby the necessity of *kenosis* is deduced philosophically. This action on God's part indeed reveals something of the "law of the immanent Trinity" but is utterly non-deducible except from the ever-greater God's self-disclosure (*GL7*, p. 215). Christ's vicarious suffering is effective because, as incarnate love, he bears human sin and therefore becomes the object and substitutionary receptacle of divine wrath (*GL7*, p. 207).

366. *GL7*, p. 225.
367. *TD4*, p. 334.
368. *GL7*, p. 223.
369. See *TD4*, pp. 334–336 for Balthasar's discussion. Here you will find his nuanced defense of Anselm—which is not uncritical itself—and his appropriation of the scapegoat insight of René Girard.
370. Although the motif of divine wrath is disturbing, Balthasar thinks that fidelity to Scripture requires its theological inclusion: "God is angry with the sinner on account of his sin. This is a constant theme of Scripture, from the first book to the last" (*TD4*, p. 339).
371. See Abraham J. Heschel, *The Prophets* (New York: Harper Collins, 2001). Much of the text of Part II has to do with the pathos of God in its different manifestations through the prophetic writings. For pathos in relation to divine wrath, see Part II, chapters five and six; in chapter six Heschel addresses Marcionism specifically.
372. *TD4*, pp. 341–344.
373. *TD4*, pp. 345–346.
374. Balthasar, *Spouse of the Word*, p. 290.
375. Michael Wyschogrod, *The Body of Faith: God in the People Israel* (Lanham, MD: Rowman and Littlefield, 1996).
376. See his *Buber*, p. 8.
377. See Buber, *Two Types of Faith*, pp. 11, 26, 32–35, 39–40, 44–47, 55, 77ff. and Wyschogrod, *The Body of Faith*, pp. 54–55.
378. *TD2*, p. 57.
379. Balthasar, *Spouse of the Word*, p. 291.
380. Ibid.
381. Ibid. For Balthasar, God's hardening of Israel's hearts is not exculpatory given that throughout the Old Testament such hardening is often used to express guilt and a moment in God's larger salvific plan.
382. Ibid., pp. 291–292.
383. Ibid., pp. 292 and 293.
384. Stories here include: Isaac, who is born of God's spiritual promise despite Sarah's infertility; and God's choice of Jacob over Esau, the younger twin over the older. Each of these stories exhibits a divine judgement that stresses God's freedom beyond physical or natural / cultural considerations. For Balthasar, the faithful remnant constitutes spiritual Israel, which has its roots deep in Israelite history and its fulfillment and future in the Church. The greater part of Israel, "fleshly Israel," comes to "grief in the desert, in exile and diaspora" showing that the "dialectic of election and reprobation did not take place only between the synagogue and the Church but was present already within Judaism and the Law" (ibid., p. 293).
385. Ibid. Obviously given these categories, the first Christians were both corporeally Jewish and members of Israel after the Spirit. We should also note that

"spiritual" or "spiritualization" does not for Balthasar mean incorporeal or lacking in concreteness; the Incarnation rules this view out.

386. Balthasar stresses the "whyless love" of God in *GL5* when speaking of the German mystical tradition as it moves from figures such as Angelus Silesius through Hölderlin and Martin Heidegger. See *GL5*, pp. 31, and 441.

387. *TD3*, p. 269.

388. *TD3*, pp. 382–383; cf. ibid., p. 391.

389. *Spouse of the Word*, pp. 291–292.

390. 2 Tim. 2:12-13, quoted by Balthasar in *TD3*, p. 385. From the Old Testament, Balthasar has in mind Dt. 28:62-63 and Hosea 11:8-11.

391. *TD3*, p. 399.

392. *TD3*, p. 385; Balthasar is obviously drawing upon Romans 11:26.

393. *Buber*, p. 92; cf. p. 93.

394. *TD3*, p. 389.

395. *TD4*, pp. 216 and 348.

396. Ibid.

397. Ibid. Balthasar repeats this view in *TD3*: "He [Christ] shows solidarity with the latter [Israel] precisely in that, in his person, he embodies the role allotted to all Israel in the poems of the 'Suffering Servant': he suffers on behalf of others" (p. 398).

398. *TD3*, p. 367.

399. *TD3*, p. 368.

400. *TD3*, p. 398.

401. *TD3*, p. 369.

402. *Buber*, pp. 100–101.

403. *Buber*, p. 101. Balthasar's position is not novel here, and in fact he is largely advocating a position held by Paul Démann. See *Buber*, pp. 99–102.

404. *Buber*, p. 101.

405. *Spouse of the Word*, p. 294.

406. Ibid., p. 296.

407. Ibid., p. 297.

408. *Buber*, p. 93.

409. Ibid.

410. That Christian theology of Judaism has not really progressed farther than Balthasar's book on these issues is evident in the dialogue between Avery Dulles writing in *First Things* 157 (November 2005), pp. 16–21 and Philip Cunningham writing in *Commonweal*, vol. 133: 13 (July 14, 2006): pp. 11–15. Cunningham believes that Dulles is arguing for a mission to the Jews, and he repudiates such a claim. I confess to not finding precisely that implication in Dulles' article.

411. See *Buber*, pp. 7–8.

412. See *Buber*, pp. 15–16. "Indeed one might justifiably ask whether relations between the two peoples had ever advanced beyond the point at which the Christian felt called upon to enlighten his blind and stubborn brethren and help them on the

right path; whether they ever advanced to the point of becoming an intellectual and spiritual relationship and what Buber calls a dialogue; so that the Christian might expect to receive something vital and alive from the Jew, something more than the letter of the Scriptures as they were handed down, something that could not be divorced from the living voice, very necessary perhaps, and bearing upon salvation" (p. 15). Balthasar then proceeds to give a scathing account of supercessionism and observe that gentiles are admonished by Paul to humility in that they are grafted into the holy root *para physein* or against nature and not through their merit. See ibid., pp. 15–19.

413. *Buber*, pp. 7–8.

414. Martin Buber, *Two Types of Faith*, pp. 11, 26, 32–35, 39–40, 44–47, 55, 77ff.

415. *Buber*, p. 109 and *TD3*, pp. 366–367.

416. Hans Urs von Balthasar, "Liberation Theology in the Light of Salvation History," in James V. Schall (ed.), *Liberation Theology in Latin America* (San Francisco: Ignatius Press, 1982), pp. 131–146.

417. See also *TL2*, p. 88.

418. *TD4*, p. 440.

419. Yet he also sees Marx as a much-needed corrective to Christian nonchalance with respect to human need and a crucial Jewish riposte to Hegelian anti-Semitism. See *GL5*, p. 596.

420. *TD4*, p. 440.

421. Balthasar notes, for instance, Buber's own support for a utopian Israel; he is careful to note, however, that Buber repudiated Marxism *per se*, and supported a kind of agrarian, cooperative socialism based on the period of the judges.

422. This is the gist of my "Contesting the World and the Divine: Balthasar's Trinitarian Response to Gianni Vattimo's Secular Christianity," in *Modern Theology* 23, no. 4 (October 2007), pp. 525–559.

423. *TD2*, p. 427.

424. Ibid.

425. *Buber*, p. 108.

426. *Buber*, p. 107.

427. *Buber*, p. 109.

428. He notes, for instance, that Stalin was a former Christian. *TD4*, p. 440.

429. *Buber*, p. 23.

430. *TD2*, p. 426.

Chapter Four

431. See, for example, Luke Timothy Johnson's *Among the Gentiles: Greco-Roman Religion and Christianity* (New Haven: Yale University Press, 2009). One reason for this is Balthasar's use of Martin Hengel's work, considered essential to the elimination of the Judaism-Hellenism dichotomy by his arguments that in fact

Palestinian Judaism is already rife with Hellenistic influence; another is Balthasar's own extensive reading in the original literature. Johnson adverts to the importance of Hengel's work (p. 28).

432. *ET1*, p. 44. Balthasar removes the patristic view that Plato learned from Moses, but he follows Clement of Alexandria, for instance, in his view that "alongside the Jewish revelation history in its clearly visible course, there proceeded a gentile salvation history whose course was obscure...."

433. *GL1*, p. 26. See also D. C. Schindler's very helpful discussion of Balthasar's concept of form in his *Hans Urs von Balthasar and the Dramatic Structure of Truth* (New York: Fordham University Press, 2004), pp. 12–17.

434. *GL1*, p. 122.

435. *ET1*, p. 161.

436. *GL4*, pp. 11–12.

437. *GL1*, p. 151.

438. *TL1*, pp. 38–39. D. C. Schindler argues against Ben Quash that, for Balthasar, the dissolution of form is the central problem of modernity, and that only with form can there be drama. See Schindler, *Hans Urs von Balthasar and the Dramatic Structure of Truth*, pp. 22–23.

439. *GL1*, p. 145.

440. *GL6*, pp. 99–100.

441. Balthasar argues that the objectivity of the form of revelation, which will give it somewhat of an extrinsic feeling, comes in part from the fact that humanity is distanced from God in sin and will feel this revelation, whether in the Old Testament as law and prophecy or in the New as the Incarnation and the ecclesial Word, also as judgment (*GL1*, p. 452). Balthasar reads Thomas to say that in the prelapsarian state, God's voice comes through grace in the voices of "nature" and the "heart" (ibid.).

442. In this sense, Balthasar's engagement with pre-Christian metaphysics (myth, philosophy, and religion) calls to mind a number of contemporary approaches. Balthasar's apologetic, designed to tell the story of Western metaphysics in such a way as to disclose the *aporias* in these metaphysical discourses for which Christianity can provide both an account and an answer, recalls Alasdair MacIntyre's view of how one might argue across philosophical-ethical traditions in his *Whose Justice? Which Rationality?* (Notre Dame, IN: University of Notre Dame Press, 1989). One difference might be pointed out. Whereas Balthasar explicitly grounds his view of integration in Catholic tradition and its general *ethos*, MacIntyre would seem to divorce the *kind* of argumentation he advocates from any tradition and grounds it in rationality itself. Balthasar also agrees with Francis Clooney, S.J. and Paul Griffiths that truth issues are essential to inter-religious discourse and not to be sidelined through appeals to mystical experience or epistemically thin accounts of religion. See Clooney, *Hindu God, Christian God: How Reason Helps Break Down the Boundaries between Religions* (Oxford: Oxford University Press, 2001) and Paul Griffiths, *An Apology for Apologetics:*

A Study in the Logic of Interreligious Dialogue (Maryknoll, NY: Orbis Books, 1991).

443. *GL4*, p. 15.

444. It is quite inaccurate to say that Balthasar sports a "blindness to the idea that all natural and social realities already exist within God and manifest God in the specific details of their natural and social reality" unless this means that somehow all social formations are, as such, representations of grace beyond theological criticism. This passage is quoted from Francis X. Clooney, S.J., *Hindu God, Christian God: How Reason Helps Break Down the Boundaries between Religions* (Oxford: Oxford University Press, 2001), p. 90. While I am tempted to accept Clooney's judgments on Balthasar's treatments of Hinduism (that is, that they are *a priori* caricatures, limited to a particular school of Non-Dualist Hinduism, and that Balthasar shows little experience with Hindu texts), I hesitate to do so because at least one of Clooney's claims actually supports Balthasar's view. Clooney is right to say that Balthasar differentiates between the seeking of God (extra-biblical religion) and God's finding of humanity (Judaism and Christianity); but Clooney confirms this basic idea in his own discussion: "Unlike von Balthasar, Desika and Arul Nandi do not formulate the argument for true religion and the recognition of the true God in terms of an encounter with the revealing God.... Rather, they seek the best possible explanation of the world in relation to God and accordingly the most adequate identification of the God who is explanatory of the world" (ibid., p. 89). Balthasar of course recognizes the importance of theologizing about God from the world (and *Theo-Logic* 1 is where he does so at length). Thus the "upward" movement of human reason is to be embraced and judged by the "downward" movement of divine glory and revelation. Clooney also discusses Balthasar's claim that non-Christian mysticism will always suffer a demythologization of its revelatory texts by way of some form of philosophy. Thus, it will not integrate, as does Christ, the form of the divine and finite form (and thus aesthetics). Instead, Balthasar is claiming, philosophical religion will de-mythologize and religion will die away. It is not clear that Clooney sees what Balthasar is saying here. Balthasar is arguing that outside of Christianity, the intense unification of God with a particular historical form that can be recognized as an eschatological revelation, and, therefore, as an unsurpassable revelation, does not occur; consequently, representations of revelation in Hindu myths will be more nearly allegorical than incarnational. Allegory will then yield to theological rationalism, and perhaps some form of identity philosophy. Whether this progression actually takes place or not, I do not know; Clooney is correct to say that Balthasar does not make a substantial argument through a reading of Hindu texts (though Balthasar does cite Hindu theological terms more frequently than Clooney thinks). But neither does Clooney's discussion militate against this point. Indeed, his movement between Non-Dualist and Desika's brand of monotheism that does not discuss Divine self-disclosure as a personal encounter would tend toward Balthasar's position.

445. *GL4*, p. 32. See also his claim that "The biblical eros-motif, expounded in the relation to Christ and his Bride (Church-Mary-the soul), leads both to the heart of the distinctively Christian mysteries ... and also to the deepest justification of the *spolatio Aegyptorum*, i.e., *Platonicorum*" (ibid., p. 322). See also *TD3*, p. 167: Jesus' universal mission is the "point of convergence of all the particular missions that aim towards this universality, of all the *logoi spermatikoi*, especially of the Old Covenant."

446. *GL4*, p. 14.

447. *GL4*, p. 18. See also Balthasar's essay, "The Christian Form," in *ET4* where he names the Hegelian dialectic as the principle form-dissolving system and the chief challenge to Christianity. See pp. 50–51 and 63.

448. *GL4*, p. 19.

449. *TL1*, p. 129.

450. Ibid.

451. See Jürgen Moltmann, *The Crucified God: The Cross of Christ as the Foundation and Criticism of Christian Theology* (San Francisco: Harper, 1991), p. 7. Moltmann seems to think of contradiction as the ground for likeness or communion, whereas Balthasar posits analogy as the ground for the perception of ever-greater dissimilarity. It is the latter, I would argue, that better protects against an identity philosophy.

452. I have argued elsewhere, for instance, that Balthasar incorporates elements of Jewish criticisms of Christianity into his own criticisms of Christian philosophy and theology. See Anthony Sciglitano, "Hans Urs von Balthasar and 'The Jewish Critique': Intramural Appropriation and Response," *Toronto Journal of Theology* 14, no. 2 (1998), pp. 177–196.

453. This assessment of modern philosophy does not mean for Balthasar that glory has found no one to represent it in modernity. But the representatives of glory will more often come from the areas of poetry, art, and the natural sciences than from philosophy and theology (*GL5*, p. 27). Rilke, Claudel, and Péguy each offer a reflection of glory or at least the contemplative stance necessary to represent glory through their work.

454. *GL5*, pp. 247, 249, and 261.

455. *ET4*, p. 16.

456. *GL4*, p. 101.

457. Balthasar writes, "But in Euripides, there stand beyond all these who are given up to their fate, those who give themselves up, who willingly sacrifice themselves" (*GL4*, p. 112); "But the major emphasis ... is peculiar to Euripides: that of a willing, sacrificial death" (*GL4*, p. 142).

458. Important in this regard is one of Balthasar's favored exegetes, Martin Hengel, and his book on the Atonement. See Hengel, *The Atonement: The Origins of the Doctrine in the New Testament* (Eugene, OR: Wipf and Stock, 2007).

459. *GL4*, p. 70.

460. *GL4*, p. 50.

461. *GL4*, p. 102.
462. *GL4*, p. 77.
463. We should point out that for Balthasar Greek metaphysics still remain a "whole level down" vis-à-vis the Old Covenant. This is because the Old Covenant maintains much more strongly its commitment to divine transcendence and freedom, to monotheism, and has a discernible movement towards the New Covenant that is pre-eminent in giving the form of Christ its legibility. We will discuss this later in the chapter.
464. *GL4*, p. 78.
465. *GL4*, p. 79.
466. *GL1*, pp. 143–144.
467. We should be careful here. Both the epiphanic moment without an essential ground in Being and the universal that does not present itself in some particular form are abstract. Hegel too speaks of sense knowledge as the most abstract kind of knowledge. What Balthasar is moving toward is the idea, expressed in *TL1*, that in a particular form, the essence gives itself to the knower and the particular form surrenders itself to reveal its own essence, its universality; from the side of the knower, the knower must surrender himself to the thing known, as this thing gives itself to be known. In other words, knowing the world is a mutual dialogue between the world that gives and surrenders itself to be known (and always gives more than we can absorb at any one time, for the potential in a species is never exhausted by a particular of the species, and so remains unknown in its giving) and the knower who is given over to the world, to being. Thus, it is not merely the image that is epiphanic, nor merely the essence, but both, together, and the act of knowing that form an analogy to the God who surrenders his Son, the Son who surrenders himself, takes on the formlessness of sin, but then gains a new form in the resurrection, and so can carry the world into the ground of his image, into the Father and assume time into eternity. In this analogy between the world and the economic Trinitarian relations, which presupposes an analogy to the immanent Trinity, Balthasar shows us how the world itself is dialogical and theophanic, not in isolated moments or in static essences alone, but in Being's giving itself over and letting itself be known, and in the knower's performing of an analogous kind of self-forgetting in service to this order to bring this disclosure to fruition in knowledge and action. So, God has made a covenant with Being, with all the world, through Christ so that the world can be properly seen in Christ and shows Christ in everyday, prosaic life, in each act of knowledge and in each being.
468. *GL4*, p. 218.
469. *GL4*, p. 12.
470. *GL1*, p. 145. Balthasar argues that this is the fate of theology that takes up the direction of nominalism and divorces itself from metaphysical thought. Of course nominalism threatens form. See *GL5*, pp. 16–21.
471. Richard Viladesau gives this impression in his book *Theological Aesthetics: God in Imagination, Beauty, and Art* (Oxford: Oxford University Press, 1999).

472. *GL4*, p. 156. Martin Heidegger's commentaries on Parmenides and Heraclitus extol the "strife" inherent to Being as it arises in the early Greek thinkers (normally called pre-Socratic). Heidegger approves of this agonistic interpretation of Being because it does not allow Being to become the less wondrous and more technologically domitable reality of essence. Balthasar seems to be in agreement with Heidegger's reading, but against his evaluation of the pre-Socratics. Jacques Derrida sees violence in the origins of philosophy as well: " ... that philosophy died one day, within history, or that it has always fed on its own agony, on the violent way it opens history by opposing itself to nonphilosophy... " (*Writing and Difference*, trans. Alan Bass (Chicago: University of Chicago Press, 1978), p. 79).

473. *GL4*, p. 156. Balthasar cites Plato's LawsIII.701C for this passage.

474. *GL4*, p. 182.

475. *GL4*, p. 156; cf. *GL4*, p. 182: "Again, prayer falls away...."

476. *GL4*, p. 155.

477. *GL4*, p. 156. Cf. p. 213 where he is summing up the terminus of Plato's philosophy of beauty: "This rounds off an aesthetic ethic immanent in the world in which the divine as well as the human appears in a final identity as a harmony of balance; the last glimmer of a revelation from above ... fades, or rather passes over into the macrocosmic harmony which is accessible to philosophical inquiry." This too will have important and disturbing political consequences. See 213 n. 404 and p.175 where Balthasar critiques Plato's inner-worldly vision of utopia in *The Republic*. The critique is of course not new. Balthasar notes that on Plato's view the "freedom of the individual and the worth of love must be overridden in the interests of a merciless systematic" (p. 175).

478. In *Introduction to Metaphysics*, Heidegger is concerned to reject a modern and contemporary philosophical tendency to read Platonic and Aristotelian thought as the proper ground for and perfection of earlier Greek thinking on Being. This means for Heidegger that *physis* must be related to *logos* in such a way that *logos* does not become an atemporal reality or series of blueprints of which beings in time are only copies. Idea then becomes the "sole and decisive interpretation of being," and this represents a "falling off" (p. 182). The move of *physis* into Latin (both Rome and Christian middle ages) and from that translation into modern philosophy, for Heidegger, represents a movement of decline, "deformation" and "decay," from *physis* as emergent energy or "blossoming-forth" to *natura*, a movement by which "the actual philosophical force of the Greek word is destroyed" (p. 13). Modern and contemporary philosophy and science, he thinks, consider Being in terms of beings and thinking in terms not of contemplation or wonder or questioning, but in terms of calculation and clever quantification. Emergence and epiphany, surprise, and becoming all become devalued (see esp. pp. 46–49 and p. 63). A movement to interpret *physis* as *ousia* / substance is equally detrimental on Heidegger's view. See Martin Heidegger, *Contributions to Philosophy (from Enowning)*, trans. Parvis Emad and Kenneth

Maly (Indianapolis: Indiana University Press, 1999), p. 156 #113. The movement into Latin is not incidental to this decline for Heidegger. He views Greek and German as properly philosophical languages; Latin is not, and presumably the same can be said for English and Russian. Heidegger, then, sees himself as engaged in a "vocation" to bring Western civilization back to its primordial energies in the early "pre-Socratic" Greeks by connecting the Greek language of Being with German and dispensing with whatever intervened—a destruction for a re-construction. *Physis* designates a kind of power of emergence and *logos* the limitation or "gathering" of that power to a particular *essent*. Balthasar shares many of Heidegger's concerns, but not his philhellenism, philo-Germanicism, or his reading of the Western tradition.

479. *GL4*, pp. 178 and 200.

480. *GL4*, p. 179.

481. One could also point out Balthasar's reading of Moses as a mediator who goes up the Mountain to receive the word of God, and then descends to bring this to his people.

482. *GL4*, pp. 173, 183, 206–208.

483. *GL1*, p. 144. Balthasar's discussion of Plato is complex. There is no doubt that he sees in the philosophical *eros* toward total knowledge a need to enclose reality in a pre-made system that reason can comprehend. The human will take on a divine aspect in Platonic philosophy to justify a kind of noetic or epistemological still point by which the philosopher can judge the realm of becoming. In this sense, philosophy will often be the enemy of genuine revelation and divine-world difference.

484. *GL4*, p. 245: "It cannot be said that in the human longing to succeed in saying an unconditional 'Yes' there is concealed the kind of arrogance that cannot put up with a defective world, or that is confident in its own power to perfect it. Even for the philosophers the contemplation of the 'starry heavens above,' which is primary for the classical mind, is not connected with the secondary sense of the 'moral law within' in such a way that the individual as such is allowed to claim, in Promethean style, any sort of identity, internal or external, with the order of the cosmos.... " This is important for Balthasar because it means that pre-Christian thought forms are in fact redeemable; any system that argues against the divine-world difference, and this will be true of many post-Christian Western thought forms, is unredeemable.

485. *GL4*, pp. 195–196.

486. *TL1*, p. 7. Balthasar goes on to deepen the point: "In order to be a serious theologian, one must also, indeed, first, be a philosopher; one must—precisely also in the light of revelation—have immersed oneself in the mysterious structures of creaturely being ... " (ibid., p. 8).

487. *Theology of Karl Barth*, p. 291. Balthasar makes the same point in *TL1*, pp. 11–12: " ... the supernatural has impregnated nature so deeply that there is simply no way to reconstruct it in its pure state (*natura pura*)."

488. Ibid, p. 280. Emmanuel Levinas' *Totality and Infinity* comes to mind as an important example here.
489. Ibid, p. 257.
490. Ibid. See also pp. 251 and 252.
491. *TL1*, p. 50.
492. *TL1*, p. 217.
493. Interestingly, Balthasar calls upon science to support his view that a meaningful substratum lies beneath and within surface appearance, although he views the laws of science as finite. See *TL1*, p. 84.
494. *TL1*, p. 50.
495. See Heidegger, *Introduction to Metaphysics*, p. 13. There is a parallel here with Derrida's view, expressed in a number of places. See, for instance, Derrida's discussion of Greek philosophical patrimony in *Writing and Difference*, p. 81. See also *Of Spirit: Heidegger and the Question*, trans. Geoffrey Bennington and Rachel Bowlby (Chicago: University of Chicago Press, 1989), pp. 4–5, 29, 32.
496. The theme of ontological excess permeates the entirety of *Theo-Logic*. See *TL1*, pp. 85, 107, and 142 for examples.
497. *TL1*, pp. 49–50.
498. *TL1*, p. 87.
499. *TL1*, p. 141.
500. *TL1*, p. 39.
501. Ibid.
502. *TL1*, p. 47.
503. *TL1*, p. 159.
504. *TL1*, pp. 158–159.
505. *TL1*, pp. 149–153. Balthasar is here working with the Thomistic *conversio ad phantasma* but giving it a spiritual sense reading.
506. *TL1*, p. 54.
507. *TL1*, p. 164.
508. *TL1*, p. 51.
509. *TL1*, p. 53.
510. *TL1*, p. 55.
511. *TL1*, pp. 147–148.
512. *TL1*, p. 145.
513. *TL1*, pp. 142–143.
514. *TL1*, pp. 172, 173, 202.
515. *TL1*, p. 145: "The truth is in motion; it presses upon the mind and calls the conscience to decision."
516. *TL1*, p. 136.
517. *TL1*, p. 137.
518. Ibid. "Since the world provides only formless material, consciousness seeks salvation in itself and looks to itself to give form."
519. *TL1*, p. 145.

520. *TL1*, p. 127.
521. Ibid.
522. *TL1*, p. 124.
523. *GL4*, p. 216.
524. *GL4*, p. 218.
525. *GL4*, p. 86.
526. *GL4*, p. 243.
527. Ibid. Balthasar observes "syncretism" inherent in the biblical use of various forms of contemporary discourse (i.e., Stoic diatribe, the Johannine Logos, first-century uses of political conceptions such as *parousia* and *epiphaneia*).
528. *GL4*, p. 244.
529. *GL4*, pp. 216–220.
530. From a completely different point of view, Jonathan Israel makes essentially the same claim regarding Spinoza in his work on the Enlightenment. See Jonathan I. Israel, *Enlightenment Contested: Philosophy, Modernity, and the Emancipation of Man, 1670–1752* (Oxford: Oxford University Press, 2006), p. 45. For Israel, there is no sense in which Spinoza's God-as-Nature can be theistic.
531. *GL4*, p. 238.
532. *GL4*, p. 241.
533. Ibid.
534. Ibid.
535. Of course Plotinus is not chronologically pre-Christian, but in Balthasar's view Plotinus is untouched by Christian revelation and so is philosophically pre-Christian.
536. *GL4*, p. 291.
537. It is important to recognize, however, that Balthasar is willing to take up this Neo-Platonic schema only conditionally, that is, under critique from New Testament revelation. This leads him, in his book on Barth, to praise Thomas and criticize Origen for insufficiently adjusting his neo-Platonism (*Theology of Karl Barth*, pp. 67 and 261). Whereas Patristic theology, he argues, had yet to formally differentiate nature from grace, and enacted its theology from the concrete order of revelation, Thomas helps foster the conceptual differentiation not only between nature and grace, but also between philosophy and theology. Thomas, however, does not escape unscathed, as he structures his thought upon an egress-regress philosophical foundation rather than upon those doctrines central to theology, namely, the doctrines of Trinity, Christ, and Church. On Balthasar's reading, it is not the events of revelation themselves that are most significant to Thomas, but the eternal wisdom to which these events point, which for Thomas is the real object of theology. *Theology of Karl Barth*, pp. 262–264.
538. Balthasar takes the idea of "situation" very seriously, as one can see from *TL1*. "Situation" designates the deep contingency of knowing and the importance of context for all understanding. In this sense, for Balthasar no appeal to "nature" or "essence" as a separated reality that merely judges or imposes itself on the particulars of a context can be appropriate.

539. *In the Fullness of Faith*, p. 27.

540. *GL7*, p. 13.

541. Although inclusion of the material in *TD1* would take us too far afield, here too Balthasar shows the integrative nature of his enterprise. Lyric and Epic are not to cancel each other out for him, but rather ought to be integrated and maintained in a higher form of dramatic theater. D. C. Schindler makes this important point against Ben Quash, who reads Balthasar's use of Hegel's categories as a kind of acceptance of Hegel's view of those categories and their relation. The contrast between the Hegelian dissolution of form in an evolutionary dynamic and Balthasar's integration of form is important to *Theo-Drama*. See Schindler, *Hans Urs von Balthasar and the Dramatic Structure of Truth*, p. 23.

542. *GL1*, pp. 142, 182–183.

543. *TD3*, p. 417.

544. *TD3*, pp. 417–418. Balthasar quotes Augustine to the effect that the "Christian religion had always existed in ancient times, and was never unknown, right from the beginning of human history until Christ appeared in the flesh" (*TD3*, pp. 417-418 n. 37, quoting Augustine, *Retractions*. I. 13, 3).

545. *GL1*, pp. 184–185.

546. *GL1*, pp. 182–184.

547. *ET4*, p. 89.

548. *ET4*, p. 92.

549. *GL4*, p. 243.

550. *TL3*, p. 255 (Jn. 3:16, 17:2, 12:32, 10:16 and Acts 2:17). He also cites Joel 3:1f. but notes that this may refer to Israel alone.

551. *TL3*, p. 255. He cites DS 1880, 2428ff. In the current English edition, the numbers are DS 993 and 1378ff.

552. *TL3*, p. 258. Balthasar cites a number of scripture passages here. For Acts 10:2, 10:44–47 it is clear that the Holy Spirit is not restricted to Jewish believers or to the Church already constituted but descends upon the gentiles prior to baptism. Balthasar also cites Acts 11:18 and 15:8.

553. *TL3*, p. 257.

554. Balthasar cites the French Revolution and Karl Marx, among others, as holding to truths originally Christian but frequently lost sight of in Christianity and detached from what gives them their fullness.

555. So far as I know, this term is not found in Patristic material, but it makes perfect sense as an extension if indeed the Spirit is the Spirit of Christ.

556. Friedrich Schleiermacher, *The Christian Faith* (Philadelphia: Fortress Press, 1976), pp. 60–62, §12.

557. See Kant's *Religion within the Limits of Reason Alone*, trans. Theodore M. Greene and Hoyt H. Hudson (New York: Harper and Row, 1960), pp. 116–117. Franklin H. Littell's *The Crucifixion of the Jews: The Failure of Christians to Understand the Jewish Experience* (Macon, GA: Mercer University Press, 1996) offers

similar criticisms of Kant and Schleiermacher based on a modern aversion to particularity and the singularity of events.

558. In his renowned book, *An Interpretation of Religion: Human Responses to the Transcendent*, Hick writes, "A key premise for me is the (so far as we can tell) salvific parity of the great world religions ... " (p. xxxiii).

559. *TD3*, p. 422.

560. *ET4*, p. 92.

561. Ibid.

562. Ibid., p. 93.

563. *ET4*, p. 97; see also *TL3*, pp. 50–54.

564. *ET4*, p. 89.

565. See also Christopher Morse, *Not Every Spirit: A Christian Dogmatics of Disbelief* (Valley Forge, PA: Trinity Press International, 1994), pp. 34–37. Morse presents a sermon in which Israel's role is replaced by a mythical Germany that provides the "prehistory" for their new messiah.

566. *TL3*, p. 264. A new book called *The Aryan Jesus: Christian Theologians and the Bible in Nazi Germany* (Princeton, NJ: Princeton University Press, 2010) by Susannah Heschel observes the extent to which the German Christians felt a need to exclude "the Old Testament, John's Gospel, and all references to Jesus as servant or lamb of God." (See John Connelly's February 26, 2010 *Commonweal* review entitled "Hitler's Gospel"; the quote is from his text). See also Michael Burleigh's *Sacred Causes: The Clash of Religion and Politics, from the Great War to the War on Terror* (London: HarperCollins, 2006).

567. Balthasar points to "Christendom" as another example of the loss of prophetic critique; the issue here is a "statist" view of Christian culture (*ET4*, pp. 95 and 276). For a similar ecclesial self-criticism, see *TL3*, pp. 265–266. And he also warns against the danger of seeing the city of Rome as having any kind of theological significance. This would be another conflation of culture and covenant. For Balthasar, Rome should not be considered a homeland akin to that of Jerusalem in the Old Covenant. No such Holy Land is possible for Christians in the wake of the New Covenant and the Resurrection (*ET4*, p. 65).

568. Balthasar believes that if religions prior to Christ had been given a "supernatural existential," it would seem that they would be more likely to maintain a "personal" understanding of God. But he does not think that in fact this is what happens, even though it is obvious that in many religions a personal view finds expression. Often, this personal view is seen as a stage to get beyond, just as philosophers in the West will frequently view mythology as a form to be thoroughly rationalized. (See *TD3*, 414–415.) This claim strikes me as a difficult one to verify. While it would be true that the philosophical schools in Hinduism, for instance, seek to "purify" ritual philosophically or speculatively, the relation between this philosophical Hinduism and Vaishnavism would not be analogous to that between Christianity and Gnosticism in the West, but rather two very different religious traditions. So far as I know, Vaishnavism never moves toward the impersonal divine.

569. See Karl Rahner, *Hearer of the Word: Laying the Foundation for a Philosophy of Religion*, trans. Joseph Donceel (New York: Continuum, 1994), pp. 52–53.

570. See Rahner, "Anonymous Christians," in *Theological Investigations*, vol. VI, trans. Karl-H. Kruger and Boniface Kruger (Baltimore: Helicon Press, 1969), pp. 391–392. Rahner here discusses the possibility of degrees of membership in the Church in terms of a "descending order from the explicitness of baptism into a non-official and anonymous Christianity which can hold and should yet be called Christianity in a meaningful sense" (p. 391). Elsewhere, he also recognizes that Christianity in its "full sense" does involve as one of its factors a conscious awareness of faith, an explicit creed, and a constitution of the Church as a society. See "Anonymous Christianity and the Missionary Task of the Church," *Theological Investigations*, vol. XII, trans. David Bourke (London: Darton, Longman and Todd, 1974), p. 165.

571. See Lucas Lamadrid, "Anonymous or Analogous Christians? Rahner and von Balthasar on Naming the Non-Christian," *Modern Theology* 11, no. 3 (July 1995), p. 373; cf. Rahner, "Christianity and the Non-Christian Religions," *Theological Investigations*, vol. V, trans. Karl-H Kruger (Baltimore: Helicon Press, 1966), pp. 119, 121, and especially 125–126.

572. See Rahner, *Foundations of Christian Faith: Introduction to the Idea of Christianity*, trans. William Dych, (NY: Seabury, 1978), pp. 126–133.

573. See especially his discussion in *ET*4, pp. 74–77.

574. *ET*4, p. 75.

575. Another way to think of this is to say that a philosophical *apophaticism* comes to govern biblical content and *cataphatic* revelation, even if that revelation reveals a *mysterium* beyond conceptual grasp. Of course Rahner believes the Trinity is behind this revelation, but Balthasar worries that, once again, the Kantian conceptual pairing endangers the mystery that is also the God of revelation. Balthasar's discussion of Negative theology, to which he gives a decidedly biblical thrust in *Theo-Logic* 2, is among his most thought-provoking discourses.

576. *TD*4, pp. 274–277; Rahner thinks that this doctrine is problematic on the same grounds that Kant thought so, namely, that it endangers moral responsibility, and also on the grounds of divine immutability. Rahner is concerned not to see God as having his mind changed from angry to reconciled through Christ's obedience. See *Foundations of the Christian Faith*, trans. William Dych (New York: Crossroad, 1989), pp. 219, 254–255. The Pauline notion of expiation, Rahner contends, should be viewed as a "legitimate but secondary interpretation of the fact that in the death and resurrection of Jesus God's salvific will reaches its historical manifestation as victorious and irreversible, and thereby is itself definitively present in the world" (p. 255).

577. Balthasar, *The Theology of Karl Barth: Exposition and Interpretation*, trans. Edward T. Oakes, S.J. (San Francisco: Ignatius Press, 1992), p. 287.

578. The phrase "literate spokespersons" is taken from Paul Griffiths' *An Apology for Apologetics*.

579. Balthasar is aware that if Jews adhere to the Covenant, and thus to the transcendent God of Israel revealed throughout their life of worship and practice,

then there can be a kind of harmonious form of vertical and horizontal; the problem is that, as Michael Wyschogrod, for an entirely different purpose, notes, one need not adhere to this covenant to be Jewish. One can be an atheist and remain Jewish. Balthasar thinks that modern utopian movements sometimes take advantage of the Jewish futural thrust and dispense with covenantal norms including a transcendent God.

580. *ET4*, pp. 228 and 237.

581. *No Bloodless Myth: A Guide through Balthasar's Dramatics* (London: Continuum International Publishing Group, 2000).

582. I have written about this previously. See "Contesting the World and the Divine: Balthasar's Trinitarian 'Response' to Gianni Vattimo's Secular Christianity," in *Modern Theology* 23, no. 4 (October 2007), pp. 525–559.

583. I get this image from Aeschylus' *Prometheus Bound*.

584. Hans Urs von Balthasar, *Bernanos: An Ecclesial Existence*, trans. Erasmo Leiva-Merikakis (San Francisco: Ignatius Press, 1996), p. 179.

585. *TD3*, p. 368.

586. *Buber*, p. 101.

Index

a posteriori xv, 81, 111, 145, 159
a priori xxiv, 81, 106, 117, 118, 125
Aletheia 127, 131
Altizer, Thomas 90, 91, 103, 105
Analogy, *analogia entis* 2, 51, 138, 141
Anthropocentrism 50, 65, 78
Anti-Christian 2, 102
Anti-Gnosticism 32
Anti-humanism 63
Anti-Judaism xv, xvi, xvii, 3, 6, 16, 21, 40, 41, 72, 108
Anti-Marcionite x, xvii, xviii, 1, 5, 6, 24, 25, 33, 44, 50, 67, 85, 93, 126, 127, 149, 155
Anti-Marcionism ix, xx, 26, 32, 41, 127
Anti-Promethean 44, 63, 79, 90, 126
Anti-Semitism xv, xvi, xvii, xx, 6, 33, 45, 102, 108
Anti-theism 13, 17, 102
Apocalyptic 12, 14, 20, 36, 40, 45, 53, 54, 62, 73, 77, 78, 79, 91, 139, 155
Apokatastasis 78
Apophatic xiv, 26, 30, 37, 38, 42, 50, 58, 131, 132, 160
    Extreme, pp. 132; pedagogy, pp. 6, 37, 81, 151
Architectonic xi
Atheist 2, 24, 29, 102
Balthasar, Hans Urs von ix
Barth, Karl 12, 32, 36, 44, 47, 52, 55, 65, 97, 125, 133, 137, 151, 152, 160
Begriff 26, 28, 42
Biblical integrity 3
Bloch, Ernst 24, 33
Buber, Martin 82, 94, 98, 99, 100, 105
Bultmann, Rudolf 28, 36, 121, 133
Camus, Albert 4, 23
Canon 3, 6, 7, 28, 44, 50, 54, 65, 74, 128, 151, 155
Cataphatic 30, 37, 38
Catholicism 1, 136, 163
Chesed 59, 61, 88, 89

Christ xi, xiii, xiv, xv, xvii, xix, xxiii, xxiv, 4, 5, 11, 13, 14, 15, 19, 25, 31, 32, 33, 35, 36, 38, 39, 44, 45, 46, 51, 54, 56, 59, 63, 64, 70, 71, 72, 73, 76, 77, 79, 81, 82, 83, 85, 86, 88, 90, 92, 93, 95, 96, 97, 98, 99, 100, 102, 103, 106, 107, 108, 109, 112, 113, 114, 115, 116, 120, 133, 137, 138, 139, 140, 141, 142, 143, 146, 147, 149, 150, 151, 152, 155, 156, 157, 158

Christian theology ix, x, xiv, xvii, xxi, 2, 23, 30, 76, 100, 107, 114, 122, 136, 145, 158, 160

Christian triumphalism 2

Christian-Jewish relations 3, 150

Christocentrism xvi, 111, 118, 146, 150, 152, 155

Christology x, xii, xv, xvi, xviii, xxii, 3, 4, 35, 36, 37, 58, 83, 104, 111, 126, 139

Circumincessio 61

Clement of Alexandria xviii, 6, 27, 111

Clooney, Francis x, xi

Correctness (*justesse*) 67

Cosmocentric 8, 9, 11, 13, 17, 23, 41, 146

Cosmos theion 11

Covenant ix, x, xvi, xvii, xviii, xix, xx, xxi, xxii, xxiv, 3, 5, 10, 12, 13, 16, 23, 24, 28, 31, 32, 37, 38, 39, 40, 41, 42, 48, 51, 52, 53, 54, 55, 56, 57, 58, 59, 60, 61, 62, 64, 65, 66, 67, 68, 69, 70, 71, 72, 73, 75, 78, 79, 81, 85, 87, 93, 95, 98, 102, 106, 107, 112, 113, 116, 118, 126, 127, 131, 138, 140, 141, 149, 155, 156

Dabar, see: Word (*dabar*)

De Lubac, Henri xx, xxi, 1, 4, 12, 17, 19, 21, 44, 63, 103

Dialogue x, xvi, xvii, xviii, 11, 22, 62, 67, 100, 106, 107, 108, 113, 114, 118, 119, 121, 123, 126, 129, 130, 134, 141, 142, 151, 159, 160

Dinoia, Joseph xi

Disclosure xiv, 23, 46, 54, 57, 58, 60, 62, 66, 68, 69, 71, 73, 87, 88, 89, 91, 113, 114, 116, 123, 130, 136, 137, 150, 155, 160

Disenchantment 10, 14, 17

Divine **Grace**, xii, 27, 66; **kenosis**, 10, 39, 82, 83, 84, 88, 91; **mystery**, 19, 20, 22, 58, 62; **personality**, 3, 20; **plurality**, 58; **sovereignty**, 55, 58, 95; **transcendence**, xiv, xvii, xx, xxii, 2, 4, 5, 8, 11, 12, 15, 21, 23, 25, 41, 49, 50, 53, 60, 76, 79, 82, 89, 90, 92, 93, 94, 103, 119, 120, 121, 123, 125, 130

Doxa 87, 91, 92, 115, 118, 134

Doxological 41, 67, 78, 126

    Existence, pp. xxiii

Dualism xix, xx, xxi, xxii, xxiii, 21, 32, 33, 36, 39, 91, 100, 105, 121
Dupuis, Jacques xv
Ecclesial **Faith**, 3, 5, 31, 34, 39; **theology**, 5, 155
Ecclesiocentric xii
El Shaddai 56
Elohim 56
Emeth 59, 88, 127, 128, 131, 132
Emptying (*kenosis*) 2, 10, 13, 14, 17, 23, 39, 82, 84, 85, 89, 90, 91, 92, 93, 108, 125, 148
En Christoi 90, 104, 105
Epicureanism 65
Eros 63, 83, 85, 114, 119, 124, 128, 135, 136
Eschatology 87, 105, 158; **Absolute**, 14, 16, 21, 22; **Judaeo-Christian**, 101; **Jewish**, 142; **messianic**, 125; **relative**, 14, 22; **realized absolute**, 14, 21; **unrealized**, 20, 103, 104; **unrealized absolute**, 14, 16;
Eternal **Reconciliation**, 52; **truth**, 51
Excess 42, 128, 130, 160
Exclusivist xi, 75
Exegesis 36, 44, 45, 83, 92, 155
Expropriate 28, 62, 65, 66, 67, 70, 71, 86, 128, 131, 149, 155
Extrinsicism 29, 30
Ezekiel 70, 71
Feuerbach, Ludwig 8, 9, 13, 15, 36
Forgiveness 86, 87, 107, 153
Form (*Gestalt*) xi, 3, 5, 6, 28, 36, 113, 137, 139, 140, 144
Freedom xxiii, 2, 3, 4, 5, 8, 9, 11, 12, 13, 14, 15, 16, 18, 19, 20, 21, 22, 30, 31, 32, 37, 38, 41, 49, 55, 57, 58, 59, 60, 62, 64, 68, 69, 75, 83, 84, 85, 87, 92, 93, 95, 101, 113, 117, 121, 141, 146, 148, 152; **Divine**, 4, 21, 38, 41, 49, 55, 83, 119, 132, 151; **human**, 5, 9, 11, 12, 15, 31, 37, 38, 64, 69, 84, 122
Frei, Hans 46
Gawronski, Raymond ix
Gestalt, see: Form (*Gestalt*)
Glory xii, xxii, xxiv, 2, 3, 7, 9, 11, 12, 16, 17, 18, 19, 22, 23, 24, 25, 26, 28, 29, 37, 38, 39, 40, 41, 42, 43, 44, 45, 46, 48, 49, 50, 53, 54, 56, 57, 58, 59, 60, 64, 65, 66, 68, 70, 71, 72, 73, 74, 75, 76, 77, 78, 79, 81, 82, 87, 88, 89, 90, 91, 92, 98, 108, 114, 115, 121, 122, 124, 125, 126, 133, 134, 135, 137, 151, 157, 159

Gnosis, see: Knowledge (*gnosis*)
Gnostic xx, 4, 5, 7, 20, 21, 24, 27, 28, 32, 58, 73, 76, 78, 79, 106, 156
God of the Jews xxii, 1, 2, 155
Grillmeier, Alois 4
Halakah xvii, 103
Hegel, Georg Wilhelm Friedrich 10, 14, 15, 19, 20, 21, 22, 26, 27, 28, 30, 45, 50, 51, 52, 53, 56, 57, 61, 62, 84, 90, 132
Heidegger, Martin 10, 11, 23, 77, 123, 127, 128, 160
Hermeneutics xiv, xxiv, 3, 5, 7, 20, 25, 26, 28, 32, 33, 34, 53, 79, 137, 145; **Biblical,** xvii, 3, 53, 54
Heterodox 105
Heteronomous xxii, 18, 69
Hick, John xiii, xvi, 140, 159, 160
Historical Jesus 35, 36
Holy Spirit ix, 89, 133, 139, 157
Homer 64, 119, 120, 121, 122, 123, 151
Hubris 5, 8, 78, 90, 91
Human autonomy xxii, 2, 3, 8, 9, 12, 15, 18, 19, 20, 41, 42, 62
Humanism 9, 18, 63
Hypostases 58
Idealism xxii, 9, 128; **German,** 18, 21, 49; **pantheistic,** 136; **Promethean,** 128, 129
Identity metaphysics 2, 41, 49, 53, 55, 57, 77, 78, 79
Imago dei 62, 85
Incarnation xiii, xv, xxiv, 4, 5, 9, 13, 14, 15, 17, 18, 19, 20, 22, 24, 36, 37, 40, 42, 45, 54, 55, 67, 68, 69, 71, 77, 78, 79, 82, 83, 85, 89, 92, 99, 100, 101, 102, 103, 104, 105, 106, 108, 111, 112, 114, 133, 134, 136, 137, 138, 145, 147, 148, 149, 150, 151, 158
Inclusivism 111
Integration 54, 55, 58, 60, 67, 68, 111, 112, 114, 115, 116, 117, 118, 122, 124, 125, 135, 136, 146, 151, 152, 158
Irenaeus xviii, 6, 7, 17, 32, 71
Israel ix, xvi, xvii, xix, xx, xxi, xxiv, 3, 5, 10, 11, 12, 13, 14, 17, 23, 27, 32, 36, 37, 38, 39, 40, 45, 46, 47, 48, 50, 54, 55, 56, 57, 58, 59, 60, 61, 62, 63, 64, 65, 66, 67, 68, 70, 71, 72, 73, 74, 75, 76, 77, 78, 81, 83, 84, 85, 86, 87, 88, 90, 94, 95, 96, 97, 98, 99, 101, 102, 104, 105, 107, 113, 114, 140, 141, 142, 143, 144, 152, 155, 156, 157, 160

Jesus xiii, xiv, xv, xvii, xviii, xix, xx, xxi, xxii, xxiv, 3, 11, 21, 24, 30, 32, 33, 34, 35, 36, 37, 40, 45, 52, 54, 77, 85, 86, 87, 88, 89, 92, 93, 94, 95, 96, 99, 100, 107, 116, 146, 147, 148, 149, 155, 156

Jewish xvi, xvii, xix, xx, xxi, 3, 4, 5, 7, 8, 9, 10, 13, 15, 18, 20, 22, 24, 25, 27, 33, 43, 44, 50, 55, 59, 75, 77, 87, 95, 99, 100, 102, 103, 104, 105, 106, 108, 109, 112, 141, 142, 147, 152, 156, 159, 160

Joachim di Fiore 19, 102

Joachimite 20, 41

Judaism ix, xv, xvi, xvii, xviii, xix, xx, xxii, 1, 3, 4, 10, 15, 16, 17, 20, 21, 22, 23, 33, 37, 41, 43, 45, 50, 68, 72, 73, 74, 76, 77, 78, 79, 82, 83, 94, 95, 96, 100, 101, 102, 103, 104, 105, 106, 107, 108, 109, 112, 135, 140, 141, 142, 144, 145, 147, 150, 152, 155, 156, 157; **Post-biblical Judaism**, 22, 37, 45, 68, 78, 81, 82, 94; post-exilic Judaism, 72, 76, 79; **secularized**, 20, 101, 102, 103, 104

Kabod 11, 57, 60, 70, 74, 87, 91, 131

Kant, Immanuel xiii, xiv, 46, 69, 140

Kantian xiii, 58, 143, 144, 152, 160

Kenosis, see: Emptying (*kenosis*)

Kerygma 36, 47

Knitter, Paul xvi

Knowledge (*gnosis*) 22, 24, 25, 27, 28, 29, 53, 79

Küng, Hans xvi

Liberation theology 101, 105

Lindbeck, George 46, 65, 72, 75, 77, 107, 108

Logos, *logos spermatikoi* 85, 111, 116, 126, 136, 137, 138, 139, 148, 151, 157, 158, 160

Löwith, Karl 4, 101, 106

Marcion xvii, xviii, xix, xxi, xxii, 1, 3, 6, 7, 19, 21, 24, 28, 39

Marcionism ix, x, xviii, xxi, xxii, 1, 2, 4, 6, 7, 9, 10, 19, 25, 32, 37, 40, 41, 44, 45, 50, 62, 106, 108, 118, 160; **Ancient**, xxii, 2, 8, 9; **modern forms of**, xxii, xxiii, 5, 6, 8, 9, 21, 23, 40, 45, 119, 155; **anthropocentric**, pp. 8, 23, 24, 34, 40, 41; **cosmocentric**, 9, 41; **Promethean**, 13, 17, 23, 24, 27, 37, 46, 160

Marcionite ix, xx, xxi, xxii, 1, 2, 4, 5, 6, 10, 14, 15, 17, 21, 22, 23, 27, 28, 32, 33, 35, 37, 41, 43, 50, 79, 82, 90, 105, 127, 155, 156

  As heresy, pp. ix

Marx, Karl 19, 20, 21, 22, 102

Mary 49, 69, 82, 87, 129

Merton, Thomas 63
Messianic xv, xvii, 16, 24, 40, 45, 62, 73, 77, 79, 82, 97, 101, 102, 125, 155, 157
Messianism 12, 16, 20, 24, 73, 77, 79, 140, 142
Metaphysics xxiv, 2, 17, 18, 41, 49, 50, 53, 55, 57, 77, 78, 79, 92, 111, 112, 115, 125, 127, 132, 160
Mishpat 59, 61, 88
Moira 11
Mongrain, Kevin ix, xi, 15, 26, 149
Monism 33, 105
Monotheism xvi, xix, 4, 5, 83
Myth 11, 12, 13, 112, 116, 118, 119, 121, 122, 123, 124, 125, 132, 133, 134, 148
Nature
  and grace, pp. 12, 63, 70, 134, 151; human, pp. 38, 41, 63, 64, 83, 85, 143; divine, pp. xxiii, 8, 16, 58, 93, 151
Negative theology xiv, 18, 37, 40, 42, 160
Neo-scholasticism 49
New covenant xxvi, xx, xxi, xxiii, xxiv, 1, 3, 5, 6, 16, 21, 25, 27, 29, 32, 39, 42, 44, 46, 47, 48, 53, 54, 56, 57, 58, 63, 64, 67, 70, 73, 79, 84, 85, 86, 89, 90, 91, 92, 105, 107, 108, 113, 136, 141, 152
Nostra Aetate ix, xiii, 99
O'Regan, Cyril 20, 53, 92, 131
Old covenant xvii, xix, xx, xxi, xxii, xxiii, 1, 2, 3, 5, 6, 8, 10, 11, 12, 13, 14, 15, 16, 17, 18, 19, 20, 22, 24, 25, 26, 27, 28, 29, 32, 33, 37, 38, 39, 40, 41, 42, 43, 44, 45, 46, 48, 49, 50 53, 54, 55, 56, 57, 62, 67, 68, 69, 70, 71, 73, 75, 77, 79, 81, 83, 84, 85, 86, 87, 88, 89, 90, 91, 92, 93, 94, 95, 103, 105, 107, 108, 111, 112, 113, 119, 120, 121, 123, 125, 127, 131, 134, 135, 140, 141, 144, 155
  God of, pp. 2, 29, 37
Old Testament xviii, xix, xxi, xxii, 2, 3, 6, 21, 22, 32, 38, 40, 44, 46, 47, 48, 54, 71, 73, 83, 86, 91, 92, 96, 103, 113, 121
Ontology 11, 14, 38, 59, 69, 70, 116, 117, 121, 123, 125, 126, 127, 128, 130, 131, 132, 137, 141, 149, 159, 160
Origen xviii, 27, 78, 79
Otto, Rudolf 59
Patristic xi, xv, xvii, 4, 27, 44, 46, 63
Paul xix, 22, 27, 88, 94, 95, 96, 98, 100, 107
Perichoresis 59, 69
Phenomenology 18, 50, 69, 78, 79, 82, 117, 126, 128, 129, 141

Plato 4, 16, 44, 122, 124, 125, 128, 141, 151
Plotinus 135
Pluralist xii, xiii, xiv, xv, xvi, 142
Porphyry 135
Pre-history 55, 56, 68
Primitive history 55, 56, 68
Prometheanism xxii, xxiii, xxiv, 1, 2, 3, 4, 5, 6, 7, 8, 9, 10, 16, 17, 19, 23, 24, 25, 37, 38, 43, 44, 45, 50, 62, 63, 72, 76, 79, 100, 118, 119, 121, 127, 131, 151, 160
Prometheus xxii, 7, 43
Prophetic staircase 12, 45, 62, 68, 70, 83, 85, 141
Quash, Ben ix
Rahner, Karl xi, 48, 52, 112, 142, 143, 144, 145, 152
Recapitulation 85, 86, 87, 89, 116
Relative autonomy 12, 13, 44, 76
Resurrection ix, xiv, xv, xix, xxiii, xxiv, 13, 15, 16, 19, 31, 34, 35, 39, 40, 57, 89, 95, 105, 107, 115, 137, 148, 149, 151, 161
Revelation x, xii, xiv, xvi, xxi, xxii, xxiii, 2, 3, 4, 7, 9, 11, 12, 13, 14, 17, 18, 19, 21, 22, 25, 26, 27, 28, 29, 30, 31, 32, 33, 34, 35, 36, 37, 38, 39, 42, 44, 45, 46, 47, 48, 51, 52, 53, 54, 55, 56, 57, 58, 61, 62, 63, 65, 66, 67, 69, 71, 74, 77, 78, 79, 81, 82, 83, 84, 88, 89, 91, 92, 93, 102, 103, 105, 107, 108, 112, 114, 115, 116, 118, 119, 122, 125, 126, 127, 131, 132, 133, 136, 138, 139, 140, 141, 142, 143, 144, 145, 146, 148, 152, 155, 158, 160
Romans 82, 94, 95, 98, 99, 156, 157
Ruether, Rosemary Radford xv, xvi, xvii, 83
Salvation xii, xiii, xiv, xvi, xvii, xxi, xxii, xxiv, 4, 6, 7, 16, 18, 22, 37, 39, 41, 42, 46, 52, 54, 55, 56, 60, 61, 66, 67, 68, 70, 71, 72, 73, 77, 78, 82, 83, 86, 87, 89, 93, 95, 96, 97, 99, 100, 105, 107, 116, 118, 140, 142, 143, 145, 147, 152, 156
Sapiential 45, 62, 73, 155
Schillebeeckx, Edward xii, 53
Schindler, David 113
Schleiermacher, Friedrich 36, 46, 140
Scripture 2, 3, 4, 6, 16, 27, 30, 31, 34, 36, 38, 39, 44, 46, 47, 49, 51, 65, 67, 72, 79, 83, 139, 160
Second Vatican Council xii, 99
Secular autonomy 64
Secularism 2, 5, 12, 13, 20, 43, 44, 77, 79, 101, 102, 103, 104, 107, 142

Sedeqah (Sedekah) 59, 60
Shalom 59, 89
Shema xvi, 57
Shoah xvii
Soteriology xxiv, 55, 78, 97, 105, 139, 142
Sovereignty xiv, xvi, 2, 3, 5, 8, 10, 12, 22, 39, 47, 55, 57, 58, 60, 63, 75, 87, 95, 96, 116, 134, 156, 158
Spolia Aegyptorum 111, 116
Stairway of obedience 68
Subjectivism 29, 30, 36
Suffering Servant 40, 42, 97, 121, 141
Supercessionism xvi, 107, 108
Tertullian xviii, xix, 1, 6, 7, 23
Theo-Drama 14, 35, 82, 97, 101, 103, 105, 113
Theologian xi, xiv, xv, xxiv, 46, 72, 100, 125, 146
Theology of glory 71, 73, 76
Theology of religions ix, x, xii, xxiii, 115, 121, 132, 137, 146; **Balthasar's**, ix, x, 111, 114, 137, 150; **Christian**, 111, 112, 113; **Rahner's**, 143; **Ruether's**, xv
Theophany 45, 53, 54, 57, 58, 59, 61, 62, 63, 66, 87, 91, 92, 120, 131, 155
Thomistic xi, 18
Torah 10, 74, 75, 79, 92, 103
Transcendence xiii, xiv, xxi, xxiv, 9, 10, 11, 12, 19, 21, 22, 24, 25, 28, 37, 53, 55, 66, 73, 90, 94, 103, 106, 108, 121, 123, 124, 132, 137, 139, 158, 159, 160 **Divine**, xvii, xx, xxii, 2, 4, 5, 8, 11, 12, 15, 21, 23, 25, 41, 49, 50, 53, 60, 76, 79, 82, 89, 90, 93, 94, 103, 119, 120, 121, 123, 125, 130; **human**, 18, 112, 113, 121, 157; **self**, xiii, 113, 114, 143
Trinitarian theology xvii, 3, 24, 103
Trinity xiv, xvii, 3, 5, 13, 42, 52, 67, 85, 93, 148, 152, 160
Triune xiv, xxi, 5, 13, 25, 33, 68, 91, 160
Universalism 56, 133
Valentinianism 7
Vatican II x, xv, xvi
Vattimo, Gianni 19, 90, 103, 105
Von Harnack, Adolf xxi
Von Rad, Gerhard 47, 48, 55
Vorstellung 26, 27, 42

Wholly Other 57, 59
Wilken, Robert Louis 4
Wisdom xxiii, 48, 49, 53, 54, 64, 73, 79, 91, 141
Word (*dabar*) 12, 69, 85
Yahweh xx, 11, 19, 20, 22, 24, 25, 74, 87, 88, 101, 102, 105, 113, 134
YHWH 48, 49, 52, 56, 61, 75

About the Author

Anthony C. Sciglitano, Jr. is Chair of the Department of Religion and Director of the University Core Curriculum at Seton Hall University. His interests include theological hermeneutics, the relation of Christianity to modernity and post-modernity and inter-religious dialogue. He was raised by Anthony and Jeanine Sciglitano, who generously shared their Catholic and culinary traditions without which he would be, well, someone else.

Acknowledgements

A first book must present the most difficult challenge for an acknowledgements, for one's making explicit of debts comes so belatedly that there is seemingly no end to the list. Selection, then, is both invidious and necessary. From Saint John's, in Collegeville, MN, I learned a capacious, intellectual, and deeply prayerful Catholicism to which, someday, I hope to do justice. William T. Cahoy, or Bill as we know him, incarnated this spirit with remarkable energy, humility and hospitality. I hope that in some small measure his intellect and critical eye for the pretentiously obscure has rubbed off just enough here. At Saint John's, I also had the good fortune of meeting Kevin Mongrain in what began a now decades-long friendship and theological conversation that informs every page of the present work, which he graciously read and re-read always lobbying for clarity of thought and expression. I don't know that Elizabeth Johnson would approve of Balthasar's theology or my appreciation for it, but possible theological differences notwithstanding, she taught me that fidelity to the tradition called for creativity and cultural engagement and encouraged her students to find their own theological voice. She also went some lengths to help me find my first academic job and for that I am forever grateful. Out of some combination of fraternal love and Christian charity that eludes me, my brother, Chris, proofread every last iota of this manuscript. I remain in awe of his generosity. Tom Guarino read and commented on the entire manuscript. His comments are invaluable, his friendship an unexpected gift. Cyril O'Regan gave me the confidence to engage Balthasar in the first place and this book would never have happened had he not graciously invited me to his Yale seminars on *Glory of the Lord* and *Theo-Drama* in what seems like a distant age. John Jones at Crossroad was a simply wonderful editor who helped me find my post-dissertation voice and get it onto the page. His patience shamed the angels (May he rest in eternal peace). I must also thank John Zmirak, editor at Crossroad, for seeing this manuscript to publication and to Seton Hall undergraduate, Nathan Caldwell, who with great attention to detail on a tight schedule created the index.

Finally, I must thank my wife, Julie, whose fully incarnate love lends joy and energy to all my days.

You Might Also Like

Cyril O'Regan

Anatomy of Misremembering: Von Balthasar's Response to Philosophical Modernity. Volume 1: Hegel

Paperback, 688 pages, 978-0-8245-2562-0

This compelling work is the most comprehensive and sophisticated account to date of the relationship between Hans Urs von Balthasar—a Swiss theologian and Catholic priest—and the German philosopher Georg Hegel. While underscoring the depth and breadth of Balthasar's engagement with the philosopher, author Cyril O'Regan argues that Balthasar is the most concertedly anti-Hegelian theologian of the 20th century. For him, it is essential to engage Hegel because of his corrections of sclerotic forms of premodern Christian thought, but even more importantly to resist and correct his systematic thought, which represents a comprehensive misremembering of the Christian thought, practices, and forms of life. An important and original work, this book addresses a topic that puts the possibility of an authentic postmodern theology at stake.

You Might Also Like

Rodney A. Howsare and Larry S. Chapp, editors
How Balthasar Changed My Mind
15 Scholars Reflect on the Meaning of Balthasar for Their Own Work
Paperback, 312 pages, 978-0-8245-2569-9

Addressing the widespread and growing interest in the thought of Catholic theologian Hans Urs von Balthasar—whose influence on Popes John Paul II and Benedict XVI has been enormous—this collection, by a team of established theologians and intellectuals, reflects on Balthasar's impact. Not a collection of scholarly articles, this book offers essays on the way in which Balthasar's theology is being taken up into other theological and philosophical projects, as well as thoughts on how Balthasar has influenced the authors personally. Key themes include the importance of beauty, the dramatic nature of truth, the centrality of revelation, the uniqueness and universality of Christ, and the intrinsic relationship between theology and sanctity. Contributors include Robert Barron, Martin Bieler, Anthony DiStefano, Raymond Gawronski, S.J., Michael Hanby, Nicholas J. Healy, Rodney A. Howsare, Francesca Murphy, Danielle Nussberger, Cyril O'Regan, Russell Reno, Tracey Rowland, David C. Schindler, David L. Schindler, and Adrian Walker.

You Might Also Like

Scott W. Hahn and Benjamin Wiker
Politicizing the Bible
The Roots of Historical Criticism and the Secularization of Scripture 1300-1700

Paperback, 624 pages, 978-0-8245-9903-4

Penetrating the pretense of objectivity often presented in secular studies, Hahn and Wiker track the sources of current assumptions about scriptural interpretation and show that what we hold to be neutral, fact-based approaches actually originate in the political wrangling of 13th and 14th centuries. This wide-ranging volume covers the development of historical criticism and the resulting undermining and fracturing of the integrity of the church. The authors look at the role of the revolutionary writings of Marsilius of Padua and Machiavelli, the political projects of Henry VIII, Thomas Hobbes, and John Locke, and the quest for an empire of science that emerges in the work of Descartes and Spinoza. A formidable revisioning of how we understand scripture.

Support your local bookstore or order directly from the publisher at www.CrossroadPublishing.com

To request a catalog or inquire about quantity orders, please e-mail sales@CrossroadPublishing.com

www.ingramcontent.com/pod-product-compliance
Lightning Source LLC
Chambersburg PA
CBHW032315230426
43666CB00032B/180